ON SANDY SHORES

Teacher's Guide

Grades 2–4

Skills
Observing, Organizing, Sorting and Classifying, Communicating, Comparing, Recording, Making Inferences, Writing, Drama and Role-Playing

Concepts
Classification Systems, Erosion, Rocks and Minerals, Composition of Sand, Seasonality, Waves, Currents, Habitat, Community, Camouflage, Predator/Prey Relationships, Pollution, Conservation, Environmental Ethics, Social/Personal Responsibility

Themes
Unity and Diversity, Patterns of Change, Scale and Structure, Evolution, Systems and Interactions

Mathematics Strands
Number, Measurement, Pattern, Logic and Language

Nature of Science and Mathematics
Scientific Community, Interdisciplinary, Cooperative Efforts, Creativity and Constraints, Objectivity and Ethics, Real-Life Applications, Science and Technology

by
Craig Strang
Catherine Halversen
Kimi Hosoume

Great Explorations in Math and Science
Lawrence Hall of Science
University of California at Berkeley

Cover Design
Lisa Haderlie Baker

Illustrations
Lisa Haderlie Baker
Rose Craig

Photographs
Richard Hoyt
Laurence Bradley
Craig Strang
Catherine Halversen

Lawrence Hall of Science, University of California, Berkeley, CA 94720-5200

Chairman: Glenn T. Seaborg
Director: Ian Carmichael

> **Publication of *On Sandy Shores* was made possible by a grant from the McDonnell-Douglas Employee's Community Fund and the McDonnell-Douglas Foundation. The GEMS Project and the Lawrence Hall of Science greatly appreciate this support.**

Initial support for the origination and publication of the GEMS series was provided by the A.W. Mellon Foundation and the Carnegie Corporation of New York. Under a grant from the National Science Foundation, GEMS Leader's Workshops have been held across the country. GEMS has also received support from: the McDonnell-Douglas Foundation and the McDonnell-Douglas Employee's Community Fund; the Hewlett Packard Company; Join Hands, the Health and Safety Educational Alliance; and the people at Chevron USA. GEMS also gratefully acknowledges the contribution of word processing equipment from Apple Computer, Inc. This support does not imply responsibility for statements or views expressed in publications of the GEMS program. For further information on GEMS leadership opportunities, or to receive a catalog and the *GEMS Network News*, please contact GEMS at the address and phone number below. We also welcome letters to the *GEMS Network News*.

©1996 by The Regents of the University of California. All rights reserved. Printed in the United States of America.

Printed on recycled paper with soy-based inks.

International Standard Book Number: 0-912511-98-2

COMMENTS WELCOME !

Great Explorations in Math and Science (GEMS) is an ongoing curriculum development project. GEMS guides are revised periodically, to incorporate teacher comments and new approaches. We welcome your criticisms, suggestions, helpful hints, and any anecdotes about your experience presenting GEMS activities. Your suggestions will be reviewed each time a GEMS guide is revised. Please send your comments to: GEMS Revisions, c/o Lawrence Hall of Science, University of California, Berkeley, CA 94720-5200.
The phone number is (510) 642-7771.
The fax number is (510) 643-0309.

Great Explorations in Math and Science (GEMS) Program

The Lawrence Hall of Science (LHS) is a public science center on the University of California at Berkeley campus. LHS offers a full program of activities for the public, including workshops and classes, exhibits, films, lectures, and special events. LHS is also a center for teacher education and curriculum research and development.

Over the years, LHS staff have developed a multitude of activities, assembly programs, classes, and interactive exhibits. These programs have proven to be successful at the Hall and should be useful to schools, other science centers, museums, and community groups. A number of these guided-discovery activities have been published under the Great Explorations in Math and Science (GEMS) title, after an extensive refinement and adaptation process that includes classroom testing of trial versions, modifications to ensure the use of easy-to-obtain materials, with carefully written and edited step-by-step instructions and background information to allow presentation by teachers without special background in mathematics or science.

Staff

Principal Investigator: Glenn T. Seaborg
Director: Jacqueline Barber
Associate Director: Kimi Hosoume
Associate Director/Principal Editor: Lincoln Bergman
Science Curriculum Specialist: Cary Sneider
Mathematics Curriculum Specialist: Jaine Kopp
GEMS Sites and Centers Coordinator: Carolyn Willard
GEMS Workshop Coordinator: Laura Tucker
Staff Development Specialists: Lynn Barakos, Katharine Barrett, Kevin Beals, Ellen Blinderman, Beatrice Boffen, Celia Cuomo, Gigi Dornfest, John Erickson, Stan Fukunaga, Philip Gonsalves, Cathy Larripa, Linda Lipner, Laura Lowell, Debra Sutter
Administrative Coordinator: Cynthia Eaton

Distribution Coordinator: Karen Milligan
Workshop Administrator: Terry Cort
Distribution Representative: Felicia Roston
Shipping Assistants: Ben Arreguy, George Kasarjian
Trial Testing Coordinator: Stephanie Van Meter
Public Information Representative: Gerri Ginsburg
Senior Editor: Carl Babcock
Editor: Florence Stone
Principal Publications Coordinator: Kay Fairwell
Art Director: Lisa Haderlie Baker
Designers: Carol Bevilacqua, Rose Craig, Lisa Klofkorn
Staff Assistants: Kasia Bukowinski, Larry Gates, Nick Huynh, Steve Lim, Nancy Lin, Michelle Mahogany, Karla Penuelas, Alisa Sramala

Contributing Authors

Jacqueline Barber
Katharine Barrett
Kevin Beals
Lincoln Bergman
Beverly Braxton
Kevin Cuff
Celia Cuomo
Linda De Lucchi
Gigi Dornfest

Jean Echols
John Erickson
Philip Gonsalves
Jan M. Goodman
Alan Gould
Catherine Halversen
Kimi Hosoume
Susan Jagoda
Jaine Kopp

Linda Lipner
Laura Lowell
Larry Malone
Cary I. Sneider
Craig Strang
Debra Sutter
Rebecca Tilley
Jennifer Meux White
Carolyn Willard

Reviewers

We would like to thank the following educators who reviewed, tested, or coordinated the reviewing of *this series* of GEMS materials in manuscript and draft form (including the GEMS guides *On Sandy Shores, Secret Formulas,* and *Learning About Learning*). Their critical comments and recommendations, based on classroom presentation of these activities nationwide, contributed significantly to these GEMS publications. Their participation in the review process does not necessarily imply endorsement of the GEMS program or responsibility for statements or views expressed. This role is an invaluable one; feedback is carefully recorded and integrated as appropriate into the publications. **THANK YOU!**

ALASKA

Iditarod Elementary School, Wasilla
Tacy Carr
Cynthia Dolmas Curran
Carol Lowery
Bonnie Tesar

ARIZONA

Hualapai Elementary School, Kingman
Nora Brown
Catherine Ann Claes
Traci A. D'Arcy
Rhonda Gilbert
Lisa Julle
Barbara McLarty
Stephanie L. Murillo
Rose Roberts

Northern Arizona University, Flagstaff
Lynda Hatch

CALIFORNIA

Albany Middle School, Albany
Jenny Anderson
Chiyo Masuda
Kay Sorg
Janet Teel

Anna Yates Elementary School, Emeryville
Aron Cargo*
Cecile L. Carraway
Sally Gallinger
Peggy Jones

Beacon Day School, Oakland
Deborah Ellis

Berkeley Arts Magnet, Berkeley
Sam Frankel
David Freedman*
Sandra Guerra
Janice Kohler

Claremont Middle School, Oakland
Susan Cristancho
Malia Dinell-Schwartz
Sheila Lucia
Mike Predovic

Cleveland Elementary School, Oakland
Cathy Chan
Jan Greer
Vivian Lura*
Patti MacFarland
Kathy Wong

Dover Middle School, Fairfield
Rebecca Hammond
Sarah Yourd

Fairmont Elementary School, El Cerrito
Nancy Buckingham
Carrie Cook
Karen DeTore
Sandi Healy
Linda Lambie
Katy Miles
Laura Peck
Nancy Rutter-Spriggs

Foshay Learning Center, Los Angeles
Stephanie Hoffman

Golden State Middle School, West Sacramento
Natasha Lowrie

Jefferson Elementary School, Berkeley
Mary Ann Furuichi
Linda Mengel
Fern Stroud
Gaye Ying

John Muir Elementary School, Berkeley
Anne Wihera Donaker*
Kathleen Giustino
Julie Koehler
Molly Shaw

Lafayette Elementary School, Oakland
Barbara B. Anderson*
Sue Capps
Veronica Rivers
Eleanor Tyson

Malcolm X Intermediate School, Berkeley
Arden Clute
DeEtte LaRue
Mahalia Ryba

Marina Middle School, Los Angeles
Leticia Escajeda

Markham Elementary School, Oakland
Eleanor Feuille
Sharon Kerr
Ruth Quezada
Audry Taylor
Margaret Wright

Moffett Elementary School, Huntington Beach
Patsy Almeida*
Mary Green
Nancy Hanan
Georgie Williams

Nelson Elementary School, Pinedale
Julia Hollenbeck
Vicki Jackson
Erla Stanley
Phyllis Todd

Nobel Middle School, Northridge
Margie Hickman

Oxford School, Berkeley
Anita Baker
Joe Brulenski
Barbara Edwards
Judy Kono

Park Day School, Oakland
Aggie Brenneman
Karen Corzan
Michelle McAfee Krueger
Suzie McLean-Balderston

Parker Elementary School, Oakland
Lorynne Dupree
Linda Rogers
Zerita Sharp
Marian Wilson

Thousand Oaks Elementary School, Berkeley
Ray Adams*
Liz Fuentes
Sharon Strachan
Mario Zelaya

Washington Irving Middle School, Los Angeles
Mary Lu Camacho
Bernadette J. Cullen
Joe Kevany
Thomas Yee

Westside Science Center, Los Angeles
Nonnie Korten

Willard Junior High School, Berkeley
Kathy Evan
Clydine James

COLORADO
Franklin Elementary School, Sterling
Vickie Baseggio
Marty Belknap
Barbara Nelson
Shelly Stumpf

Hotchkiss Elementary School, Hotchkiss
Roy Cranor
Kevin Elisha*
Sheryl Farmer
Margie Hollembeak
Becky Ruby

DISTRICT OF COLUMBIA
Anne Beers Elementary School, Washington, D.C.
Elizabeth Dortch
Fredric Hutchinson
Gloria McKenzie-Freeman
Connie Parker
Gregory Taylor
Gloria Warren Tucker

Park View Elementary School, Washington, D.C.
Olive Allen
Carol R. Corry
Michelle Davis
Barry G. Sprague*
Mary P. Tunstall

IOWA
GMG Elementary School, Green Mountain
Nadine McLaughlin*
Todd Schuster
Catherine Vint
Lynne Wallace

MAINE
Coastal Ridge Elementary School, York
Nancy Annis
Rick Comeau
Julie Crafts
Patricia Gray
Carol A. Moody

York Middle School, York
Andrew Berenson
Deborah J. Bradburn
Rick Comeau
Jean Dominguez
Susan E. Miller
Robert G. Vincent

MICHIGAN
Marine City Middle School, Marine City
Peggy Brooks
Gina Day
Laura Newton
Alan Starkey

NORTH CAROLINA
C. W. Stanford Middle School, Hillsborough
Leslie Kay Jones
Tom Kuntzleman
Christopher Longwill
Dawn M. Wills

Grady Brown Elementary School, Hillsborough
Lisa A. Crocker
Audrey T. Johnson
Sandra Kosik
Sandra L. McKee
Tonya L. Price
Karen Sexton

WASHINGTON
Orchards Elementary School, Vancouver
Mary Jane Boyle
Debbie Doden
Heidi Graumann*
Debra Palmer
Fay Stewart

WEST VIRGINIA
Flinn Elementary School, Charleston
Sharon Adkins
Ann B. Edele
Kathy Kemper*
Louise St. Clair

* On-Site Coordinators for *On Sandy Shores*

Acknowledgments

The authors would like to thank Katharine Barrett, Director of the Biology Education Department at the Lawrence Hall of Science, for her support, guidance, and encouragement over many years as we developed the MARE program. Roberta Dean, MARE Program Coordinator, was integrally and creatively involved in the development of all activities in this guide. Her input and expertise was essential to our approach to the entire project. Victor Candia, MARE Program Coordinator, provided invaluable input as he helped to field test and refine many of the activities in schools across California.

Special thanks to mentor and friend, Dr. Stephanie Kaza, University of Vermont, who wrote "Sandy's Journey to the Sea," found in the activity, The Sights that Sand has Seen, and who originally inspired us to organize the MARE curriculum around marine habitats. We would also like to offer special thanks to our respected colleagues and friends, Francisca Sanchez and Marcus Martel at Alameda County Office of Education who so greatly influenced our thinking about language acquisition theory, cultural diversity, and equity issues. They gently guided our discovery of the compelling role that science education can play in creating success among language minority students. Several of the language development activities found in this guide are based on activities developed by Francisca Sanchez.

Dr. Jere Lipps, Professor of Integrative Biology and Director of the Museum of Paleontology at the University of California at Berkeley provided expert scientific review of the marine science content in the guide. We are particularly pleased that Dr. Eugene C. Haderlie, long admired by the MARE staff for his contributions to the field, was kind enough to look over this guide.

Jacqueline Barber, GEMS Director, provided extremely helpful guidance at several key points along the path to shaping and refining the activities. Lincoln Bergman, GEMS Principal Editor did more than edit our many drafts—he provided wise counsel and insight about the content of the activities themselves, and artfully guided the entire publication process with patience, good humor, and exceptional wit. We would also like to thank Stephanie Van Meter, GEMS staff, for her "beyond-the-call" job of assembling kits heavy with rocks, sand, and smelly beach wrack (though many of us LIKE that smell) for our trial tests. Florence Stone, GEMS Editor, assembled the quite comprehensive "Resources" and "Literature Connections" sections, and also scrutinized the fine details of our final draft before it went off to the printer. Lisa Baker painted the beautiful cover that adorns this book and illustrated the organisms, Rose Craig created the other illustrations, and Lisa Klofkorn designed the book.

Finally, we would like to thank the many, many teachers and students who trial tested and provided valuable suggestions for improving these activities. We have been constantly inspired to publish these activities by the thousands of students whose faces we have seen brighten with startled wonder upon seeing the beauty of sand grains through a microscope. Thanks to Gaye Ying and her third grade class at Jefferson Elementary in Berkeley who helped in the initial testing phase. Those teachers involved in the GEMS trial test process are listed at the front of this guide. In addition, hundreds of dedicated teachers in MARE schools throughout California, Nevada, Texas, Colorado, Oregon, and Michigan have taught and tested the original MARE activities that were adapted for this guide. We owe them all a great debt. Their input provides an authenticity and reliability to these activities that we could never otherwise have achieved.

Table of Contents

Acknowledgments..vi

Introduction..1

More About MARE...7

Time Frame...9

Getting Ready Tips (for the entire unit)..10

Activity 1: Beach Bucket Scavenger Hunt....................................13
    Session 1: Planet Ocean Brainstorm/My Buddy Says
    Session 2: Beach Explorations
    Session 3: Make a Mini-book

Activity 2: Sand on Stage...27
    Session 1: Partner Parade/Anticipatory Chart
    Session 2: Comparing Sands
    Session 3: Observing and Recording
    Session 4: The Experts Meet

Activity 3: The Sights that Sand has Seen...................................45
    Session 1: My Buddy Says/Story Chart
    Session 2: A Postcard Story
    Session 3: Postcard Game Show

Activity 4: Build a Sandy Beach..59
    Session 1: Partner Parade/Classroom Field Trip
    Session 2: Drawing Organisms and Habitats
    Session 3: Making the Organisms
    Session 4: Arranging the Displays
    Session 5: Class Presentations
    Information for the Displays..77

Activity 5: Oil on the Beach..91
    Session 1: Partner Parade/Anticipatory Chart
    Session 2: Brief Oil Talk/Fouled Feathers
    Session 3: Oil on the Beach/My Buddy Says
    Session 4: Cleaning the Oil Spill/Debriefing the Results

Behind the Scenes..109

Resources...117

Assessment Suggestions..131

Literature Connections...135

Summary Outlines..141

On Sandy Shores was developed by the Marine Activities, Resources & Education (MARE) program of the Lawrence Hall of Science. MARE (pronounced as in the Latin word for ocean: mär´ ā) is an exciting whole-school, interdisciplinary, marine science program for elementary and middle schools. This GEMS guide is excerpted and adapted from the *MARE Teachers' Guide to the Sandy Beach* for second grade that includes activities in Earth and Physical Science, Biological Science, and Environmental Issues.

Please see page 7 for more on the MARE program. In adapting portions of the MARE activities, this GEMS guide features a number of the teaching strategies and "activity structures" developed by MARE and embedded in the MARE approach. These special methods are designed to encourage the acquisition of both science and language, especially among English language learners. They also foster cooperative learning. They are discussed in more detail in the main introduction to this guide and are described in step-by-step fashion as part of the activities.

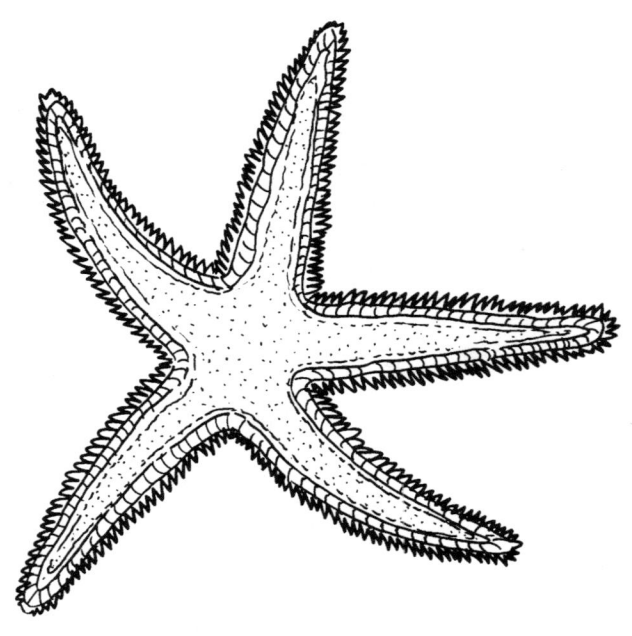

Introduction

The activities in this GEMS guide transport your students to the sandy shore, one of the most fascinating ecosystems on our planet. At this special ecological juncture, where the sea (or lake or river) meets the sand, a rich multiplicity of life forms find ways to survive, thrive, and interact with each other. The sandy shore can also inspire natural curiosity in your students, leading them to key scientific and environmental understandings.

Using a wide variety of learning formats, students explore and deepen their understanding of many aspects of the "sandy shore," from the grains of sand themselves to characteristic plants, animals, and more complex biological and ecological interactions. As students acquire information and construct their knowledge, they gain respect for the environment and all living things, fostering an enhanced sense of personal and social responsibility.

You don't need to live near the ocean or be a marine science expert to present this guide to your students. Concise background information is woven into each lesson. The "Behind the Scenes" section and a wealth of illustrations of sandy beach organisms provide plenty of information to bring you up to a comfortable knowledge level. Besides, *On Sandy Shores* provides fun opportunities for you to learn right along with your students!

This guide is truly interdisciplinary. There's no need to confine the activities to any given "science time" as they extend far and wide across the curriculum, providing depth of learning in many areas. The "Mini-books" that students make in several of the activities, and all of Activity 3: The Sights that Sand has Seen, strengthen and support language arts instruction. Many aspects of Activity 5: Oil on the Beach lend themselves to further discussion in social studies or current events about the responsibilities of individuals and groups in a community. Your students won't be able to complete Activity 4: Build a Sandy Beach unless they have considerable "art time" to create and construct their organisms. The more you find various disciplines blending together in this mutually beneficial way, the better we predict your students will learn, grasping key concepts and applying them to new situations.

We recommend that you read through both this introduction and the entire guide before you begin to teach *On Sandy Shores*. This will give you a sense of the unit as a whole and its unique activity structures, and will help you foresee special needs. You may also find that issues and questions raised in early activities are more fully explored and responded to in subsequent ones.

Session-by-Session

This is a substantial unit, with five main activities, each of which contains multiple class sessions. You will want to plan accordingly, and/or adapt or tailor some of the activities to suit your curricular needs and scheduling constraints. The many scientific and environmental concepts and processes that are explored, along with the creative, artistic, writing, and language arts opportunities make this unit well worth the time educationally. The entire unit helps build and reinforce many key concepts for your students, but does take time. We cautioned our trial test teachers, for example, to be sure to save time for Activity 5 (Oil on the Beach) because Activity 4 (Build a Sandy Beach) can lead in so many creative directions. Here's a look at *On Sandy Shores:*

In Activity 1: Beach Bucket Scavenger Hunt, students working in small cooperative groups explore a simulated sandy shore in a plastic tub that is littered with "beach drift" and debris. Through a sorting activity, students discover that objects found on the sandy shore can be further grouped into those that show: evidence of plant life, evidence of animal life, and evidence of humans. They also discover the differences between once-living (biotic) and never-living (abiotic) objects.

In Activity 2: Sand on Stage, students with hand lenses work in small groups to compare the color, size, and shape of grains from several sand samples. Based on their observations, students make guesses, or inferences, about the origins of the samples. Students discover that sand grains can be made of animals, plants, rocks, or minerals and that these differences can be clues about where the sand came from and how it got to its present location.

In Activity 3: The Sights that Sand has Seen, students listen to a story about the journey of a sand grain from high on a mountain to a sand castle on a beach. They work in small groups to write and illustrate a series of "postcards" that re-tell the story of the sand grain's journey. Through hearing and re-creating the story, students discover that sand is created by erosion, and can be transported long distances by streams, rivers, and ocean currents.

In Activity 4: Build a Sandy Beach, students discover that most of the life on a sandy beach is actually hidden in the sand. They first color in one of the line drawings of sandy beach organisms provided at the back of this guide and draw a habitat for that organism. Then they construct three-dimensional models of organisms to place into three displays that provide views of different parts of the same sandy beach. One of these displays is a panoramic view of the beach and its surroundings called "Above the Sand." The second display, "Under the Sand," focuses on the many organisms that live below the sand. The third display, "Beach Wrack," is a magnified look at the living and dead organisms that make up the "beach wrack" washed ashore by the waves. The class is organized into three large groups for these activities. **We strongly recommend that you recruit some adult volunteers or older students to assist you in presenting these exciting activities.**

Older students may pay special attention to making their organism models to appropriate scale, depending on which display is involved. A special "Information for the Displays" section on page 77 provides concise information on the organisms that students build and place in the displays, along with tips for making three-dimensional models of them. If names of organisms or other terminology used in the main text of the guide (such as "holdfast" or "beach wrack") are unfamiliar to you, please consult the "Information for the Displays" and "Behind the Scenes" sections. Please be aware that this activity could easily extend over many class sessions. Depending on your scheduling and time constraints, you may want to modify it to best suit your needs. It would make a wonderful unit in and of itself!

In Activity 5: Oil on the Beach, students learn where oil comes from, how people use oil, ways to conserve it, and why conservation is important. They help make a classroom "sandy beach" in a tub, and observe how the beach is affected by oil spilled offshore that washes onto the beach with simulated tides. Students then work in small groups to attempt to clean up an oil spill using a variety of methods. Through experimentation, students discover that oil spills are almost impossible to clean up—people can help prevent them through conservation measures, such as reducing the use of oil. This activity builds upon what students have learned in this unit to make a strong connection to environmental issues in our daily lives.

Into, Through, and Beyond

This GEMS guide features activities developed by the Marine Activities, Resources & Education (MARE) program at the Lawrence Hall of Science, and highlights several unique aspects of the MARE curriculum. For example, each activity in this guide is composed of three main pieces:

INTO THE ACTIVITIES helps students recall how much they already know about the activity topic. Teachers may be pleasantly surprised by the wealth of knowledge students bring to the classroom, and may also become aware of significant misconceptions (or a lack of prior knowledge) that need to be addressed.

THROUGH THE ACTIVITIES contains experiments, simulations, demonstrations, games, and facts to help students build on their prior knowledge, and acquire, construct, and reflect on new concepts and information.

BEYOND THE ACTIVITIES provides opportunities for students, usually in groups, to explore the content further, applying what they have learned to new situations through self-designed projects, research, home activities, etc.

These three sections are described in the "Overview" to each of the five main activities, and are also playfully represented by these icons in the margin.

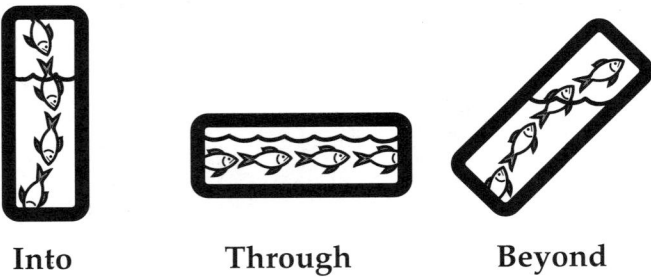

Into   Through   Beyond

Activity Structures and Teaching Strategies

Several key "activity structures" or teaching strategies developed by the MARE program are utilized in this guide. These are designed to help students talk, write, and draw about their related prior knowledge of a topic, or to distill and summarize what they have recently learned. They have names like "Partner Parade" and "My Buddy Says." In general, these activity structures emphasize short, small group discussions, cooperation, and social skills development. They create opportunities for students to use language in a non-threatening and highly relevant setting in which the focus is on science content, not on the language itself.

These activity structures support current research in second language acquisition. Research shows that students acquire language most quickly by using, hearing, reading, and understanding it—in context and in non-threatening settings. Contrary to what might be expected, students acquire language when they are focused on the *meaning* rather than the *form* of the language they are using. It is better not to correct grammar or pronunciation at this time, and instead let students who are English language learners strive to use English in these exciting science activities and observe you and others using language correctly. Constructivist learning theory maintains that students acquire language skills and construct new concepts in science only when the new information builds on, is compared to, and is sifted through, students' prior knowledge.

These activity structures are meant to be simple and accessible, and to simultaneously help students build their knowledge of science and their language skills. You also may find the activities help students to begin working in cooperative groups by developing their social skills. We hope you will also find them useful in other subject areas as well as in *On Sandy Shores*.

In Culturally Diverse Classrooms

This guide is especially designed to be used with no modification in culturally diverse classrooms with large numbers of English language learners. The activities were created with high-quality science content and language development in mind. They meet the criteria established by linguists and language acquisition experts for Specially Designed Academic Instruction in English (SDAIE), also sometimes known as sheltered instruction. SDAIE refers to curriculum and courses in content areas (science, mathematics, social studies, etc.) designed to be delivered in English to students whose native language is not English but who have reached intermediate proficiency in English. These students will find *On Sandy Shores* activities comprehensible and academically challenging at or above their grade level. They will also find that the activities help build their English language skills.

Students already fluent in English will of course enjoy the activities themselves, as well as the richness and depth of understanding that comes with integrating poetry, literature, discussions, art, music, video, journal writing, brainstorming, graphics, and cooperative projects with their study of science.

A "Summary Outlines" section is included, to assist you in guiding students through the activities. Additional, removable copies of student data sheets are provided at the end of the book. These data sheets, as well as the line drawings of organisms with brief text (also at the back of the book) are meant to be duplicated for students (and for teacher's workshops) so you do not have to request permission for their duplication for these educational purposes. To *publish* any of these sheets, however, in any form, including on an electronic network, and/or to copy, reprint, or publish any other text, permission must be requested in writing from GEMS at the Lawrence Hall of Science.

Sections highlighting resources, assessments, and literature connections are also included. We welcome your and your students' suggestions for books that connect well to the activities in this guide. GEMS guides are revised frequently, to incorporate new ideas and teacher feedback.

We hope you and your students, wherever you may be, thoroughly enjoy your sojourn on these sandy shores!

AT THE SEASIDE

by Robert Louis Stevenson

When I was down beside the sea
A wooden spade they gave to me
To dig the sandy shore.
My holes were empty like a cup,
In every hole the sea came up,
Till it could come no more.

MORE ABOUT MARE

MARE is a program of the University of California at Berkeley's Lawrence Hall of Science. MARE is a year-long, whole-school program, highlighted at each school by an Ocean Week or Ocean Month. It engages the entire staffs and student bodies, parents, and communities of hundreds of schools in a comprehensive study of the ocean. In addition to providing curriculum, MARE offers teacher education in-services and summer institutes based on the most up-to-date scientific and educational research. The program focuses specifically on helping culturally, linguistically, and academically diverse schools to implement high-quality science education that is accessible to all students. Customized, whole-faculty in-services introduce teachers to new methods for developing their own integrated instructional plans based on the MARE curriculum, present marine science content, and help the entire school plan for their Ocean Week. At MARE's two-week, residential Summer Institute, teacher leaders sample hands-on activities, plan school-wide programs, learn from leading scientists and educators, and participate in exciting field experiences.

MARE's Ocean Week is a whole-school/whole-school-day "immersion" experience that transforms an entire school into a laboratory for the discovery and exploration of the ocean. This intensive educational event creates an exciting atmosphere school-wide and serves as the centerpiece for year-long ocean studies. Ocean Week builds a sense of inclusion throughout the school community and improves the general climate and educational culture of the school. Special education, language minority, and mainstream students work side-by-side across grade levels, peer teaching and tackling special projects. Students have long uninterrupted blocks of time to explore areas of interest in depth. Teachers receive on-site support from MARE staff, who work at the school every day of Ocean Week, coaching, model teaching, coordinating, and dispensing materials from MARE's extensive multi-media library. Parents are directly involved in the school's academic program.

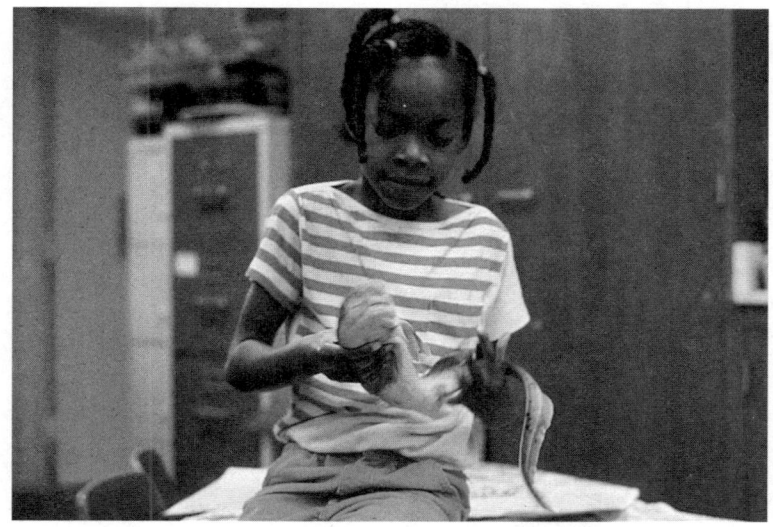

The MARE curriculum focuses each grade on a different marine habitat and integrates language arts, language development, social studies, and art with science and mathematics. Many key science themes and concepts are explored. Integrating disciplines and linking subject areas, the curriculum helps students understand the overarching themes of science. Within each curriculum guide, you will find in-depth teacher reference information, hands-on activities, teaching strategies, children's literature connections, planning materials for developing a comprehensive whole-school science program based on the study of the ocean, and suggestions for assembling student portfolios and conducting performance tasks to assess student achievement. Each activity in the MARE curriculum identifies and develops students' related prior knowledge through a rich variety of language experiences, before introducing new topics. Each of the MARE guides can be used, minimally, as a six- to eight-week science unit, or can be expanded and integrated into a comprehensive, year-long science curriculum covering the disciplines of earth, physical, biological, and environmental sciences. If you're interested in more information about MARE, please contact:

MARE
Lawrence Hall of Science   phone: (510) 642-5008
University of California   fax: (510) 642-1055
Berkeley, CA 94720-5200   e-mail: mare_lhs@uclink4.berkeley.edu

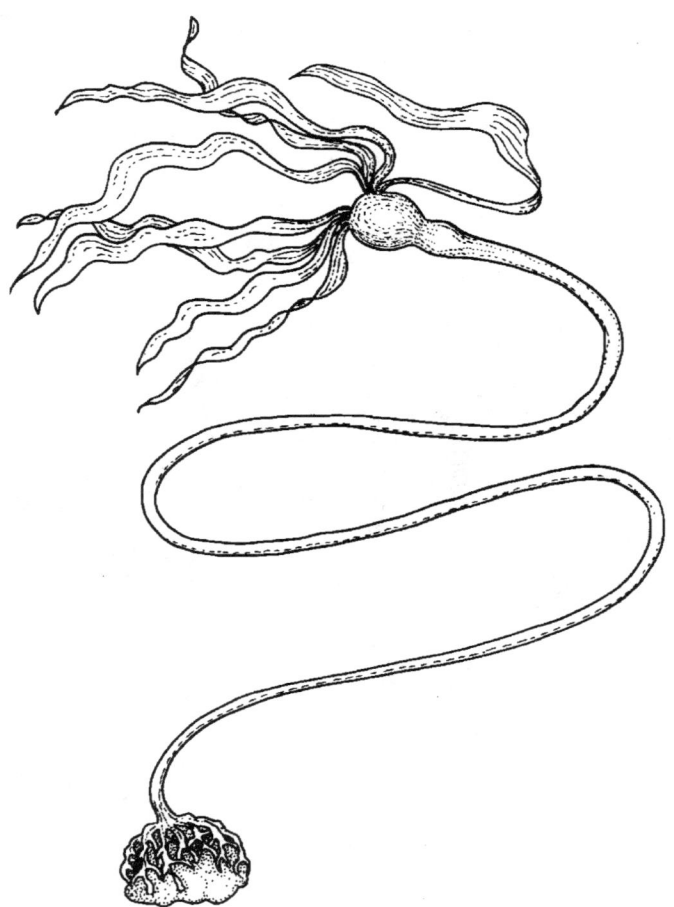

Time Frame

Activity 1: Beach Bucket Scavenger Hunt
    Session 1: Planet Ocean Brainstorm/My Buddy Says   (45–60 minutes)
    Session 2: Beach Explorations   (60 minutes)
    Session 3: Make a Mini-book   (45 minutes or more)

Activity 2: Sand on Stage
    Session 1: Partner Parade/Anticipatory Chart   (60 minutes)
    Session 2: Comparing Sands   (60 minutes)
    Session 3: Observing and Recording   (45–60 minutes)
    Session 4: The Experts Meet   (45 minutes or more)

Activity 3: The Sights that Sand has Seen
    Session 1: My Buddy Says/Story Chart   (60 minutes or more)
    Session 2: A Postcard Story   (45 minutes)
    Session 3: Postcard Game Show   (45 minutes)

Activity 4: Build a Sandy Beach*
    Session 1: Partner Parade/Classroom Field Trip   (60 minutes or more)*
    Session 2: Drawing Organisms and Habitats   (60 minutes or more)*
    Session 3: Making the Organisms   (60 minutes or more)*
    Session 4: Arranging the Displays   (60 minutes or more)
    Session 5: Class Presentations   (60 minutes or more)

Activity 5: Oil on the Beach
    Session 1: Partner Parade/Anticipatory Chart   (60 minutes)
    Session 2: Brief Oil Talk/Fouled Feathers   (60 minutes)
    Session 3: Oil on the Beach/My Buddy Says   (45–60 minutes)
    Session 4: Cleaning the Oil Spill/Debrief the Results   (45–60 minutes)

*You will be able to at least introduce these activities in the amount of time estimated here. However, students will need a considerable amount of extra time working individually and in small groups to "build" their three-dimensional organisms.

Getting Ready Tips (for the entire unit)

Materials lists ("What You Need") and preparation steps ("Getting Ready") for the five main activities in this guide are included in the instructions for each activity. In order to prepare for the *On Sandy Shores* unit, however, some materials and resources require advance planning and/or ordering at least several weeks before the unit. These are highlighted here so you'll be aware of them before beginning the unit.

Photos and Pictures of the Sandy Shore

You'll need to gather **photographs or pictures of sandy beaches and beach organisms** (plants and animals) from magazines and other sources. These pictures are used in Activity 1, when you'll need at least one for every student, and several times thereafter, with new pictures added. In Activity 2, for example, many of the pictures used in Activity 1 could be used again and you should also make sure you have some others that focus on the sand itself. In Activity 4: Build a Sandy Beach, additional sandy beach images, including slides and videos, are used for a simulated field trip. Pictures of oil-based products, such as plastics, or of oil being used in cars, trucks, refineries, etc. are needed in Activity 5: Oil on the Beach.

To build up a nice collection of photos and pictures, contact parents, ask each student to bring in several images, and gather some yourself. Assorted old magazines are likely to yield many useful pictures. You could mount the pictures on construction paper and/or laminate them for durability. The "Resources" section on page 117 includes some suggestions for obtaining slides and videos.

Beach Bucket Items

You will need to collect items for the beach buckets in Activity 1. If you live in a land-locked city, don't worry! There are many ways to obtain beach material without having to visit an ocean, lake, or river shoreline. Send notes home and to friends to save crab claws, clam shells, and dried fish skeletons from their seafood dinners. Seaweed can be collected from some beaches or it is available dried in many grocery and health food stores and in Asian markets. Sand can be purchased from hardware or building supply stores, or ordered from other sources (see the "Resources" section). Beach materials will also come in handy for the three displays the class creates in Activity 4 and for the beach model in Activity 5. Please see the

"What You Need" lists for Activities 1, 4, and 5 for more detail.

Resource Books

For all the activities, and most especially for Activity 4: Build a Sandy Beach, it will prove very helpful to have some nicely illustrated resource books available for your students to consult as they create their three-dimensional organisms and learn about interactions on the sandy shore. See the "Resources" section for some suggestions.

Sand Samples/Rock and Mineral Kits

For Activity 2: Sand on Stage, you will need to obtain rock and mineral kits. You may be able to borrow these from existing kits in your school, or from a nearby school, find them at a local hobby store, or order them from a scientific supply house (see the "Resources" section).

You will also need to acquire a diverse collection of sand samples. As much as several months before conducting this activity, alert students, parents, and friends that the class will be studying sand, and they should be on the lookout wherever they travel for samples of sand. On trips to the coast, lakes, rivers, deserts, or even playgrounds, have students collect small bags of sand. Does anyone have a friend in another state or country who can send an exotic sample? Discuss each sample as it arrives. Be sure to label each sample with information on where and when it was collected, and who collected it. Alternatively, the "Resources" section includes information on purchasing sand kits.

Sand Table

You may want to encourage younger students to "get a feel for sand." Set up a sand table or tub for free exploration, and encourage students to explore it individually or in small groups when they have free time. You might put out water, funnels, sieves, spoons, or cups. Have them look at the sand closely, run it through their fingers, make sand sculptures, or look for evidence of life. Put out drawing paper and pens for students to spontaneously write descriptions or illustrate sand-related images. Every day or so, add a new item: a shell, feather, rock, or piece of litter. This would make a nice pre-teaching exploration station before presenting the activities in this guide.

Activity 1: Beach Bucket Scavenger Hunt

Overview

A sandy shore reveals evidence of nearly everything that has been washed onto it from the land or the adjacent ocean. Rocks and minerals are carried from tall and distant mountains to beaches through streams and rivers. Waves and wind push sediment and "beach drift" from the ocean onto beaches around the world. Marine debris (garbage that ends up in the ocean or at the seashore) is carried from land by the millions of visitors to the world's beaches and dumped from the world's fleet of boats and ships. As waves crash against the shoreline, all these objects are ground into sediments—rough edges are progressively smoothed and rounded into sand grains.

Look closely at sand and you might see pieces of rocks and minerals that have broken free from the rocky seashore, cliffs, ocean floor and even from the distant mountains. There might be shells or shell fragments from animals that once lived on nearby reefs, bones from animals living in the ocean and on land, algae, coral fragments, glass, driftwood, plastics, feathers, and much more.

In this activity, students are introduced to the vastness of our planet's ocean and to the characteristics of one type of shoreline we call a beach. In Session 1, two activity structures, Planet Ocean Brainstorm and My Buddy Says, guide students "**Into** the Activities" by sharing what they already know, value, and enjoy about the sea and beaches.

In Session 2, students go "**Through** the Activities" as they work in small cooperative groups to explore a simulated sandy beach in a plastic tub that is littered with beach drift and debris. Through a sorting activity, they discover that biotic objects found on the sandy beach can be grouped into those that represent: evidence of plant life, evidence of animal life, and evidence of humans. They discover the differences between once-living (biotic) and never-living (abiotic) objects. Also introduced in this activity is the concept that sand is made up of tiny bits of everything that is found on the beach. In Session 3, students go "**Beyond** the Activities" by making mini-books about visiting a beach.

"Beach drift" is anything that washes up on the beach, whether it came from living or non-living materials. Later in the unit, your students learn about "beach wrack" in great detail. At that time you may want to clarify the distinction between beach drift and beach wrack for them. Beach drift generally refers to the washed up items, not to living organisms. Beach wrack is the line of kelp, other seaweeds, or sea grasses that often forms across an entire beach at high tide. It includes other organisms, shells, beach drift, and debris. Many organisms—such as snails, crabs, and limpets—that live on the kelp stipes and fronds are carried into the beach wrack along with the kelp. Worms, flies, and birds are attracted as the kelp begins to decay. Most of the animals of the beach wrack are hidden underneath the seaweed to avoid bird predators and the hot sun. The beach wrack is a temporary ecosystem on the sandy shore.

For more information about the formation of sand, see "Behind the Scenes," page 109, as well as Activities 2 and 3.

The Center for Marine Conservation reports that the following twelve types of trash were found most often in the United States during a 1994 clean up: cigarette butts; plastic pieces; foamed plastic pieces; plastic food bags/wrappers; paper pieces; glass pieces; plastic caps/lids; glass beverage bottles; metal beverage cans; plastic straws; plastic beverage bottles; and metal bottle caps.

There is a saying, "Take only pictures and leave only footprints." This is a wise practice for learning about and enjoying the outdoors and leaving it unspoiled for those who come later. However, many of our children do not have the opportunity to visit beaches and as teachers we can bring the ocean and an environmental ethic to them. When collecting for the classroom, take only a small amount of beach drift, the dead animals and plants washed up on the shore. On the other hand, collect as much human litter and debris as you can carry. It is important that we tell our students why we collected our beach drift [many, many students will have the opportunity to learn from it], that we only collected drift and debris (no living organisms), and when we are done with it we will return the drift to the beach where we found it and dispose of the litter in the trash. Nothing may be taken or collected from a reserve, preserve, or National Seashore, not even beach drift or sand. We suggest that you do not purchase shells and other dead animals such as sea stars or sea horses because most are collected alive and reefs may have been dynamited to find them.

Posters, drawings, photos, and pictures are especially helpful for students who are English language learners.

What You Need

For the class:
- ❏ 1 classroom globe
- ❏ 4–6 sheets of chart paper (approximately 27" x 34")
- ❏ markers (4–5 colors, wide tip)
- ❏ masking tape
- ❏ (*optional*) miscellaneous posters or calendar pictures of beach scenes and/or beach animals

For each group of 4–6 students:
- ❏ 1 plastic tub or dishpan, 12" x 9" x 4"
- ❏ enough beach sand to fill each tub 2" deep
- ❏ fine-point markers or crayons
- ❏ 4–6 sheets of 11" x 17" or 8 1/2" x 11" construction paper (and copy of template on page 25 for simple version of mini-book)
- ❏ 4–6 photos, pictures, or drawings of beach organisms or sandy shores with and without marine debris
- ❏ pieces of beach drift and marine debris—**at least two from each of the following groups:**

___ evidence of plants: driftwood, twigs, leaves, seaweed, seaweed holdfasts attached to rocks

___ evidence of animals: shells; feathers; bones; dried fish parts; shark, skate, or ray egg cases (often called "mermaids' purses"); crab parts; tracks in the sand

___ evidence of humans: cans, bottles, candy wrappers, six pack rings, plastic straws, bottle caps, juice boxes, fishing line, balloons, plastic toys, coins, chicken bones

___ non-living material: rocks, "beach glass" (broken glass worn smooth), plastic, metal

Getting Ready

1. Several weeks before beginning this unit, plan your strategy for gathering a large number (at least one for every student in your class) of photographs, pictures, or drawings of sandy beaches and beach organisms (plants and animals). These pictures are used early on in this first activity and again later in the unit. For the second activity, some of these pictures should focus on the sand itself. You can contact parents, ask students to bring several photos or illustrations in, and gather some yourself.

2. Collect items for the beach buckets. If you don't live near a beach, don't worry! See the "Getting Ready Tips" on page 10 for ideas.

3. Assemble the beach buckets by adding two inches of sand to the bottom of each plastic tub, and randomly placing marine debris and beach drift items on top of or in the sand.

4. Have chart paper, markers, and masking tape at the front of the room. Duplicate mini-book template as needed.

5. Divide one piece of chart paper into three columns, each one headed by simple drawings of a plant, an animal, or a human. On another piece of chart paper, draw a large question mark as heading.

6. *(Optional)* Hang the posters or calendar pictures of beach scenes and/or beach animals.

7. Write out each of the Key Concepts for this activity in large, bold letters on separate sheets of chart paper and set aside.

- **Objects found on the sandy beach can be grouped into: evidence of plant life, evidence of animal life, evidence of humans, and non-living material.**

- **Sand is made up of tiny bits of everything that is found on the beach.**

Later in the unit, in Activity 4: Build a Sandy Beach, additional sandy beach images, including slides and videos, are used for a simulated classroom field trip, so be on the lookout for slides and videos. See "Resources" for suggestions.

Some teachers use sentence strips to write out and display the key concepts horizontally. You could also do this by cutting butcher or chart paper in half lengthwise and using these as sentence strips.

Activity 1   15

Session 1: Planet Ocean Brainstorm

The ocean is so vast that it is difficult to study or understand all of its parts at once. Many students will have some prior knowledge of and experience with the sandy shore. Beginning with something familiar, such as a beach, will help students create a context within which they can later place new ideas and concepts about the ocean. This process of identifying prior knowledge and beginning from a point of strength and confidence is especially important for English language learners. It will speed their acquisition of English vocabulary and grammar, as well as their grasp of science concepts.

1. Ask students to brainstorm all the ways that people use and depend on the ocean. Use a globe to show a "traditional" map view of the world—that is, with the continents in full view with the Americas in the center. Now turn the globe to show the "Pacific Ocean view"— half of the world with almost no land showing. What does this view tell about the world? [Most of the earth is covered by oceans.] Depending on the level of your students, introduce and discuss the following ideas:

- Most of our planet is covered by ocean.
- People get food and water from the ocean.
- Over half of our oxygen comes from plants in the ocean.
- The ocean plays a major role in moderating our climate. Without an ocean the surface of our planet would burn up or melt during the day and freeze at night.

2. Tell students that in the next few weeks they will be learning more about the ocean and in particular, about the place where the water meets the land. Ask if anyone knows what this place is called? [beach, shore, shoreline]

My Buddy Says

This teaching strategy or activity structure helps students talk about their related prior knowledge. It emphasizes short conversations, cooperation, and good listening skills. It creates opportunities for students to use language in a non-threatening, highly relevant setting where the focus is on the meaning rather than the form of the language. In My Buddy Says, students are introduced to articulating their thoughts and to active listening by responding to questions and prompts about the beach.

1. Quickly introduce the topic of a beach to your class by asking, "Has anyone been to a beach?" "What kinds of things are at a beach?" Remind students that a beach could be next to a river or creek as well as the ocean.

2. Tell them that the first thing they're going to do is an activity called My Buddy Says. They'll be learning more

Listening skills are critical for language development. Students learn to speak a new language by hearing it used correctly. By using a language naturally, even if they make lots of errors, students invite others to speak back to them, and that is when new language is acquired.

about beaches from each other. Discuss with students what it means to really listen to a classmate. How does active listening look? [you look directly at the person, nod your head, you don't interrupt]

3. Form student buddy pairs at their seats and assign each student to be either #1 or #2. Pass out a picture of a beach or a beach organism to each student. Have the students look at the pictures closely. The pictures will help them think about beaches and respond to a few questions with their partner.

4. Ask a question from the list below, and give Buddy #1 30–60 seconds to talk about their response to Buddy #2 (who listens only).

5. Ask several Buddy #2's what their Buddy #1 said about the question. They can answer, "My Buddy, DeMarco, says..." Buddy #1 may correct misstatements by the reporting buddy, but cannot add new information. As they share, list their responses in words or pictures on the board.

6. Switch roles and pose a question for Buddy #2 to answer. If time allows, repeat the process so that each buddy gets to respond to at least two questions. Remind the students that only one person in each pair is talking at a time—the other person is actively listening.

If you have more than one language spoken in your room, ask students the words for "water," "ocean," "beach," or "shore" in other languages. What other related words do students know in their native language? Write the words down and have everyone practice repeating them. Try to use these words as you teach the rest of the unit. You will not only be showing respect for your students' languages, you will also be reminding students that they each have a wealth of knowledge, although it may not all be in the language of English.

My Buddy Says prompts and questions:

- Close your eyes and imagine you are sitting on a beach. Look down the beach. Now open your eyes and describe what the beach looked like.

- Where are some beaches you have visited?

- What are some things you like best about beaches?

- If you walked along a sandy beach looking very carefully, what types of things do you think you might find?

7. Spend some time discussing this last question with your students. You may want to write down their responses on chart paper (or the chalkboard), using words and simple drawings. You may also organize the responses into categories, such as: evidence of plants, evidence of animals, evidence of people, and non-living things.

For younger students, you may want to define evidence or explain it in other words. You could talk about "clues" that we can observe because they've been left behind on the beach. These clues can give us information about the plants, animals, people, and things that live on or visit the sandy beach.

8. Ask the students to think about two or three of the following questions and then lead a class discussion.

- When you were speaking, how did you know if your buddy was listening?

- Did you learn anything new?

- What did it feel like to talk while your buddy only listened?

- What did it feel like to listen without answering back?

- What helped you to remember what your buddy said? What could help you remember more?

- Did anyone notice that the teacher hasn't taught anything yet? You've been teaching each other!

9. Tell students that this activity will help them be better listeners and teammates when they work together on the next activity about beaches. Collect the pictures or photos of beaches and beach organisms for use later in the unit.

One teacher told us, "My students really struggled with My Buddy Says. It showed me how much they need to work on listening skills." Another said, "Developing listening skills is the most valuable part of all of these activities. I'll use this over and over again." Like any skills, students will listen better and become more respectful of their buddies with practice. We recommend that you try structures like this several times to give your students a fair chance to succeed.

Session 2: Beach Explorations

Explore-a-Beach

1. Tell students that now they will have the chance to explore a "beach" right in their own classroom! Show them the beach buckets you have prepared and ask the students to handle the items carefully.

2. Divide the class into groups of four to six students. Tell them they can feel the sand and pick up pieces of drift and debris to look at more closely. They should keep all the sand in their tub so the classroom will stay clean! Provide each group with a beach bucket and let them begin their observations.

3. Circulate among the groups. Ask focusing questions, such as: "What colors do you see?" "What do the things on the beach feel like?" [fuzzy, rough, prickly, soft, etc.] "What are some of the shapes of objects on the beach?"

"Where do you think the items came from?" "What evidence is there of living things?"

Sorting and Classifying

1. After they've made some observations, encourage them to sort or group the items into categories, based on any observable characteristic of their choice.

2. Give groups time to share and describe the categories they devised.

3. Explain that often when we go to a sandy shore, we may not see many living plants and animals at first, but if we look closely, we will always find plenty of **evidence** of living things.

4. Next, have students re-sort the items into the following four groups: evidence of plant life, evidence of animal life, evidence of humans, unknown items (or items about which they can't agree).

5. Display the piece of chart paper with three columns headed by simple drawings. Display the second piece of chart paper headed by a large question mark to record unknown items.

6. Have the groups share again. On the chart paper, record, with simple labeled drawings, the items groups share. Explain that everything in the first two categories is evidence of life (or biotic material). Evidence of humans could be biotic (chicken bones or paper) or abiotic (plastic, aluminum). Can anyone identify the unknown items?

7. (*Optional*) Point out any large pictures or posters you may have in the classroom that show examples of the whole, live animals and plants from which the biotic material came.

8. Ask students if there are things left in their beach buckets that were never alive. These things, such as rocks and most of the sand, are called non-living or **abiotic** materials. Ask if there are items that could go in more than one category. In general, things found at the beach are called "beach drift." More specifically things left by humans are referred to as "marine debris."

9. Ask the students what might eventually happen to all of this beach drift and marine debris if it were left on a real beach? If it doesn't come up in the discussion, explain that

*Recording student ideas on chart paper provides a permanent "group memory" for which the whole class is responsible. If misconceptions arise, they should also be recorded. If they are challenged by another student, add a question mark in another color next to the idea. Make sure that sometime during the unit, all misconceptions are "discovered" and corrected, preferably by students. Go back to your group memory and physically replace the misconceptions with the new information. **No individuals need be "wrong." The group's collective knowledge simply changes as it grows.***

Younger students will need adult help with the 11" x 17" mini-book. The 8 1/2" x 11" mini-book is much simpler to make.

many of the items found at the beach will be pounded by wind, waves, tides, and each other, and eventually will be ground into sand. Sand can be either biotic or abiotic, and is usually a combination of both.

10. In closing the activity, hold up the Key Concepts for this activity one at a time, and have one or more students read them aloud. Briefly discuss how these statements review the important ideas from today's activities. Post the concepts on the wall near your chart-paper record of evidence of plants, animals, and humans for students to revisit during the rest of the unit.

- **Objects found on the sandy beach can be grouped into: evidence of plant life, evidence of animal life, evidence of humans, and non-living material.**

- **Sand is made up of tiny bits of everything that is found on the beach.**

Session 3: Make a Mini-book

A mini-book is an activity structure designed to help students organize and reconstruct new information and to guide their creativity. This activity also provides opportunities for students to use written language in meaningful ways and for the teacher to assess the writing skills and science knowledge of individual students.

1. Tell students that they get to become authors of a book about visiting a beach by making a mini-book with pictures and words. First they need to make the blank book. Pass out fine-point markers or crayons and either 11" x 17" paper or 8 1/2" x 11" paper and lead them through the directions on the appropriate Mini-book instruction sheet. (Please see pages 22 and 24.) There are instructions for simple and more complex versions, depending on your preference and your students' abilities.

2. Encourage students to write their book about what they have learned by creating text and illustrations on alternate pages. They can title their book, "My Beach Book." Chapter titles for each two-page spread can be as follows: Chapter 1: Plants and Animals; Chapter 2: People at the Beach; Chapter 3: The Best Thing About Beaches.

3. Provide students with time to write and draw pictures that are appropriate for each chapter.

4. When completed, give the students time to share their mini-books informally with their cooperative group.

5. After they've completed their mini-books, ask the students to think about two or three of the following questions and then hold a class discussion:

- How did you decide what to include in your book?
- Was there anything special you did to help you remember what you learned in this activity?
- Are you proud of your book? Could you improve it?
- Do you think this book will help you remember what you learned?
- Does your book reflect the most important things you learned?

Going Further

1. Take a field trip to the beach (at a local seashore, stream, river, pond, or lake) and conduct a clean-up project. Have students explore the beach and sort what they find into the same categories used in this activity. Bring enough plastic garbage bags so every pair of students can have one. Divide the pairs into three collection groups: 1) unbroken glass and cans; 2) plastic; 3) paper and other miscellaneous trash. Students should wear gloves and be warned of picking up sharp or toxic items. If you're on an ocean beach, you could have all pairs line up from the water's edge to the dune area and sweep a half-mile section of beach. Remind students that they should collect only evidence of humans. Take all the debris they have collected and organize it into categories. Weigh or measure the volume of each. Discuss the differences between biodegradable and non-biodegradable, and recyclable and non-recyclable objects. Point out any collected items that are natural, rather than human-made, and ask students to return them so your impact on the ecosystem is minimized.

2. As appropriate, research nearby beach and shoreline conservation projects, and seek out ways your class can become involved.

Mini-books should be written in whatever language students are most comfortable using, and the focus should be on content and creativity, not grammar and spelling.

Mini-books can be introduced and begun as a whole group activity and then completed during subsequent work sessions or whenever students have extra time. Consider letting students finish during your normal writing time. Mini-books are ideal assessment tools. Collect them, develop an evaluation or scoring system, and include them in student portfolios.

The MARE Teacher's Guide to Marine Science Field Trips: Central California describes dozens of field trip sites and gives you invaluable guidelines on organizing and carrying out a customized field trip experience. Contact MARE at (510) 642-5008.

For more information about the official Adopt-A-Beach program in California, contact the California Coastal Commission (415) 904-5206 or the Center for Marine Conservation (415) 391-6204. Similar programs may be in place in other regions.

Mini-book *(11" x 17")*

1. Fold the sheet in half crosswise.

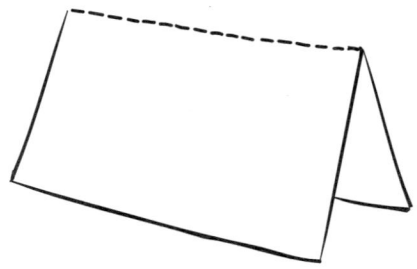

2. Fold up ends separately to form a "W" shape.

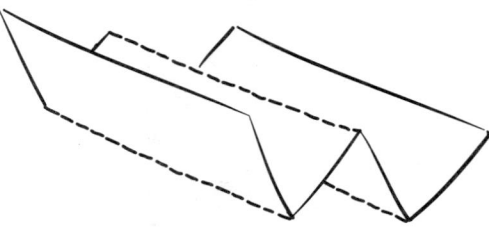

3. Fold the paper in half again to form a small rectangle. Then unfold this last fold, and fold it again back the opposite way, making good, hard creases on each side.

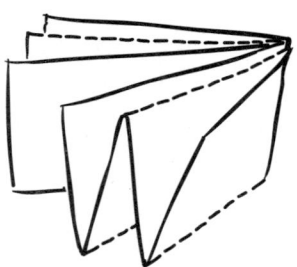

4. Unfold back to step #1, where the sheet is only folded in half.

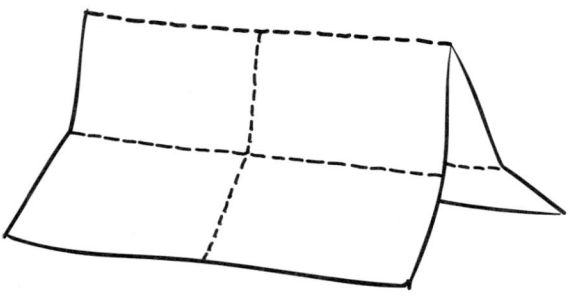

5. Face the folded edge closest to you and cut along the middle fold through both sides to the center as seen in the diagram.

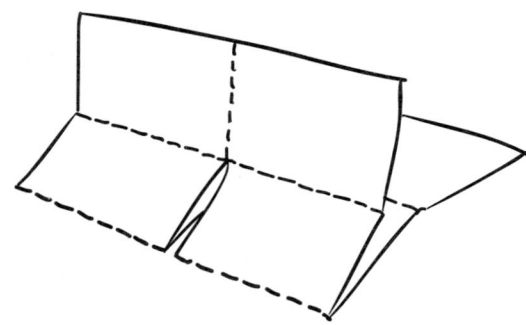

6. Unfold the sheet entirely.

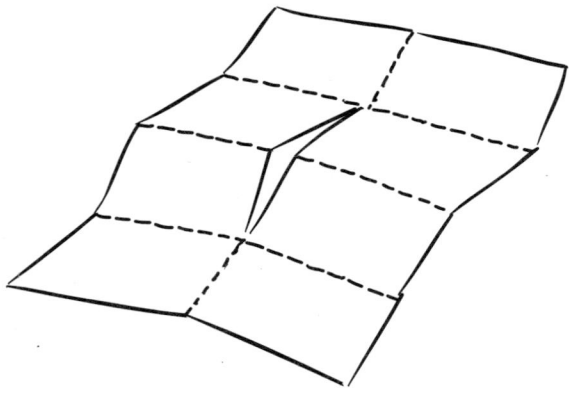

7. Refold the sheet in half, this time lengthwise.

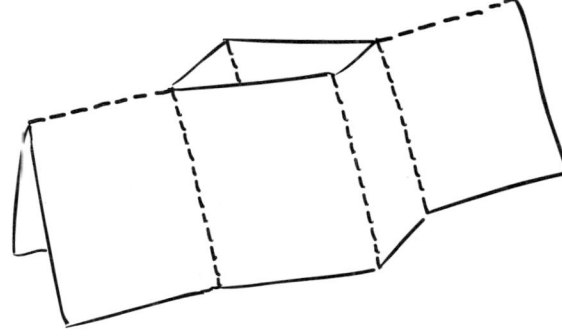

8. Grab the two outside panels and push inward. The part you cut with the scissors should open up and form a diamond.

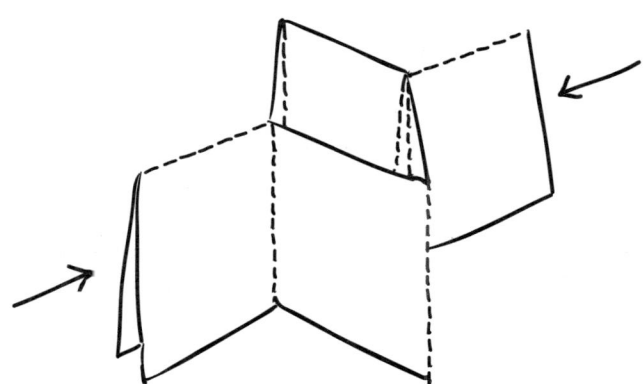
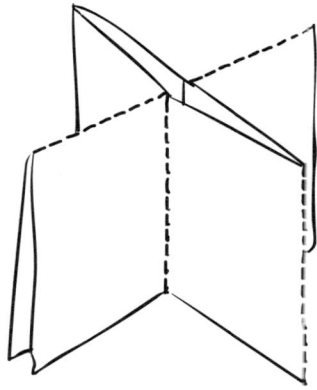

9. Finally, fold all the pages together to form a small book. Make good, hard creases on all sides.

Mini-book (8 ½" x 11")

Note: A simple template for folding and cutting this mini-book is on the next page. On the template, dotted lines show where to cut the paper and other lines show where to fold.

Fold an 8 ½" x 11" piece of plain paper in half lengthwise and then into thirds. Open it up so it is only folded in half lengthwise—with the fold on top. On the top half only, use scissors to cut along the two small folds, to form three flaps that open vertically. Then fold the right third to the center, and the left third on top of that. With the book folded shut and only the "cover" showing, have students write the title of their mini-book on the cover and illustrate it. Then have them open the cover (from right to left) and write their name as the author. Then turn the title page (from left to right) and label each of the three chapters or sections. As they flip up each of the three chapters they can use one panel inside to draw a picture and the other to write about what they've learned.

1. Fold in half lengthwise.

2. Then fold into thirds.

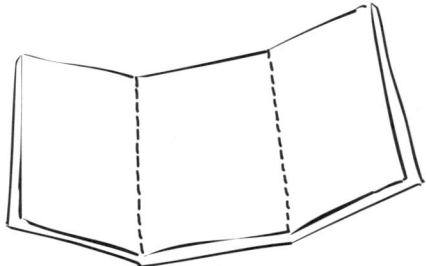

3. Cut only the top half into three sections.

4. It will now look like this.

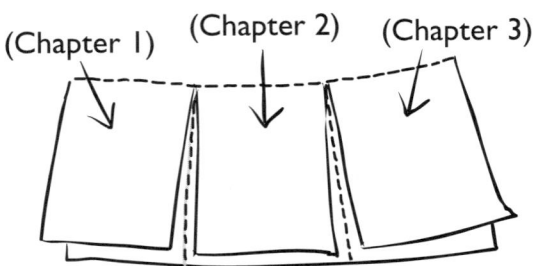

5. Fold the right third to the center and the left third on top of that.

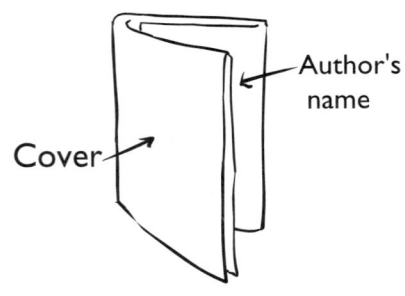

Mini-book (8 ½" x 11") *Template*

Activity 2: Sand on Stage

Overview

Nearly all solid materials in the world, both living and non-living, will eventually be eroded into sand. Mountains, rocks, minerals, shells, corals, bones, metals, and glass are all worn down over time by wind, waves, rivers, earthquakes, and other forces into smaller and smaller particles. Thousands or millions of years may pass as a rocky outcropping on a mountain top is transformed into a grain of sand on a sandy beach.

In this activity, small groups of students use hand lenses (or low-powered microscopes, if available) to compare the color, size, and shape of several sand samples and to guess about their origins. Students discover that sand grains can be made of animals, plants, rocks, or minerals. Sand grains come in many different shapes, sizes, and colors. These differences can be clues about where the sand came from and how it got to the beach.

In Session 1, Partner Parade, students get "**Into** the Activities" by working with partners to discuss and write about sand. They record their knowledge and any questions they may have on their own charts, then contribute their ideas for a class "Anticipatory Chart." In Sessions 2, 3, and 4, students go "**Through** the Activities." They compare different types of sand, observe sand with hand lenses or microscopes, and record their findings on a student sheet. Then they complete the Expert Group student sheet and draw a picture of the beach where the sand they examined might have been found. A number of "Going Further" activities are suggested for going "**Beyond** the Activities."

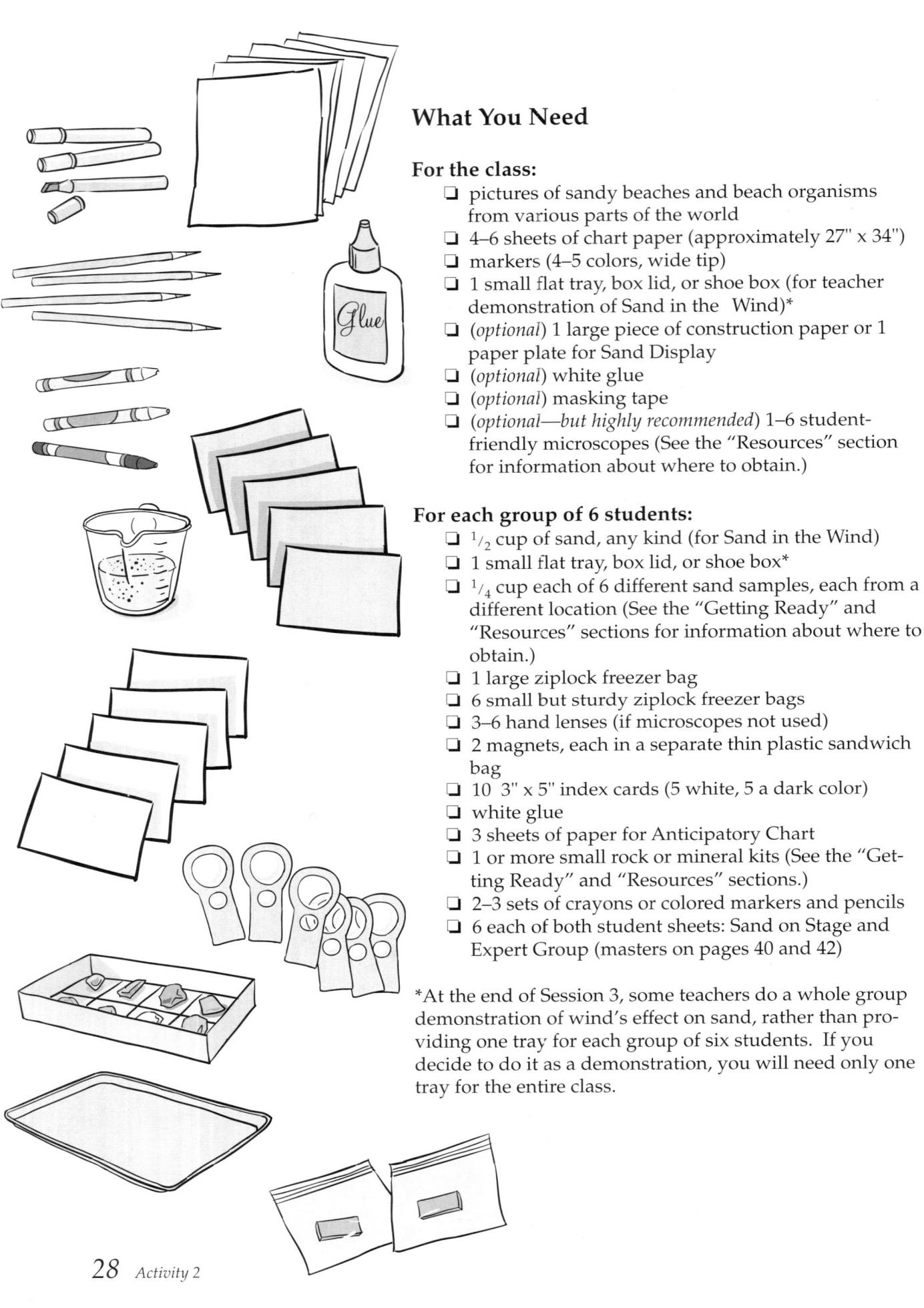

What You Need

For the class:
- pictures of sandy beaches and beach organisms from various parts of the world
- 4–6 sheets of chart paper (approximately 27" x 34")
- markers (4–5 colors, wide tip)
- 1 small flat tray, box lid, or shoe box (for teacher demonstration of Sand in the Wind)*
- (*optional*) 1 large piece of construction paper or 1 paper plate for Sand Display
- (*optional*) white glue
- (*optional*) masking tape
- (*optional—but highly recommended*) 1–6 student-friendly microscopes (See the "Resources" section for information about where to obtain.)

For each group of 6 students:
- $1/2$ cup of sand, any kind (for Sand in the Wind)
- 1 small flat tray, box lid, or shoe box*
- $1/4$ cup each of 6 different sand samples, each from a different location (See the "Getting Ready" and "Resources" sections for information about where to obtain.)
- 1 large ziplock freezer bag
- 6 small but sturdy ziplock freezer bags
- 3–6 hand lenses (if microscopes not used)
- 2 magnets, each in a separate thin plastic sandwich bag
- 10 3" x 5" index cards (5 white, 5 a dark color)
- white glue
- 3 sheets of paper for Anticipatory Chart
- 1 or more small rock or mineral kits (See the "Getting Ready" and "Resources" sections.)
- 2–3 sets of crayons or colored markers and pencils
- 6 each of both student sheets: Sand on Stage and Expert Group (masters on pages 40 and 42)

*At the end of Session 3, some teachers do a whole group demonstration of wind's effect on sand, rather than providing one tray for each group of six students. If you decide to do it as a demonstration, you will need only one tray for the entire class.

28 Activity 2

Getting Ready

1. Obtain rock and mineral kits: Track down existing kits in your school or order from a scientific supply house (see the "Resources" section).

2. Acquire sand. As much as several months before conducting this activity, alert students, parents, and friends that the class will be studying sand. Ask them to be on the lookout wherever they travel for samples of sand. On trips to the coast, lakes, rivers, deserts, or even playgrounds, have them collect small bags of sand. Does anyone have a friend in another state or country that can send an exotic sample? You can also put a notice on the internet about collecting samples—teachers in other locales may be interested in swapping samples with you—especially teachers who are also presenting *On Sandy Shores!* Discuss each sample as it arrives. Be sure to label each sample with: where and when it was collected, and who collected it. Alternatively, sand kits can be purchased from a number of sources (see the "Resources" section).

3. Organize sand samples. For each group of six students, fill six ziplock bags with a 1" layer (about $1/4$ cup) of sand. If possible, each small bag should have a different sand sample and all should be labeled with the location of the sand. Tightly seal each bag. Place the six samples into a large ziplock bag and seal. Each group should have the same six samples.

4. Decide if you will have all groups try blowing on the trays of sand to simulate wind, or if this will be done as a teacher demonstration with several student volunteers. If all groups will simulate the wind, place $1/2$ cup of sand on tray, box lid, or shoe box for each group. If this will be a teacher demonstration, then prepare one tray.

5. (*Optional*) Make a Sand Display by gluing a small amount of sand from each sample to a paper plate or construction paper. Label each sample with its location.

6. Obtain hand lenses or 1–6 low magnification microscopes (optional). Using microscopes will make this activity much more dramatic and fun. Grains of sand become huge boulders or easily discernible chunks of shells. Beautiful colors and the details of shapes that would otherwise be lost, are easy to see. See "Resources" for ideas on how to obtain microscopes. If microscopes are not available, hand lenses are adequate—just make sure they are not too scratched up.

If you plan to collect sand for your classroom samples, remember that only a very small amount is needed. A sandwich bag filled with sand is more than enough for years of use in your classroom. Also keep in mind that nothing, not even sand, is allowed to be collected or taken from reserves, preserves, and some National Seashores.

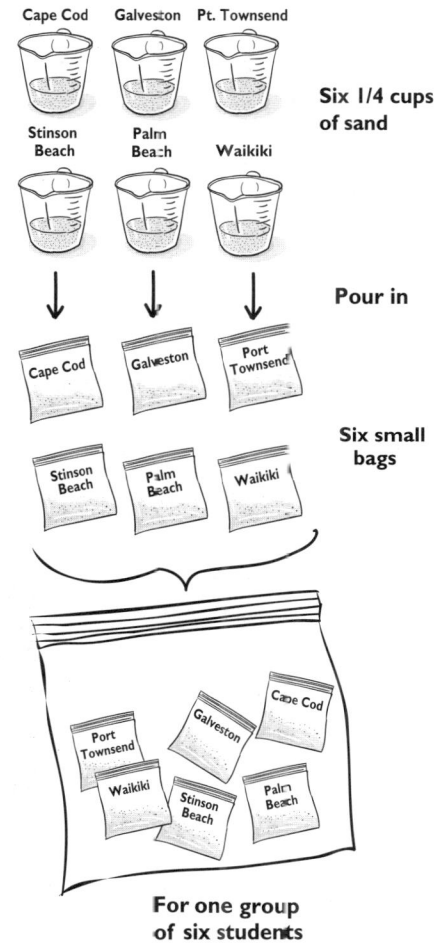

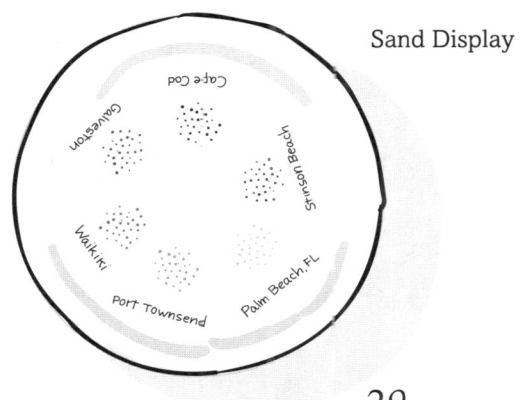

Sand Display

7. Duplicate the Sand on Stage and Expert Group student sheets for each student (masters on pages 40 and 42).

8. Start the class Anticipatory Chart. Draw a line down the middle of the chart paper to divide it in half lengthwise. At the top of one column write "What we already know about sand." At the top of the other column, write "What we want to find out about sand."

9. *(Optional)* For Partner Parade, place two strips of masking tape on the floor parallel to each other and about an arms length apart. Make each strip long enough to accommodate half the class standing side by side on the tape.

10. Write out the Key Concepts for this activity in large, bold letters on separate sheets of chart paper and set aside.

- **Sand grains can be made of animals, plants, rocks, or minerals.**

- **Sand grains come in many different shapes, sizes, and colors.**

- **Differences between sand grains can be clues about where the sand came from and how it got to the beach.**

If you're presenting these activities to younger students and/or like to have free exploration stations set up in your classroom, you may want to consider setting up a sand exploration station (as described in #1 in "Going Further" on page 38) before you present the activities.

Session 1: Partner Parade

This activity structure helps students to talk and write about their related prior knowledge. It emphasizes short discussions with different partners, cooperation, and social skills development. It creates opportunities for students to use language in a non-threatening, but highly relevant setting. In Partner Parade, students build on their active listening skills by learning how to hold short interesting discussions about sand and beaches with a variety of different partners.

1. Have students recall the activity, My Buddy Says. Tell them that Partner Parade is a similar activity in which they will get a chance to talk with different classmates. Just as in My Buddy Says, they need to cooperate, follow directions, and talk quietly with each of their partners.

2. Ask the students to recall what a good listener should do [you don't interrupt, you look directly at the person] In Partner Parade, both partners will be able to discuss each question or topic. This is called having a conversation or

discussion. To have a good discussion, each partner should be a good listener and speak clearly when it's her or his turn.

3. Pass out a picture of sand or a beach to each student. Remind the students to look at the pictures closely. The pictures will help them to think about sand and to have a better discussion with their partner. Have students stand shoulder to shoulder to form two parallel lines, so that each person is facing a partner. If you have placed strips of tape on the floor have students line up along the tape. Students standing side by side should be at least six inches apart.

4. Tell the students that you will be asking a question or giving them an idea to talk about with their partner who is facing them. They will have about a minute to talk. If they can't think of anything to say, they can discuss their pictures.

5. Pose the first question from the following list for the students to discuss:
- When was the last time you visited a sandy beach? Where was it?

- What do you think of when you hear the word "sand?"

- Describe all the different places you might find sand.

- What color is sand?

- Where do you think sand comes from? What is it made of?

- How do you think sand gets to the beach?

6. Walk along the two lines to help shy or resistant partners get started. When you call time, have a few students report something that their partner told them.

7. Before the next question, tell the students that the "parade" needs to move along. Have one of the lines move one position to the left so that everyone is facing a new person; the person at the end of that line walks around to the beginning of the line. Everyone now can greet their new partner.

8. Some students may be unhappy with the new arrangement, but tell them that this activity is to help them have

At the end of the Partner Parade, you have the opportunity to divide students up into new heterogeneous groups of two, four, or six based on where they are in line. Also, if students haven't finished talking when you call time, they can tell their partner, "Unfinished Business." At the end of the activity, you can give everyone an extra minute to go back to any previous partner and "finish their business."

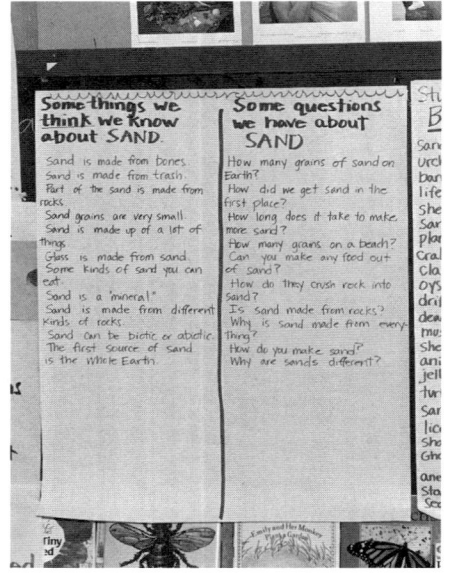

Having students record their ideas and questions on their own charts provides valuable practice organizing their thoughts in writing. It also provides the teacher with an informal pre/post survey that can become part of student portfolios. If this type of recording is not appropriate for some of your students, then verbal discussions, followed by whole group sharing, with the teacher recording on the class chart, is a fine alternative.

conversations with different people, even people they don't know very well. In a classroom, just as in a workplace, people need to be able to work together successfully with everyone, not just with a few friends. Have each student greet their new partner, then ask the next question.

9. Repeat steps 6 and 7 until you have asked all the questions.

10. At the end of the activity, ask the students to sit down with their final partner and think about some of the following questions. Then lead a brief class discussion.
- Did it seem like the whole class was cooperating?
- Did you remember to listen well to each of your partners?
- What did you learn that was new?
- Which questions were the easiest and hardest to answer?
- Did you feel comfortable doing this activity? Why?

Anticipatory Chart on Sand

Making an Anticipatory Chart is another activity structure designed to help students recall information from past experiences and to assist them in clarifying what they want to learn from the activities that follow. In the Anticipatory Chart activity, students work together in pairs and have opportunities to share their ideas with the larger group.

1. Have students continue to work with their final Partner Parade partner. Show them the beginnings of the class Anticipatory Chart. Distribute paper to each pair of students and have them create their own chart.

2. If you have them, you may want to pass out a few more pictures of different beaches to each pair to give them ideas. Ask students to discuss the two questions about sand (what we know/what we want to find out) and write notes on their own chart. If there's time, each pair can share responses with another pair and discuss again.

3. When the class is ready, call them back together to share some of their best ideas and questions with the whole group. Record the group's ideas on the class Anticipatory Chart. If the same idea comes up more than once, put a

star next to it each time it is mentioned. Display the chart and refer back to it throughout the activity. As questions are answered, check them off and record the answers on another chart. Collect the pictures of sand, beaches, and beach organisms.

Session 2: Comparing Sands

Observing Samples

1. Divide students into groups of six. Tell the groups they will now have the opportunity to observe different types of sand from many different places.

2. Give each group the large bag containing six small bags of sand. Have each of the six students take out one small bag of sand. Tell them that for now they should not open the bag; they should make their observations by looking or feeling through the bag. They should do this **gently**, being careful not to puncture the bag! Ask, "How big are the sand grains?" "Can you tell what they're made of?" "What colors do you see?" "What do the sand grains look like?"

3. Next, have each group compare their six samples. How are they similar? How are they different?

4. Bring the whole class back together for a short discussion. What did they discover about their sand? How were the samples the same? different?

5. Ask students to imagine a clam living burrowed in the sand on a beach. How might its shell end up as sand? [It dies and waves break it up into little pieces; it gets smaller and smaller as it is jumbled in the waves with other pieces of rocks, shells, and sand.] How might a rock on a mountain top become sand? [It breaks off from the mountain top and rivers carry it to the ocean.] How about coral on a coral reef? [Parrot fish eat it and crunch it into small bits or waves gradually wear it away after the coral dies and currents bring it to shore.] Why then might there be so many different colors of sand? [Different colors indicate that the sands are made of different things such as rocks, shells, bones, coral, glass.]

Use the responses to the Partner Parade and the Anticipatory Chart to assess your students' prior knowledge. If students seem generally familiar with the topics of what sand is made of, how it is formed, and how it travels to sandy shores, you can move rather quickly through the following activities and allow students to draw further conclusions and inferences. If they do not seem to have much prior knowledge of those topics, you may have to proceed more slowly and provide more directed information.

As students respond to the question about how a rock on a mountain might become sand, you may want to introduce the word and concept of **erosion.** *Or you could describe the process without introducing the word itself. Erosion is defined, and featured as a Key Concept in Activity 3: The Sights that Sand has Seen.*

6. (*Optional*) Show students your Sand Display, and ask them to look at how different some types of sand can look from others. Ask students to look for sand wherever they go to add to the display.

Making Sand Slides

1. Now students get to make a "sand slide" from their sample. Pass out index cards and glue to each group. If their sand sample is light colored, they take a dark index card; if their sand sample is dark, they take a light colored card.

2. Have students label their card with where their sand came from and their own name.

3. Demonstrate how to make a sand slide:

   a. Place a very small dab of white glue near an edge of the card and smear it in a small circle (size of a nickel) using a pinkie finger.

   b. Reach into the sand sample bag and take out a pinch of sand. Sprinkle the sand over the glue and tap any loose sand back into the bag.

4. Have students make their own sand slide. Collect the slides or have students keep them for the next session where they will make detailed observations of their sand grains. Collect the sample bags of sand.

Making a Sand Slide

3" x 5" card
(light colored card for dark sand)

3" x 5" card
(dark colored card for light sand)

Session 3: Observing and Recording

1. Regroup the students into their Comparing Sands groups of six. Give each student a Sand on Stage student sheet and their sand slide. Give each group the large bag containing the six small bags of sand. Ask each student to get the same small bag of sand they used to make their sand slide. Have available pencils, crayons/markers, magnets in bags, hand lenses (or microscopes), and rock/mineral kits for each group. Older students will be able to go through the activities in their cooperative group at their own speed after you provide simple directions. With younger students, you may need to go through the student sheet task by task with the whole class, guiding each observation. The following is one way you might guide a class of second graders through the Sand on Stage observation and recording activity (directions and questions from the student sheet are in italics):

#1—Look closely at your sand with a magnifier. List or use crayons to show all the different colors you see. Students who have difficulty writing should be encouraged to find crayon colors that match the sand colors.

#2—Draw a picture of some of your sand grains. Draw them BIG! Encourage students to draw the sand grains about the size of a quarter. They could use the grains drawn in #3 as models.

#3—Circle the pictures that have shapes like your sand. This task takes some extra concentration, so tell students to help their fellow teammates. Have students look again at their slide through a hand lens (or a microscope). This time look specifically at the shape of individual grains. Does their sand have rounded edges or angular edges? Why are some grains smooth while others have sharp (angular) edges? [Very round grains have been worn smooth for hundreds or thousands of years, while angular grains may have broken off a rock or shell quite recently.]

#4—Gently rub a magnet on the outside of your bag of sand. Are any of the grains in your sand attracted to the magnet? If so, what color are the magnetic sand grains? Distribute the magnets in bags. Have students drag a magnet gently across the outside of their bag of sand. If any grains are attracted, this is evidence that the sand contains some magnetic minerals, such as iron or magnetite. They are usually black.

#5—Which of the following things can you find in your sand? Students especially enjoy guessing/inferring what their sand grains are made of.

#6—Look at the rock kit. Does your sand have pieces of rock that match some in the kit? List the kinds of rocks that may be in your sand. Give each group a rock and/or mineral kit and have students compare their sand grains to rocks in the kit.

#7—Which sand in your group is the lightest in color? Which is the darkest? Put them in order from lightest to darkest. Have students pass their sand slides around the circle of their group, looking at each, until they have their own slide back. They should especially notice the colors of the different sands. Ask, "What can you learn by observing the color of your sand?" [Colors give you clues about what your sand is made of—dark sands are often volcanic in origin; light sands can be made of animals like shells or corals, or of quartz from granite mountains.] Now, have

each group arrange all their samples in a line from lightest to darkest and record their answers.

#8—Compare your sand slide to the size chart below. Imagine that the black dots are grains of sands. Color the group of dots that are about the size of your sand grains. If your sand is not like any of these, use the empty circle to draw how yours looks. Are your grains all about the same size or many different sizes? This may be confusing for some students. The different groups of dots represent different size grains of sand. They are clustered in a circle similar to the students' cluster of sand on their sand slide.

For older students: Ask, "What might the size of the sand grains tell you about the kind of place your sand sample is from?" [If their grains are very small, they were probably from an area with slow moving water such as a protected bay beach or a pool in a slowly moving stream. Tiny particles can stay put only where the water is moving slowly and gently. Large waves (or fast water) pick up small grains and carry them away down the river or off the beach and out to the ocean. If their sand grains are mainly large, they were probably from a wave-tossed beach where the rough water carried all the smaller grains away. Only the larger grains remained because they were not picked up by the waves.]

#9—Which sand in your group has the biggest grains? Which has the smallest grains? Put them in order from smallest to biggest. Have students pass their slides around the group again, this time observing grain size. Next, have each group sequence their sand cards, this time from the smallest grains to the largest grains and record their answers.

For older students: Ask the class to imagine they are a very tiny sand grain, about the size of the smallest grain in their group's samples. What might happen to them if they were hit by a wave or caught in a current? Do they think they would be able to stay in one place? [Small grains are kept moving by even very slowly moving water.] What about if they were one of the larger grains? [Because they are heavier they might stay put until a bigger wave or faster moving current came along.]

2. Have each group take a few minutes to compare their answers on the student sheets. Why might some people have gotten different answers? What do the differences tell you about the different types of sand?

Sand in the Wind

1. Explain that sand is almost always in constant motion, and that the sand grains on a beach one day might be entirely replaced by others in a few weeks. One way that sand moves is by the wind.

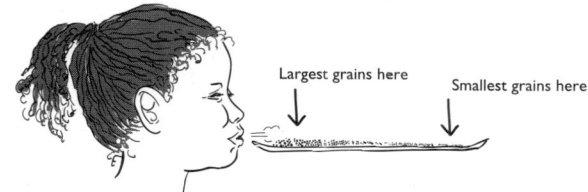

Blowing lightly on a pile of sand

2. Hand out the trays of sand to each group and give each student a chance to **gently** blow on it for five seconds or so. What happens? At a real beach, the wind blows almost all the time. What effect does this have on beach and dune sand? [The "wind" separates or sorts the grains by size—the smaller ones are blown the farthest.]

If you don't want to prepare separate trays for each group, you can do this as a whole group demonstration using one tray.

3. Have students look at their own sand slide now. If all the grains are roughly the same size, they may have come from a windy beach. If the sample is "mixed" in size, then it may have been from a beach with very little wind. Can they make a guess about whether or not their sand came from a windy place?

4. When they are finished, groups should clean up the materials at their tables. Tell them they will need their Sand on Stage student sheet, sand slide, and small bag of sand for the next session.

Session 4: The Experts Meet

1. Ask students from each group with the same type of sand to meet together in "expert groups." Have them compare their answers on their Sand on Stage student sheets and discuss any discrepancies.

2. Ask them to think about where their sand may have come from before it showed up on the beach. A coral reef? A mountain? A lava flow? Clam and mussel shells? Is the sand very old or very young? What evidence do they have for each inference? (Note: Younger students may benefit more from an informal discussion such as this, rather than completing the Expert Group student sheet.)

Some teachers have suggested completing the Expert Group sheets after doing Activity 3: The Sights that Sand has Seen. In that activity, students listen to a story of how a grain of sand is formed and makes its way to a sandy beach. Other teachers feel that the Expert Group sheet better prepares students to understand the story, so recommend that it be done as shown here, as part of Activity 2. Either order will work.

3. Have each student complete an Expert Group student sheet, working together in their groups. As they consider the questions, especially #3 and #4, you may need to focus the students' thinking by having them recall their responses to the Sand on Stage student sheets, as well as previous discussions about how rocks, shells, etc., become grains of sand.

For younger students who may have difficulty making guesses or inferences from the evidence they've collected, drawing and discussing an imaginary beach is fine. Notice whether they include descriptions of color, the types of material that became their sand, and the age of the sand as identified by being sharp or smooth. These characteristics are the most visible and therefore the most concrete, and this helps students in deriving simple cause-and-effect statements about them. For example, a student might describe their beach this way: "My beach has white and pink sand from clam shells. The sand is young sand because the sand grains are sharp and pointy. My beach has a lot of people swimming because the waves are small."

For older students, provide some clues to draw their beach such as: if they think they have coral sand, the water will probably be clear and blue, and the animals living around the coral reef will be brightly colored. If they think there is lava in their sand, there must be a volcano nearby. If the grains are very large, the waves are probably big, and maybe it would be a good beach for surfing. If the grains are small, the water is probably calm, and it may be a good beach for swimming and snorkeling. They could also label the drawings to point out features that they think contributed to the type of sand they have.

Inferring roughness and calmness of the water from the sand grain size is a difficult "leap" to make, even for adults! To help students, ask them to think about what size grains could calm, gentle waves push onto a beach? What about big, strong waves?

4. Now ask them to imagine the beach where their sand may have come from. What does it look like? Is it a sunny warm place with tropical animals or a cold place? Have each student draw a picture of what they think this beach may look like.

5. Students can present their drawings and evidence to the class. Collect the student sheets, artwork, sand slides, and bags of sand. Post the student art around the room next to the sand sample it illustrates.

6. Discuss with students why sand is important to people. [It creates fun and beautiful places for us to walk and play. It is an important home to many, many plants and animals. Many things that we use are made from sand.] Ask, "What are some items made from sand?" [It is important for oil and cement production. Glass is made from melted and reformed sand. Sand is used for sand painting, sandblasting, sandpaper, in hourglasses, and of course, in playgrounds and sandboxes. In fact, if it wasn't for sand, we might not have paved streets, tall buildings, concrete sidewalks, or glass windows.]

7. Hold up the Key Concepts for this activity one at a time, and have one or more students read them aloud. Post them near your sand table or Sand Display for students to refer to later.

- **Sand grains can be made of animals, plants, rocks, or minerals.**
- **Sand grains come in many different shapes, sizes, and colors.**
- **Differences between sand grains can be clues about where the sand came from and how it got to the beach.**

Going Further

1. Encourage younger students to "get a feel for sand." Set up a sand table or tub for free exploration, and encourage students to explore it individually or in small groups when they have free time. You might put out water, funnels, sieves, spoons, or cups. Have them look at the sand closely, run it through their fingers, make sand sculptures, or look for evidence of life. Put out drawing paper and pens for students to spontane-

ously write descriptions or illustrate sand-related images. Every day or so, add a new item: a shell, feather, rock, or piece of litter. As mentioned in the "Getting Ready Tips" (see page 11) this would make a nice pre-teaching exploration station before presenting the activities in this guide.

2. Students can compare their individual sand samples to the sand in the Beach Buckets from Activity 1.

3. Bring in old stuff to make sand, such as rocks, shells, bones, plastic, and pencils. Wrap them in pillowcases or towels and have a few students take turns breaking them up outside with hammers. (Use old towels or pillowcases—they may end up with holes and rips!) Make sure you keep a secret list of all your "ingredients," and see if students can discover what they are by examining the new sand. Make exhibits in class to display the new sand samples next to a list or picture of the ingredients.

4. Have students explore some geography related to their sand samples. Use wall maps, globes, atlases, and encyclopedias to locate the places from which the sand came. Measure with string and latitude lines to determine how far each place is from where you live. Is there anything special that anyone knows or can find out about each location? Are there mountains or volcanoes nearby? What languages do the people living there speak? Is the ocean there cold or warm?

5. Have students continue to collect sand samples. Find a class in another region of the state, country, or world to be pen pals with, and send each other sand samples. Create a sand exhibit or museum, with descriptions of each sample.

You can communicate with other LHS MARE schools via e-mail. Call or write MARE, Lawrence Hall of Science, U.C. Berkeley, Berkeley, CA 94720-5200, (510) 642-5008, mare_lhs@uclink4.berkeley.edu

6. Students can go to the library and find books about sand and sandy beaches. After they have read a few, they can classify them into groups: fiction, non-fiction, about people, about other animals.

7. Take a field trip to a sandy place. Students can act as detectives to determine if the sand has a source which is close by or far away. Sometimes sand is brought in by people from other places to "make" a sandy beach. What evidence can they find about its origin and evolution? What clues are observable [rocks, cliffs, shells, streams, etc.] Is the beach "cleaned?" By who or what? [people, birds, currents, high tides]

Name _____

SAND ON STAGE!

1. Look closely at your sand with a magnifier. List or use crayons to show all the different colors you see.

2. Draw a picture of some of your sand grains. Draw them BIG!

3. Circle the pictures that have shapes like your sand.

not rounded   a little rounded   very rounded

 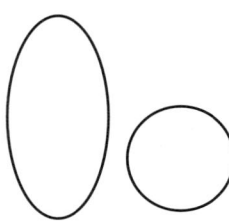

4. Gently rub a magnet on the outside of your bag of sand. Are any of the grains in your sand attracted to the magnet?

If so, what color are the magnetic sand grains?

5. Which of the following things can you find in your sand?
- ○ small rocks
- ○ pieces of glass
- ○ pieces of plants
- ○ other things. They are:
- ○ pieces of shells
- ○ pieces of wood
- ○ pieces of plastic

6. Look at the rock kit. Does your sand have pieces of rock that match some in the kit? List the kinds of rocks that may be in your sand.

7. Which sand in your group is the lightest in color?

Which is the darkest?

Put them in order from lightest to darkest.

8. Compare your sand slide to the size chart below. Imagine that the black dots are grains of sands. Color the group of dots that are about the size of your sand grains. If your sand is not like any of these use the empty circle to draw how yours looks.

  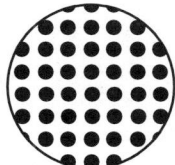 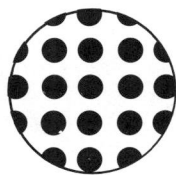 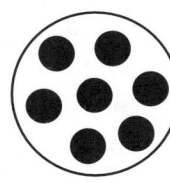 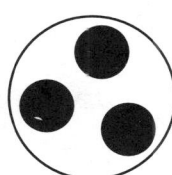 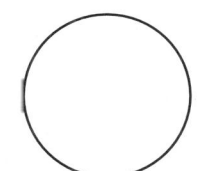

Are your grains all about the same size or many different sizes?

9. Which sand in your cooperative group has the biggest grains?

Which has the smallest grains?

Put them in order from smallest to biggest.

© 1996 by The Regents of the University of California, LHS-GEMS. *On Sandy Shores.* **May be duplicated for classroom use.**

Name _____

EXPERT GROUP STUDENT SHEET

1. Where do you think your sand was collected from?

2. What do you think your sand is made of?

3. How do you think your sand got to the beach?

4. On the back of this sheet, draw a series of pictures to show the story of how your sand became sand. Be sure to include crashing waves, freezing mountain tops, rushing rivers, or exploding volcanoes, or anything else you think helped to form your sand.

© 1996 by The Regents of the University of California, LHS-GEMS. *On Sandy Shores.* **May be duplicated for classroom use.**

- **Part 1:** Draw a picture of where your sand came from (a clam, a mountain, a coral reef, or ?...) before it arrived on the beach.

- **Part 2:** Here's what happened next.

- **Part 3:** Look what happened next!

- My grain of sand now looks like this.

© 1996 by The Regents of the University of California, LHS-GEMS. *On Sandy Shores.* **May be duplicated for classroom use.**

Activity 3: The Sights that Sand has Seen

Overview

Sandy beaches are the result of erosion and deposition. Every sand grain started its process of change as something other than a bit of sand and somewhere other than the beach where you see it today. Powerful forces of erosion break up rock formations high in the mountains and carry them to the ocean. Once these rocks reach the beach, they may be hit by as many as 8,000 ocean waves a day! It is no wonder that they are kept in constant motion and ground up into sand. A single sand grain may move up and down the beach many times in a day in the wash of crashing waves, while at the same time it is pushed along the beach in the long shore drift current. Sandy shores are one of the most unstable marine environments—better thought of as rivers of sand than anything permanent.

In this activity, students get "**Into** the Activities" with My Buddy Says, focusing on sand. Then students go "**Through** the Activities" as they listen to a story, "Sandy's Journey to the Sea," and make a story chart about the journey of a sand grain from high on a mountain to the top of a sand castle. In Session 2, they work in small groups to write and illustrate a series of "postcards" that re-tell the story of the sand grain's journey. Using the Heads Together activity structure, students play the Postcard Game Show to respond to questions about the story. Several "Going Further" activities are suggested for going "**Beyond** the Activities."

Through hearing and re-creating the story, students learn that sand is created by erosion, and can be transported long distances by streams, rivers, and ocean currents. This activity introduces the concept that erosion is the gradual wearing away of objects by glaciers, water, wind, or waves. Waves and currents constantly move sand on and offshore and along the coastline to form beaches which change with the seasons.

What You Need

For the class:
- ❑ 9 sheets of chart paper (approximately 27" x 34")
- ❑ markers (4–5 colors, wide tips)
- ❑ a few real postcards with messages on them
- ❑ at least 10 extra 4" x 6" blank index cards

For each group of 6 students:
- ❑ 7 4" x 6" blank index cards to make into postcards
- ❑ 2–3 sets of crayons, fine-point markers, or colored pencils
- ❑ 6 regular ball-point pens or pencils
- ❑ clear tape to connect the finished index/postcards

Getting Ready

1. Have students bring in postcards from home. Arrange a time before the activity for students to share their postcards with others.

2. Make the skeleton for the Story Chart. At the top of one sheet of chart paper, write the name of Part 1 of the story "Sandy's Journey to the Sea." On another write the name of Part 2, etc., until each of the following six story parts is on its own sheet of chart paper:

   Part 1: The High Mountains in Winter

   Part 2: The River Journey in Spring

   Part 3: Oceanside Rest in Summer and Fall

   Part 4: The Winter Storm

   Part 5: The Kelp Wrack in Spring

   Part 6: The Summer Beach

3. Write out the Key Concepts for this activity in large, bold letters on separate sheets of chart paper and set aside.

- **Erosion is the gradual wearing away of objects by water, wind, waves, or glaciers.**

- **Sand is created by erosion, and can be transported long distances by streams, rivers, and ocean currents.**

- **Waves and currents constantly move sand on and offshore and along the coastline to form beaches which change with the seasons.**

Session 1: My Buddy Says/Story Chart

My Buddy Says

1. Have students recall My Buddy Says from Activity 1: Beach Bucket Scavenger Hunt. Review with students what it means to really listen to a classmate. How does active listening look? [you look directly at the person, nod your head, you don't interrupt]

2. Conduct My Buddy Says (following the same procedure as described in steps 3–6 on page 17) having partners share information and switch roles, but this time focusing on sand, using questions such as the following:

My Buddy Says prompts and questions:

- Where does sand come from?

- If sand could talk, what might it tell you?

- If sand had eyes, what are some things that it might see?

- What is the most interesting, best, coolest thing you have learned about sand?

- What do you still want to know about sand?

- We are going to read a story called "Sandy's Journey to the Sea." What do you think it is going to be about?

Depending on your time constraints, you may want to focus on some, not all, of these questions. In the same way, you may want to select several of the class discussion questions listed, rather than all of them.

3. Spend a moment discussing this last question with your students. You may want to comment on how many different ideas they have.

4. At the end of the activity, ask the students to think about some of the following questions and then lead a class discussion focusing on them:

- When you were speaking, how did you know your buddy was listening?

- Did you learn anything new?

- How much of what your buddy said did you remember?

- What helped you to remember what your buddy said? What could help you remember more?

- Did you do better this time at remembering what your buddy said than you did the first time we did this activity?

- Did anyone notice that the teacher hasn't taught anything yet? You've been teaching each other!

5. Tell the students that this activity will help them to be better listeners and to recall details of the story they are about to hear.

Journey of a Sand Grain: Creating a Story Chart

The Story Chart activity structure helps students summarize and talk about information they have just learned. It helps them learn how to organize and reconstruct information by putting it into language and pictures that they have contributed and understand. This strategy is also useful as an assessment of what the students have learned. As with many activity structures in this guide, the Story Chart is helpful for all students, and will be particularly beneficial to English language learners—those students with limited or intermediate proficiency in English.

1. Gather the class into a listening circle and tell them they are going to listen to a story about a sand grain named Sandy. The story is divided into short chapters or parts just like a book. Let them know they will have to listen carefully so they can summarize what happens to Sandy on her journey.

2. Turn to the story "Sandy's Journey to the Sea" on page 55. Read aloud Part 1: The High Mountains in Winter. Post the first chart paper of the Story Chart with the title of Part 1 on it. Then ask students what the most important things were that happened in this part of the story. For example, your students might recall that Sandy was stuck in a crack; she was smooth on one side and rough on the other; and that the crack was getting wider. Record their ideas on the chart paper just the way they describe them.

If some responses are not quite accurate, ask others to help out with the description. Your students will understand and remember the important concepts presented in the story better when the Story Chart they create is in their own words.

3. Repeat this process for each part of the story so that students have a written outline of the story to refer to later. Move the discussion along by taking only a few minutes to outline the main concepts of each part on the Story Chart. Spending too much time can cause the activity to lose momentum.

4. At the end of the story, ask the students to quickly review the Story Chart. Do they have any questions or clarifications? Is there anything they want to add to any part of the Story Chart?

Session 2: A Postcard Story

1. Ask students if they have ever been on an exciting trip. Sometimes people tell others about a special trip or journey by writing them a postcard. Ask questions, such as: "Have you ever written or received a postcard?" "When do people send them?" "What types of messages or pictures are on them?"

2. If it doesn't come up in the discussion, describe how postcards usually have a photograph or picture on one side to show the friends or family of the traveler scenes from the journey. On the other side of the card, the trip is described by relating stories about experiences they are having, saying what the weather is like, and if they are enjoying the trip. It can also include anticipation of where they will visit next.

If you don't have quick access to some real postcards, here's an example you or a student could read out loud to the class:

Dear Mom,
We arrived in San Francisco Tuesday after an all-day flight from Chicago. The flight was fine but our luggage, including my toothbrush, went to Hong Kong. We were hoping to do some sun-bathing on the beach in our new surf jams—it IS summer, but yesterday it was foggy and cold. Tomorrow we're headed to Santa Cruz! Wish you could be here with us.
 Love, Francisca

It will help your students if you create the Story Chart carefully using the same format for each part of the story. Each part should have its own sheet of chart paper. Use the same color marker for all six titles of parts. Then alternate at least two other colors to separate and distinguish ideas that students contribute to the chart. Set each contribution apart with a different color bullet. If another student repeats an idea you have already recorded, put a star next to it on the chart to acknowledge the student and to remind her/him to listen carefully to others. It is not necessary to use only complete sentences, but you might want to highlight key words and ideas. Though you may want to record ideas as closely to how students say them as possible, you also may want to paraphrase or re-phrase them verbally to give language minority students another chance to understand the idea.

If you have students in your class whose native language is not English, you may want to show pictures from magazines as you read to illustrate various scenes described in the story. Better yet, several teachers told us that they drew a simple poster on butcher paper as they read the story, to illustrate a mountain, a waterfall, a stream, a beach, etc.

If you had students bring in postcards, arrange a time before this session for several students to read some postcards to the rest of the class.

Many teachers find one session enough time to read the story and to create postcards. Some classes take longer, however. You may want to read the story in one session and devote another to writing and drawing postcards.

3. Tell the class that they are going to imagine they are Sandy and are writing a postcard home describing one part of their journey to the sea. Divide the class into groups of six. Give each student a blank 4" x 6" index card. Explain that each of the cards will be a scene from Sandy's journey. Distribute a seventh card to each group to be a title card. Review the six parts of the story with the class.

4. Pass out crayons, markers, or colored pencils to each group. Assign each of the six students in each group a part of the story to illustrate. Tell them to imagine that they are Sandy on her journey and writing a postcard home. Have students use crayons or markers to draw where they are in their journey, and be sure they include Sandy in each picture.

Students can address their postcards to whomever they choose. Here are some options: their "mother rock," their former neighbor, the lodgepole pine tree, a friend or relative, themselves. Many teachers have found that students ask about how to write a street address, where the stamp goes, etc. You may want to review general letter writing practices.

5. Pass out ball-point pens or pencils to each group. On the back of each card, have students write a postcard message from Sandy. They could include something about their experiences, what has happened to them, maybe mention the weather, and whether or not they are enjoying the journey. Tell them to be as creative as they can. They can use humor, happiness, loneliness, or other emotions, but they must also include accurate information about Sandy's location and activities. Example: "Dear Mom: Hi from the mountains! It is really windy up here and I can feel the rock cracking. I keep getting blown into the wall and banging my head. The snow-capped mountains are really pretty. Bye, Sandy." Remind students that the postcards can be written in any language.

Before taping the postcards together, one teacher re-read the story asking students to hold up their postcard at the appropriate place in the story.

6. When the first person in each group finishes designing their postcard, ask them to complete the set by making a title card that says "Sandy's Journey to the Sea."

Postcard Storybook

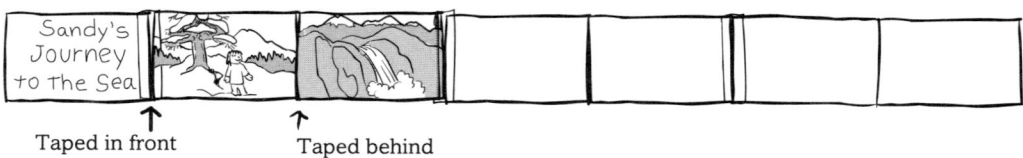

Front of postcards

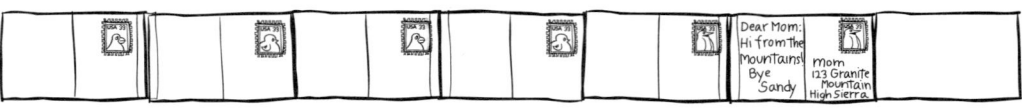

Back of postcards

7. Have the students make a postcard storybook that tells the story of the evolution of a sand grain by lining all seven postcards in a row sequentially and taping the short edges together, alternating the tape on the front and back so that it will open and close like an accordion.

8. Now have each student describe their postcard to the rest of their group. They should listen carefully, so that anyone will be able to tell about any of the postcards after everyone has shared.

9. Hold up the Key Concepts for this activity one at a time, and have one or more students read them aloud. Post them on the wall next to the Story Chart.

- **Erosion is the gradual wearing away of objects by water, wind, waves, or glaciers.**

- **Sand is created by erosion, and can be transported long distances by streams, rivers, and ocean currents.**

- **Waves and currents constantly move sand on and offshore and along the coastline to form beaches which change with the seasons.**

With younger students you may need to briefly explain what a glacier is.

Session 3: Postcard Game Show

The Postcard Game Show uses the Heads Together activity structure to facilitate small group discussions, to review previously learned information, and to informally assess student knowledge. This strategy also gives students the confidence to answer questions in front of the entire class.

1. For the next session, have students work in their original Postcard groups of six. Each group should have its postcard storybook available. Have the groups count off so each student in a group has a different number, from 1 to 6. Points will be awarded in this game. You can keep score on the chalkboard.

2. Tell the students that they are going to play the Postcard Game Show. You will ask a question about Sandy's journey and each group will first discuss the question for about a minute among themselves and decide on an answer. In this way, everyone within the group should know the answer.

This teaching strategy helps all students to be successful because they are allowed to discuss the answer before being called upon and to enhance and build on each other's responses when needed. Numbers may be chosen completely at random or if a student who does not normally offer to answer questions appears to know the answer (perhaps he had illustrated that particular card), you might want to select his number.

We have provided you with some sample questions, but you might prefer to come up with your own questions, based on the interests and backgrounds of your students. You can also play the game a second time, and have students write their own questions for other teams to answer.

One way you can decrease the emphasis on competition is by awarding bonus points to teams that encourage others. Also, since you are asking the questions and determining the completeness of the answers, it is possible for you to engineer a tie.

3. Explain that then you will pick a group, then a number, and the student with that number in that group stands up. You again ask the question and the student answers it. If she gives a "complete" answer, her group is awarded five points. If she gives a partial answer, call another number from her group and give that person a chance to complete the first person's answer. Each group will get three tries to complete the answer and get five points. Encourage students to use their postcard storybooks to help them answer the questions.

4. If three students from the group fail to give the complete answer, have the students in the group take their best guess about the part of the story where the answer might be found. Read that part of the story aloud and have the students raise their hands if they hear the answer. If they give a complete answer now, the group is awarded three points.

5. Ask if there are any questions about the rules and clarify as needed. Then begin the Postcard Game Show by asking Question #1 from the list below. Give 30–60 seconds for all the groups to discuss the answer. Then select a group and a number and ask the appropriate student to stand up. Repeat the question, ask the student to give the answer, and proceed as described above.

6. Repeat the process using a new question each time. **Make sure that each group gets called on to answer an equal number of questions.**

Sample Postcard Game Show Questions:

Question 1: Describe how Sandy left her original mountain top home. What made her leave? [The crack widened due to erosion; water from rain and snow carried her away.]

Question 2: Sandy said it seemed like there was always a party going on in the kelp wrack. Who came to the party, and why do you think it seemed like a party to Sandy? [flies, crabs, gulls, shorebirds; lots of visitors, food, and activity]

Question 3: During the winter storm, Sandy became smaller and smaller until she was just a tiny sand grain. What caused this? [The winter storm waves carried her into the ocean where she was ground up against other rocks.]

Question 4: Throughout the story Sandy was kept almost constantly on the move. What forces were moving her? [many, including winter storms, waves, and longshore current, for example]

Question 5: Remember the part of the story when the storm hit the beach at the same time as the high tide? What happened to Sandy when that happened? [She was washed out into the ocean and broken up into smaller pieces.]

Question 6: Waves in the winter are very different from waves in the summer. How are they different? [Winter waves are spaced closer together and are bigger and stronger; summer waves are spaced further apart and are smaller and more gentle.]

Question 7: How do waves affect the sand on the beach in the winter? How about in summer? [Winter beaches may be just cobblestones because all the sand has been taken offshore by large waves; summer beaches are wide, deep, and sandy because the small waves push sand onto the beach.]

7. After the Postcard Game Show, tell the students that soon they will be learning about many of the plants and animals that live on sandy shores. Ask the following questions to prepare them for the next activity:

- What were some of the plants and animals that Sandy saw on her journey? [kelp, driftwood, flies, crabs, gulls, shorebirds, people, and dogs]

- How did those plants and animals use the sandy beach? [Kelp and driftwood were just going with the flow; flies and crabs ate the kelp; gulls and shorebirds ate flies and crabs; people and dogs enjoyed the water and beach.]

- Can you think of any other ways organisms use the beach? [as a habitat in or on the sand for resting, mating, getting warm, hiding from predators, or escaping from the waves]

Going Further

1. Transform the postcard stories into dramatic presentations. Cluster the students that wrote the postcards from the same part of "Sandy's Journey to the Sea" together into "expert groups." Give the groups 15–30 minutes to develop a one- to two-minute skit about their part of the story, and to design simple costumes from materials around the room. Invite the groups to perform their skits in rapid sequence beginning with "Scene 1" until the entire story has been performed.

2. Have students act out the winter and summer wave activity. Have most of the class represent sand particles, and five students be a wave. Holding hands in a line, have the wave come back and forth quickly to represent fast winter waves, each time taking sand particles with them to the other side of the room (the ocean). Have the wave grab a pile of jackets and deposit them on the beach to represent kelp ripped from its holdfasts and washed up on shore. Now a few students can be shorebirds who peck through the kelp wrack looking for a snack—beach hoppers, kelp flies, etc. To represent summer, have the wave move slowly, quietly lapping along the shore, pushing the sand particles up onto the beach, spreading them out and leaving them relatively undisturbed.

3. Have students create their own, original postcard story. Lead a class brainstorm about all the things that may end up on a sandy beach. List all of their ideas on the chalkboard. Encourage the students to choose one of these sandy beach "things" or organisms and tell a story of its travels or life cycle from the first person perspective. Younger students may tell their whole story on one postcard; older students might like to do a series of postcards.

4. Go to the same beach to watch waves in different seasons. Compare how the beach looks in winter and late summer/fall. Draw pictures showing the differences, including landmarks that stay the same in both pictures. Where might Sandy be in each picture? If you don't have access to a sandy ocean beach, observe seasonal changes in another water habitat, such as a stream, pond, lake, or marsh.

5. Have a cooperative sand sculpture event at the beach, and see what fantastic shapes and animals you can build in small groups or as a class. If you can't make it to the beach, use your school sand box. Can students find Sandy? Why do they think that particular sand grain is Sandy?

Sandy's Journey to the Sea

by Stephanie Kaza

Part 1: The High Mountains in Winter

High in the mountains, the rivers and creeks had begun to freeze over for winter. Golden aspen leaves fluttered down along the banks, leaving the white-barked trees empty against the blue sky. Already the craggy granite peaks of the High Sierra were deep in snow. On a ledge by a gnarled lodgepole pine was a small rock named Sandy. Smooth on one side, rough on the other, the rock was about the size of your thumbnail. It had broken off from a big mountain boulder and been caught in a crack for a very long time. Year after year, the small rock watched the seasons go by. But lately as the pine tree grew, Sandy noticed that the crack was getting wider and wider. She did not seem to be quite so stuck in her place any more. She rattled a tiny bit and wondered if she would be there forever.

Part 2: The River Journey in Spring

One fine spring day, when the sun was out and beaming its hot rays onto the snow, a trickle of water crept underneath Sandy. It tickled a little bit and Sandy smiled in the warm air. As the day grew hotter, the little trickle turned to a rushing stream. Much to Sandy's surprise, she was lifted up out of her familiar crack and carried off over the edge of the granite.

Crash, bang! She tumbled down a roaring waterfall. In two seconds Sandy landed at the bottom in a deep pool, a little dazed. She barely caught her breath and was whooshed away down the racing river. She jumped and bumped through the raging rapids, sliding out of the high mountains to the foothills below.

Part 3: Oceanside Rest in Summer and Fall

After quite some time and many miles, Sandy settled out on a flat spot perched on a riverbank not far from the sea. She had drifted by leopard lilies in spring and dragonflies in summer. During the dry months of fall the river had shrunk to a narrow creek, leaving Sandy high and dry. After such an exciting journey, she thought she might just stay there awhile and rest. She hardly remembered her old crack, for she had been so many places since then.

As the season turned to winter, Sandy felt chilly in the cold night air. With all the wear and tear of going down the river, she was a little worn down. But she didn't mind, for the sky was brilliant with beautiful stars of many colors. One especially quiet night she gazed for hours at the silver dazzling full moon. In the early morning dawn she could barely hear the ocean's roar.

Part 4: The Winter Storm
Boom, crack! Just six hours later, the ocean was suddenly at her feet! It was high tide and winter storm waves were rolling in fast and hard, one right after the other. The rain pounded against the wild ocean. Before she knew it, Sandy was washed out to sea in a great churning of stones and sand. She barely caught one last look at her resting place, now so rocky and bare of sand.

Sloshing and grinding, the rocks crashed into each other in the open sea. Bit by bit, pieces broke off from Sandy until only a small sand grain was left. For days and days, Sandy tumbled around in the huge ocean, dancing on roller coaster waves and sinking in the silky blackness.

Part 5: The Kelp Wrack in Spring
After a month of gray skies and rain, the storm cleared. Sandy washed back up on the beach with many other sand grains. She herself was stuck to a big stalk of brown kelp. The waves carried her high above the tideline next to a driftwood log. She wondered if it might be her old friend the lodgepole pine.

As the sun grew hot, the kelp began to grow slimy and start to rot. Sandy was quite stuck in place, but at least she had many visitors. Flies and crabs nibbled at the kelp, while gulls and shorebirds wandered by. It seemed there was always a party going on at the kelp wrack. Out in the ocean, other sand grains waited underwater on sand bars for their time to join the party.

Part 6: The Summer Beach
As the days grew long and spring changed to summer, the beach once again grew wide and deep with sand. The kelp dried up and Sandy fell off onto the beach. People and dogs came by and scuffled the sand. Sandy hitched a ride on someone's toe and found herself at the edge of the ocean again. The waves were gentle now and spaced farther apart. At high tide she was scooped up in a quiet rocking motion and carried into the longshore current. Here Sandy drifted, pushed along by the ocean, heading south with not much to do except go with the flow.

By the end of the summer, Sandy had traveled quiet a few miles from the kelp wrack beach. Now she was near a small coastal town by a large point of land. The nearshore current caught her up and pushed her on shore right next to a child building a sand castle. Scoop! The shovel picked her up and she landed at the bottom of the bucket. Splat! The bucket dumped her onto the top of the castle. She felt the child's warm hands patting her into a beautiful shape. Oh, how lovely! She could feel the child smiling, and she was glad to be there—at least for a while.

Activity 4: Build a Sandy Beach

Overview

People have many different images of beaches, and for good reason! A California beach in winter looks quite different from a Texas beach in summer, and both differ even more from a beach around a fresh water lake. The same beach may look entirely different from one season to the next or even from day to day. But there is one thing all beaches have in common—the water and sand are in constant motion.

Ocean beaches and the seaweed that washes ashore on them are home to many kinds of organisms. How can beach life survive the crashing waves? Most of the animals living on the sandy shore are hidden from view under the sand to escape the pounding surf, drying sun at low tide, and hungry birds.

In this high-interest activity, students construct three-dimensional, magnified models of organisms that live below the sand, as well as models of the living and dead organisms that make up the beach wrack washed ashore by the waves. A special "Information for the Displays" section, starting on page 77, provides you and your students with concise information on a number of these organisms.

Your classroom will be transformed into a sandy beach habitat as you and the students arrange three displays of different views of the same beach—a panorama of the shore ("Above the Sand"), a cross-section view of the under-the-sand habitat ("Under the Sand"), and a model of beach wrack magnified 20 times ("Beach Wrack"). You will need to plan where in the classroom these can be set up.

Partner Parade and a simulated classroom field trip in Session 1 provide the "**Into** the Activities" component. "**Through** the Activities" begins with students coloring beach organisms and drawing appropriate habitats for them using the masters provided at the back of the book. In Session 3, students create the three-dimensional models of the organisms for the three beach displays, followed, in Sessions 4 and 5, by class presentations of the displays. Two games Who Am I? and Twenty Questions reinforce growing student knowledge about sandy beach organisms, their interactions, and their habitat. Several "Going Fur-

We recommend that you organize your students into three groups, each simultaneously building a different view of the beach. It will help immensely if you can organize an adult or an older student "peer teacher" to work with each group. However, if this is not possible, or if your class is not ready for such a large and independent project, you can consider other options: Build only one display and have the whole class work on it; or build all three, but build them one at a time sequentially with the whole class working on each.

Descriptions of the individual organisms mentioned here are included on the illustrations at the back of this guide and in the "Information for the Displays" section on page 77. For more detailed information refer to the "About the Habitat" section in the MARE Teachers' Guide to the Sandy Beach (see page 128 for more information on MARE Curriculum Guides.)

ther" activities provide opportunities for going "**Beyond the Activities.**"

We recommend that you read through this session's instructions thoroughly to acquaint yourself with some of the construction ideas suggested. Then you'll be able to visualize different possibilities, and add your own ideas. Students, too, may often take the lead in creating their own vision of a sandy beach habitat. Creating the three-dimensional organisms as well as planning and arranging the displays can be done in several days, but many classes find themselves taking considerably longer. You may want to set aside additional time to do this project; it is well worth the extra time and effort!

What You Need

For the class:
- ❏ 2 sheets of chart paper (approximately 27" x 34")
- ❏ crayons, colored pencils, or fine-point markers
- ❏ masking tape
- ❏ pictures, slides, or video images of sandy beaches (you can use the pictures collected for earlier activities in this guide, adding others as available, including slides and/or videos) The MARE Sandy Beach Slide Show is available for purchase. See "Resources" on page 117.
- ❏ large piece of butcher or chart paper (for simulated classroom field trip)
- ❏ a 1-gallon bucket half full of rocks the size of walnuts
- ❏ a 1-gallon bucket half full of sand
- ❏ 2 five-foot long pieces of butcher paper (to be covered with sand for displays)
- ❏ white glue
- ❏ a 2"- or 3"-wide paint brush to spread glue on butcher paper
- ❏ 5 feet of blue mural paper or blue cellophane
- ❏ one roll monofilament fishing line
- ❏ 50 feet of brown or green butcher or construction paper to make stuffed organisms (or brown or green paint and white paper)
- ❏ miscellaneous "junk" for students to design their own beach organisms including, for example: string, styrofoam, crepe paper, marbles, toothpicks, pipe cleaners, black beads, feathers, different colors of tempera paint, chopsticks, brush bristles, straws, variously colored tissue paper, plastic bags, curling ribbon, balloons

- lots of newspaper for stuffing organisms
- 1 box of facial tissues for stuffing organisms
- (*optional*) refrigerator box (instead of one piece of sand-covered butcher paper)

For each student:
- 1 piece of construction paper (used to back organism illustrations and make habitat drawings)
- 1 organism illustration (masters begin on page 165)

For each group of 10–12 students (3 groups total):
- 1–3 staplers
- 5 or more scissors
- 2–3 small bottles of glue
- masking and clear tape
- 1 lb. of modeling clay in various colors, including purple, white, and red
- 10 paper plates
- construction paper to make organisms (1 pad or 30 large sheets; various colors, including: dark green, light green, brown, black, white, and purple)
- resource books for students to use to research their organism

For the group that does "Beach Wrack" (materials in addition to above):
- 50 feet of brown butcher paper or equivalent amount of large sheets of green and brown construction paper
- 4 large (36-gallon) black, green, or brown garbage bags
- 2 cardboard boxes about 1 foot square each to make rocks
- 5–10 green balloons
- 2 rolls brown crepe paper

Getting Ready

1. Decide how you want to conduct the simulated classroom field trip. Gather videos, slides, books, or magazines with sandy beach images. (See the "Resources" section for some suggestions.)

2. Consider how and when you will divide the class into three teams for each of the three displays. It is probably wisest to decide this beforehand, so when you hand out the organism drawings for students to color you can give each group the organisms that will appear in their display.

When one of the authors of this guide taught the activities, he set up the backdrops for "Above the Sand" and "Under the Sand" while students were at recess. For the "Beach Wrack" display, the organisms are revealed under a magnified model of kelp. It's recommended that students build the kelp themselves, but they will need some assistance. An adult is often needed to help them roll the paper into tubes, but after they get started they can do it. (See Giant Kelp and Bull Kelp in the "Beach Wrack" section of "Information for the Displays" on pages 87 and 88.)

Is it reasonable to expect three large groups working at once with different materials, creating different final products to result in only an acceptable level of creative chaos? In many classrooms, we've seen it work wonderfully. However, you know your students best, and should decide how to set up the displays and orchestrate the student work. Ideally, there should be an adult with each group. A teacher can usually facilitate these activities with at least one aide/para-professional/parent and/or a group of older students, on loan from the 4th or 5th grade. Cross-age teaching, friendships across grade levels, and informal tutoring are all positive outcomes of enlisting older students.

3. Decide on your strategy for how to create the three displays that provide different views of the sandy beach. Please read the special section entitled "Three Sandy Beach Displays" on page 64 to get a better sense of what these displays involve. This should help you visualize the process of creating the displays and their placement in your classroom. There are some tasks that you or an adult assistant can do and others for which you may want to involve small groups of students.

    a. In both "Above the Sand" and "Under the Sand," for example, the teacher needs to play the main role in preparing the background before the class makes the three-dimensional plants and animals. That is, the teacher needs to hang a sandy sheet on a bulletin board ("Above the Sand") or from the backs of two chairs ("Under the Sand").

    b. To make these sandy sheets, paint two five-foot long sheets of butcher paper with watered-down white glue and sprinkle it all over with sand. Leave one side and the bottom blank if cliffs and rocks are to be painted in. It takes less than half a bucket of sand to cover two five-foot long pieces of butcher paper. Some teachers have several students paint the butcher paper with glue and sprinkle the sand—this is probably best done by a small group at recess, lunch, or after school or by students who have finished another project "early." It goes a lot faster with three or four helpers.

    c. For "Above the Sand," the teacher should put the blue paper or cellophane up ahead of time to create the beach panorama scene.

    d. Rocks, used to represent magnified grains of sand in the "Beach Wrack" display, can be obtained from building supply stores or have students bring them from home.

4. After you've familiarized yourself with the three displays, decide where in your classroom the displays should be placed, and place them. Looking at the drawings of the three displays on pages 64–66 may help you visualize them more fully. While we suggest that the three be in close proximity to each other to help students see their interrelation more easily, we are well aware that conditions and space constraints differ widely. As usual, you are the best judge.

5. Write out the Key Concepts for this activity in large, bold letters on separate sheets of chart paper and set aside.

- **Sandy beaches—and the beach wrack that washes ashore on them—provide homes to many kinds of organisms.**

- **Most of the animals living at the sandy beach are hidden from view under the sand to escape the pounding surf and hungry birds.**

Three Sandy Beach Displays

The following three displays represent distinct views of the same sandy beach. Please also see "Information for the Displays," starting on page 77.

ABOVE THE SAND

The panoramic view of the beach puts the other two views into perspective. It shows seals, birds, beach wrack, and shells. The backdrop for this view is a bulletin board mural showing a vast expanse of sandy shore and looming cliffs, with the rising and falling ocean.

Paint watered-down glue on paper. Sprinkle with sand.

1. On a large bulletin board or wall, hang a five foot long sheet of brown or white butcher paper that has been painted with watered down white glue and sprinkled with sand. "Rocks" and "cliffs" may be painted along the side and bottom of the mural.

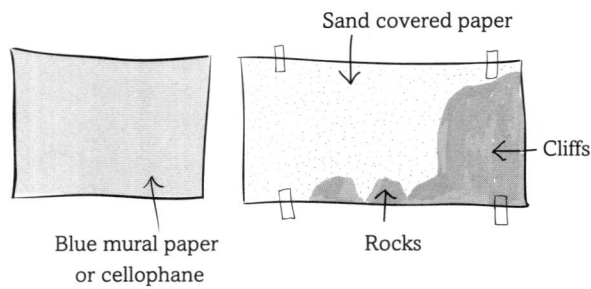

2. Add a large sheet of blue mural paper or blue cellophane to represent water covering the sand. Attach the ocean water above the upper left corner of the sandy sheet, and along the top and left side of the bulletin board, leaving the bottom and right edge free so it can be lifted up to see what lives in the sand just offshore. Cut the right edge of the water parallel to the cliffs to look like waves crashing on the beach.

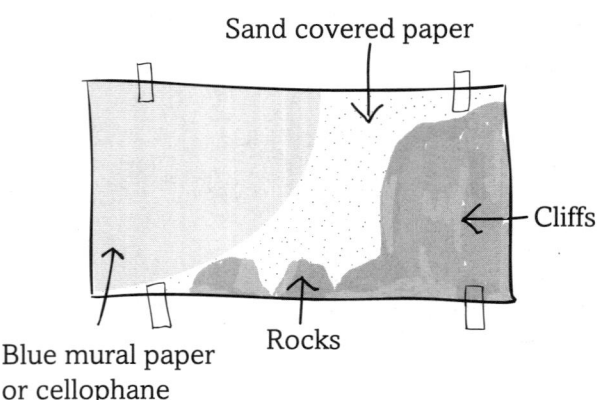

3. Some of the animals shown in this view (such as elephant seals and pelicans) should be reduced from actual size by placing them further in the distance. Some of the other organisms (such as plankton) will probably need to be magnified (show a hand lens above them to represent magnification). See the "Above the Sand" section of "Information for the Displays" on page 77 for a listing of organisms that appear in this display, with suggestions for how to construct them.

4. Some teachers have students use string and labels to connect the section of sand on their bulletin board to the "Under the Sand" model. The beach wrack shown on their bulletin board can likewise be connected to the magnified "Beach Wrack" display.

UNDER THE SAND

This display uses a cut away or cross-section model to reveal the very important part of the sandy beach that is hidden from view. It shows the myriad clams, snails, worms, and crabs that live out of sight underneath the sand, and how they react to changing tides and crashing waves.

Paint watered-down glue on paper. Sprinkle with sand.

1. Paint a large sheet of butcher paper with watered-down white glue and sprinkle with sand. (A large piece of cardboard, such as the side of a refrigerator box, can also be used and is sturdier.)

2. The display starts with the sandy sheet of butcher paper (or cardboard) taped to the edges of two tables or to the backs of chairs, so that the paper is suspended between the two tables or chairs.

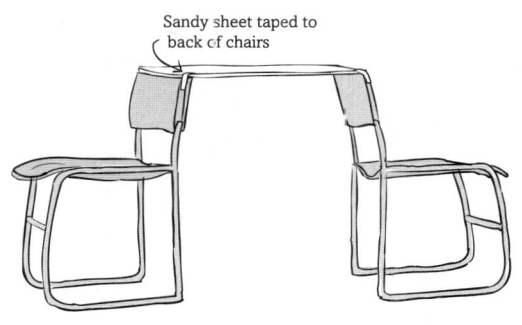

3. Attach the animals that students create to monofilament (fishing line) and hang them at the appropriate level down under the butcher paper as though they were living below the surface of the sand. These organisms and suggestions for making three-dimensional models of them are described in the "Under the Sand" section of "Information for the Displays" on page 82.

4. Make some holes in the sandy sheet to represent the tops of burrows in "the sand," showing where the organisms are living.

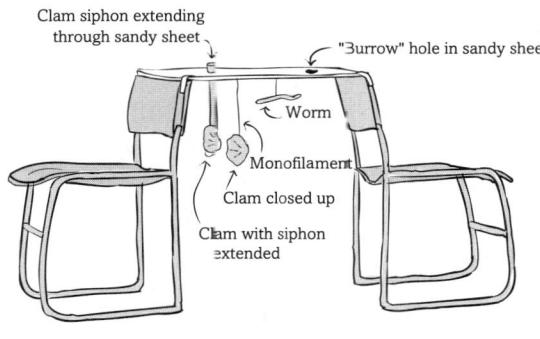

5. The display can be placed just to the side of or below the "Above the Sand" bulletin board display.

Some students working on this view have made two different versions or poses of their organisms to show them at high and low tide or when hit by a crashing wave.

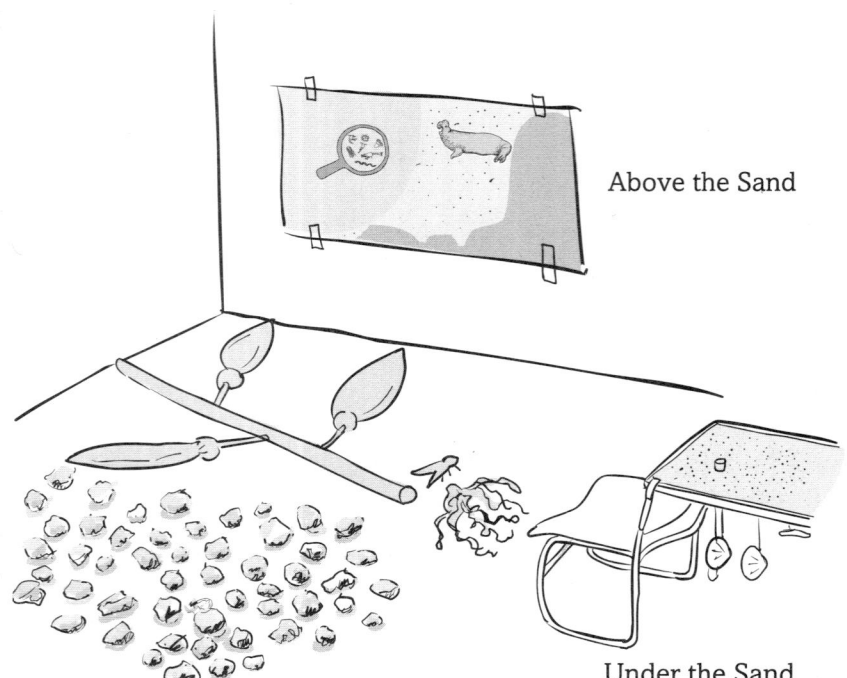

Above the Sand

Under the Sand

Rocks to represent magnified sand grains

Beach Wrack (on floor)

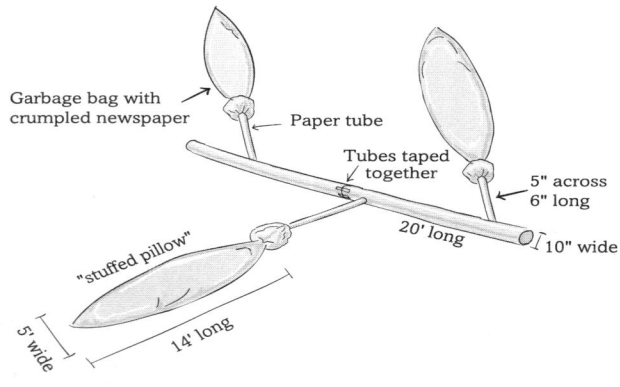

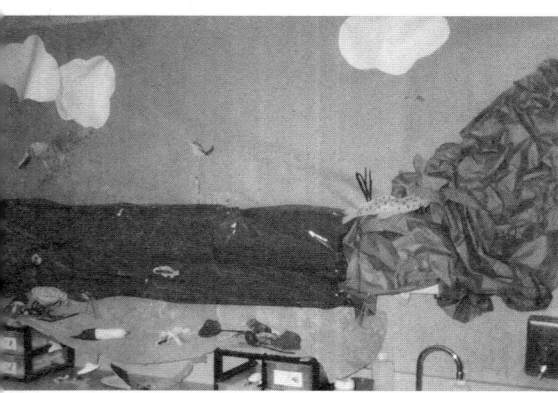

BEACH WRACK

This display is constructed at 20 times actual size so the details of many of the animals that are quite small and usually out of view can be seen more clearly. The model beach wrack can be shown as if someone just lifted up a bunch of kelp to look underneath it. Insects, worms, beach hoppers, holdfasts, and empty shells should be included. Students can also include the parts of a bird that would be visible from within the beach wrack—a pair of giant legs and a beak probing for a meal.

1. Cover the floor where the model will be with about half a bucket of rocks or cobbles about the size of walnuts to represent the sand grains when magnified 20 times.

2. You, an assistant, or older students will need to work with students to create the model of kelp that forms the background for this display. The display can only show about one foot of a piece of giant kelp (life-size kelp can be 150 feet long!) Making the model kelp includes rolling up brown paper tubes as well as making model air bladders and blades. (See Giant Kelp in the "Beach Wrack" section of "Information for the Displays" on page 87 for details.) A similar construction is suggested for Bull Kelp on page 88.

3. The other elements of the "Beach Wrack" display are detailed in the "Information for the Displays" section and include beach hoppers, pseudoscorpions, rove beetles, holdfast and rocks, barnacles, and bristle worms. All of these are also made about 20 times larger than life size.

4. The beach wrack display can be placed on the floor just to the side of the "Above the Sand" bulletin board display.

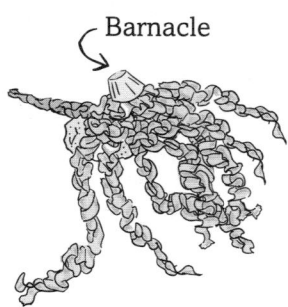

Barnacle

Holdfast

Session 1: Partner Parade

1. Recall Partner Parade from Activity 2: Sand on Stage. Remind the students that just as before, they need to cooperate, follow directions, and talk quietly with each of their partners.

2. Follow the steps for Partner Parade, as described on pages 30–32. Remind students that in Partner Parade both partners will be able to answer the questions or talk about the topic. To have a good discussion, each partner should be a good listener and speak up when it's their turn. Move along the two lines to assist as needed and when you call time have several students report on what they discussed with their partners.

3. Ask students the following Partner Parade questions:
- What would you like to do on a field trip to the beach?
- What animals or plants might we see there?
- What sandy beach animals do you think live on top of the sand?
- What sandy beach animals do you think live under the sand?
- Besides plants and animals, what else could we see at the sandy beach?

4. Have students sit down with their final partner for the simulated classroom field trip that follows.

Simulated Classroom Field Trip

1. Tell students they will now have the chance to visit a beach without leaving the classroom! Show pictures or slides of sandy beaches with little or no narrative, or video images of a sandy beach with the sound turned off. As they watch, they may talk with their partner about the different scenes. Encourage students to discuss what they see with their partner as if they were really on a field trip to the sandy beach.

2. At the end of the images, have them talk to their partner about everything they can remember that they saw on their field trip.

You may want to remind students that although they may be unhappy with the new arrangement, that Partner Parade helps them have conversations with different people, even people they don't know very well.

3. Brainstorm a class list of all the animals, plants, and physical features that students saw on their field trip. As you record them on butcher or chart paper, cluster or group together those organisms which have something in common. Possible clusters could include animal and plant groups, colors, sizes, kinds of movement, places found. You might want to add to the list with additional animals described on the organism illustrations (masters begin on page 165). Discuss the general attributes of each of the clusters to give students some background knowledge of sandy beach organisms.

4. Show the pictures, slide show, or video again, but this time present some additional content about the sandy beach habitat and the organisms living there. (See the descriptions of the individual organisms described on the organism illustrations, the text in the "Information for the Displays" section, and the "Behind the Scenes" section.)

Introducing the Sandy Beach Displays

1. Explain to the class that over the next several sessions they will be creating a sandy beach right in their classroom! First, the class will become more familiar with beach animals and plants when each student chooses one to draw in its habitat. Next they will make a three-dimensional model of an organism. Then they will place these organisms in one of three different views or displays of a sandy beach.

2. Tell students that the three displays will show the same sandy beach from three different views. The class will be divided into three teams, each of whom will work on a different display. The first display is called "Above the Sand," which is a wide, panoramic view of the sandy beach and its surroundings. The second is called "Under the Sand." It helps make the point that much of the life of a sandy beach is hidden from view under the sand or under seaweed that has washed ashore. Many people are not familiar with the organisms under the sand or under the beach wrack. The third display is "Beach Wrack," which is a magnified view of kelp and the other plants, animals, and materials washed up on the shore which together are called beach wrack.

3. Tell students that by creating the organisms and arranging the displays, they will learn a lot about how the animals live, eat, and protect themselves. Each group will become experts on the organisms living in their view of

the beach. They will also have a chance to share what they learned with the other groups. Emphasize that making the organisms and arranging them in the displays will take place over at least several days.

Session 2: Drawing Organisms and Habitats

Coloring Sandy Beach Organisms

1. If you have not already done so, divide the class into three groups: Above the Sand, Under the Sand, and Beach Wrack. Give each group the appropriate collection of illustrations for their display (see pages 165–202). Have the students choose one of the drawings to color.

2. Place construction paper, markers or crayons, glue, and scissors in the middle of each group's table. Distribute any available resource books around the room for students to use to research their animal or plant.

3. Have the students look over their drawing, read the short description, and color their organism appropriately. When they finish, they should cut out the organism and glue it onto construction paper.

Drawing the Habitat

1. Now ask the students to draw in a habitat scene around their organism, including physical aspects of the beach, such as sand, waves, and cliffs. The habitat scenes should be labeled with the name of the organism.

2. Remind students to follow the directions given on the illustration (e.g., "I am red," "I live in the sand," "I eat plankton"). In this case, students would color their animal red, draw sand around it, and draw a few plankton for their animal to eat. If students want more clues about their habitat scene, encourage them to look through the illustrations or other resource materials on hand.

3. Students may also choose to draw the animal that eats their organism.

If you have time and extra helpers in your classroom, visit each group and highlight some of the information about each organism as given in "Information for the Displays." Otherwise, there is enough information given on each drawing for the students to make the organism on their own.

Remind the students that if they have a question, they should first ask the other members of their group before calling on the teacher.

4. Ask several students to briefly describe their organism and its habitat. Ask, "What are some of the ways your organism is suited to its environment?" Explain that animals are often especially adapted to survive in a particular habitat. These ***adaptations*** are the result of thousands or millions of years of evolution.

5. Let students know that in the next session they'll get the chance to build a three-dimensional model of their organism using many interesting materials!

Session 3: Making the Organisms

Introducing Tasks and Methods

1. Remind students about the three beach view displays. Use the information under "Three Sandy Beach Displays" on page 64 and in the "Information for the Displays" section on page 77 to orient them to the task of making three-dimensional organisms for the displays.

2. Ask older students, especially, to consider size/scale differences between sandy beach organisms. For example, some plankton are one-eighth of an inch long (many are microscopic, but those are not included in this activity) while harbor seals are four feet long. As appropriate, remind students that the organisms they make are going to be placed in one of the three displays. Ask them to consider whether an organism should be magnified or reduced in size and how this might help them arrange their displays. They should consider the correct relative size—for example, life-size, reduced 50 percent, or magnified 20 times. (In the "Above the Sand" display, for example, some organisms are magnified while others are made smaller to appear more distant.)

With younger students, you may choose to de-emphasize scale and size, and focus instead on the characteristics of organisms and how those characteristics help them to survive in their specific habitat.

3. Show students the variety of art materials for them to use and ask them to think about how they might use it to build a three-dimensional model of their organism.

4. If the students have ideas on how they would like to make their organisms, they should go ahead and experiment using any of the materials available. They can make two or three individuals of their organism, and if there is time, they can design and make a different organism.

5. You may want to model some of the following techniques for making three-dimensional organisms. This will

be especially helpful for those students having trouble coming up with a design on their own:

- Bodies: mold bodies with clay, use toothpicks for legs, and pipe cleaners and construction paper for pinchers (especially useful for pseudoscorpion).

- Worms: to make really long worms, roll paper into tubes and tape several rolls together end to end; segments of the worm can be shown with painted rings or string tied around the body at intervals; chopsticks can be used for the bristles and black construction paper for jaws (for the giant bristle worms).

- Snails: one way to make snails is to spiral long "worms" of clay around a marble.

- Clams: to make clams—draw both halves of an open clam onto a paper plate, color, cut out (take care not to cut through the "hinge"), and fold at the hinge. Use straws or roll two narrow tubes of paper to form the incurrent and excurrent siphons. Add a long, pointed white foot made from two pieces of construction paper, glued at the edges and stuffed with facial tissue. Both the siphon and foot could also be made out of clay. Stuff the folded shell with facial tissue and tape shut after adding the siphon and foot.

- Most organisms can be made using the stuffed pillow technique. Draw an enlarged copy of the organism freehand onto a large sheet of butcher paper. An opaque projector can also be used to enlarge the illustrations to the appropriate size onto butcher paper taped to the wall. Cut out the drawing, then use it as a pattern to trace and cut out an exact copy. Color the outside of each of the copies. Staple the two halves of the organism together, leaving an opening just large enough to stuff with newspaper or facial tissue before stapling shut.

- Tiny organisms (such as many types of plankton) can be shown larger than life in the model by placing them under an illustration or model of a hand lens.

- You or an assistant may need to help students make the 20 times life-size giant kelp and bull kelp for the "Beach Wrack" display.

Detailed descriptions of each organism and additional suggestions for making the organisms can be found in the "Information for the Displays" section on page 77. These pages are not intended to be duplicated for students to read—rather, pertinent information can be conveyed to students as appropriate and as questions arise during the course of the activities.

6. Ask students if they have any questions about the displays or the main idea of making the three-dimensional animals for the displays.

Creating Three-Dimensional Organisms

1. Set the student groups to work making three-dimensional organisms.

2. As the students are working, you and any assistants will need to circulate around the room responding to questions about the organisms and helping students design their three-dimensional models.

3. Keep in mind the specific attributes of each of the displays, so you can assist students in creating the appropriate organisms.

4. Depending on your schedule and time constraints, you may want to extend this creative part of the activity for several class sessions.

Session 4: Arranging the Displays

Placing the Organisms

1. Tell the students that they now have the chance to arrange the wonderful three-dimensional organisms they made within the three views of a sandy beach.

2. Explain that after all groups arrange their organisms, you'd like each group to give a brief report on their display and a few of the main things they learned from it, so the groups should decide on two students to make that report.

3. Have each group work together to place their organisms in appropriate spots within their group's display of the sandy beach. (Depending on the location of each view in the classroom, you may want to stagger this activity so only one group places their organisms at a time.)

As previously noted, it is strongly recommended that you have at least one and preferably several adult assistants working with you, and/or enlist responsible older students who have done the activity in their class previously (or who have taken part in a MARE "Ocean Week" or similar all-school activities).

Many students may prefer to trace their organisms or even to simply cut out copies of the illustrations provided in this guide. Tracing is quick and easy, but not very challenging nor aesthetically pleasing. Drawing accurately is an important skill in both math and science. Drawing will help students to understand scale, spatial relationships, and proportion, as well as convey a tremendous amount about the natural history and biological characteristics of the organism they are drawing. Encourage them not to trace.

4. Once again, you and an assistant(s) or older students should help the groups of students work together and discuss placement of their organisms cooperatively.

5. Further questions about a particular organism may arise. You or an assistant can encourage students to refer to resource books you have available. You or your assistant(s) could also consult the more detailed scientific summaries in the "Information for the Displays" section on page 77.

6. Encourage students to remember any unanswered questions that arose about an organism or its placement, so they can find out more later and/or summarize some of their reasoning in the class presentations.

Session 5: Class Presentations

Group Reports and Reaction

1. Have group representatives make presentations to the class about what their group discovered.

2. After each group's report, allow about five minutes for the rest of the class to ask questions, having other members of the reporting group respond and/or add more comments of their own about what they learned in making the organisms and arranging them in the display.

3. After the final group's report, ask students for additional questions they still may have. You may want to record these on the chalkboard, and encourage students to think about how they might find out more information.

Making a Key

1. Have a student randomly choose one of the drawings of an organism with its habitat that the class made earlier and hold it up in front of the class, covering the name of the animal.

2. Students can take turns answering questions about that organism such as: "What is my name?" "What do I eat?" "What adaptations do I have to live on sandy shores?" "In what ways am I connected to other sandy beach organisms?" and "Can you find me in the sandy beach displays?"

3. As each organism is selected by a student, the selected picture could be taped up near the appropriate display, or used to create a border for the "Above the Sand" bulletin board. These pictures can then serve as the key for the displays. (Alternatively, students can write the name of their organism on a small piece of paper or a 3" x 5" card and tape this name tag near the organism within their display.)

Who Am I?

1. Using statements such as the following, plus your own, give students clues about animals featured in the three-dimensional models. When students think they have a correct answer, they should raise their hand.

Sample Clues (let class guess Who Am I? after each clue):

- I have only one foot. I use it to bury myself in the sand before the next wave hits. I have a pretty sharp name. Who am I? [razor clam]

- I hunt beach hoppers. My jaws are like a knife. All my neighbors are afraid of me—they call me "super predator." Who am I? [rove beetle]

- I stay on the beach for three months at a time without eating. I love to fight. Sharks think I taste just right. Who am I? [elephant seal]

- I swallow sand. I eat tiny bits of food stuck to each grain. I hate bird watching. I am the color of blood. Who am I? [bloodworm]

2. Call on one student to give the answer, but have every student keep track of their correct responses. The student who guesses correctly can be the next to select an organism and make up clues to give the class.

Playing Twenty Questions

1. Have students play Twenty Questions. One student comes up and selects an organism, but doesn't tell anyone except the teacher which organism it is. The rest of the class can call out questions properly phrased for yes/no answers until someone thinks they know the identity of the organism.

2. Hold up the Key Concepts for this activity one at a time, and have one or more students read them aloud. Post them near the three beach displays.

- **Sandy beaches—and the beach wrack that washes ashore on them—provide homes to many kinds of organisms.**

- **Most of the animals living at the sandy beach are hidden from view under the sand to escape the pounding surf and hungry birds.**

Going Further

1. Have students work in pairs to write their own Key Concepts that represent things they learned and want to remember. Dozens of concepts are possible from this activity. Students can take charge of their own learning by deciding for themselves what they think is important. These new Key Concepts can also become part of student portfolios used for assessment.

2. Students can create mini-books similar to those made in Activity 1: Beach Bucket Scavenger Hunt. They can title their books "Living on Sandy Shores." Chapter titles can be as follows: Chapter 1: Life on Top of the Sand; Chapter 2: Life Under the Sand; Chapter 3: Life in the Beach Wrack. Another option could be for students to focus on organisms, writing three chapters on three organisms of their choice.

3. Have the students sketch the habitat displays. They should sit quietly in front of one of the displays and sketch the habitat scene, including physical aspects (sand, ocean) and the organisms living there. Have students put numbers by each of the organisms on their drawing, and then on a separate sheet have them list the numbers and the name of the organism. This can serve as the Key to their sketch of the habitat display.

4. Have students use colored yarn to join organisms within and between models which are interconnected in some way. Different colors can be used to show different relationships, such as red for predator-prey, green for herbivore-plant, and orange for sharing a microhabitat.

5. Consider a visit to a local aquarium, museum, or oceanographic exhibit that has displays related to the sandy shore. For example, the Wild California exhibit at the California Academy of Sciences in San Francisco depicts a 50 times magnified view of beach wrack. The Monterey Bay Aquarium has a beach with living shorebirds.

6. Visit an actual sandy beach and take a trowel or shovel to dig in the sand to investigate the organisms living there. Be sure to return each of the organisms exactly where it was found. Make a Bingo board before you go using reduced versions of the illustrated organisms included in this activity. While at the beach have the kids check off the organisms they see.

Information for the Displays

The brief summaries that follow describe a number of organisms your students may wish to build for the displays, with some additional ideas for making the organisms. The information is provided under the three display headings of "Above the Sand," "Under the Sand," and "Beach Wrack."

"Above the Sand"

The birds described below are listed with common names only. For most birds, there is uniformity in how common names are used and it is not as important to also give the scientific name. There are many wonderful bird books where students can find pictures of these organisms.

On the Beach

Sanderlings: These shorebirds feed in the backwash of waves on the surface and just under the sand probing for beach hoppers and small sand crabs. They can often be seen running along the beach in large flocks, seeming to chase the waves. They are seven inches tall and nearly white to pale gray with a one-inch long bill. Peregrine falcons prey on them. **Make into a stuffed pillow.**

Gulls: There are dozens of different types of gulls seen on beaches across the United States. One of the most common on all coastlines is the Herring Gull. On the Gulf Coast, you would see more Laughing Gulls. Gulls can often be seen resting in flocks on beaches at high tide and scavenging at low tide. They will eat almost anything—sea stars, crabs, dead animals, and even picnic lunches—they are real scavengers. Herring gulls fly over parking lots and drop hard-shelled animals like clams and sea urchins to break them open. Herring gulls are 23–26 inches tall, with a wing span of 57 inches. Laughing gulls are smaller, about 16 inches tall with a wingspan of 40 inches. Peregrine falcons prey on young gulls. **Make into a stuffed pillow.**

Willets: These noisy shorebirds probe into the sand with their two and one half inch long bill looking for worms, sand crabs, and small clams. They also pick through the beach wrack looking for beach hoppers and crabs. They

Activity 4 77

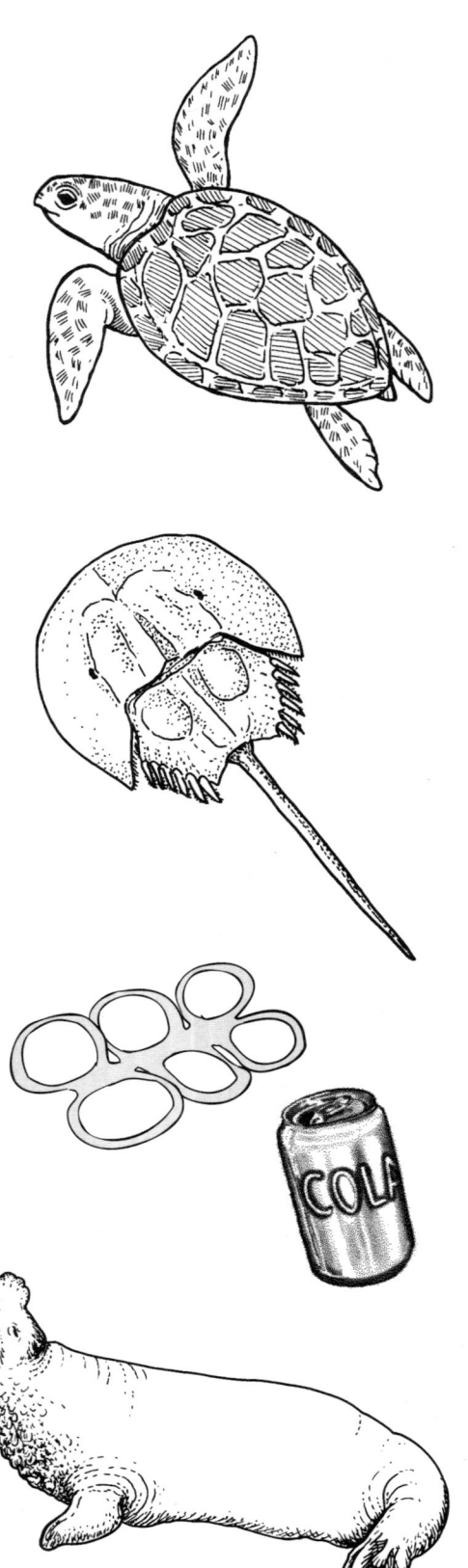

are primarily gray with a striking black and white wing pattern which can be seen when they take flight. They are 14–17 inches tall. Peregrine falcons prey on them. **Make into a stuffed pillow.**

Loggerhead Turtles: *Caretta caretta* These are the most common turtles in the United States. They nests in the tropics, including Florida, where they comes ashore at night to dig nests and lay eggs. This is a threatened species and some people dig up the nests and rebury them in more protected areas. Plastic debris and tar balls, which are mistaken for food, are serious threats to the loggerhead and all sea turtles. The most serious threat, however, is from shrimp nets in which they become entangled and drown. Near the shore, loggerheads eat crabs, clams, and urchins; offshore they eat jellyfish and the Portuguese man-of-war. **Make into a stuffed pillow.**

Horseshoe Crabs: *Limulus polyphemus* These ancient animals are actually not crabs at all, but are related to the extinct trilobites. They are a common inhabitant of sandy Atlantic shores from Nova Scotia to Florida and the eastern Gulf of Mexico. Horseshoe crabs come ashore in the spring, especially at night during the highest tides, to mate and lay eggs. Their long, rigid tails are used for balance and as an aid in burrowing. They must chew their food with the base of their walking legs since they have no mandibles or pinchers. They are scavengers, feeding on what they can find in the shallow offshore sand banks. They commonly eat mollusks, worms, crustaceans, and bits of algae. **Make into a stuffed pillow.**

Trash: Beaches, especially those on the Gulf Coast, include debris brought to the shore by currents from all over the world. In addition to its general environmental impact, such debris can also be dangerous to marine organisms. Turtles ingest plastic bags and similar items that masquerade as food. Fishing line and nets may entrap birds, turtles, and marine mammals. **Use actual items of debris, such as plastic bags, toys, cups, aluminum cans, fishing line, etc.**

Elephant Seals: *Mirounga angustirostris* These huge marine mammals, found on beaches from Central California to Baja California, can be up to 16 feet long and males can weigh 5000 pounds. Females are about half as long. They are brown and the males have a huge nose and loud bellow. Seals hind legs don't turn forward and their front flippers are very short so they can't climb on rocks easily. During breeding and molting, elephant seals may spend up to three months at a time up on the beach without eating or drinking. They are excellent swimmers and dive deeply to find fish and squid to eat. Young seals are especially vulnerable to attacks by white sharks and killer whales. **Make into a stuffed pillow. These seals are up to 16 feet long and so will have to be reduced from actual size.**

Harbor Seals: *Phoca vitulina* These marine mammals are very shy and will only come ashore where no people are around. They spend up to seven hours a day up on the beach, getting warm and escaping predators such as white sharks and killer whales. Their hind legs don't turn forward and their front flippers are very short so they can't climb on rocks easily. They are excellent swimmers and go back into the sea to find fish and squid to eat. They are silver gray with black spots and about four feet long and 250 pounds. **Make into a stuffed pillow. These seals are about four feet long, so may have to be reduced to fit on the display.**

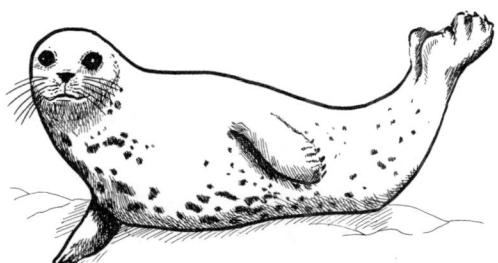

Armored Sea Star: *Astropecten* These sea stars, found on West and Gulf Coast beaches, can move above or below the sand offshore. They are sand colored or pink, about six inches across and have five arms with many spines along the edges. These sea stars don't stick out their stomach to feed like many other sea stars, but instead eat their food whole—one snail or sand dollar every day. Empty shells are spit out through the mouth. They will also scavenge dead fish and other animals. **Make into a stuffed pillow or glue sand onto paper for the rough skin.**

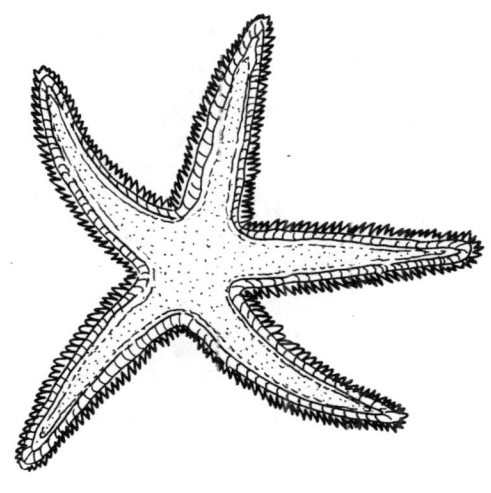

At the High Tide Line

Beach Wrack: Beach wrack is made up of seaweed (mainly kelp) and anything else (such as empty shells, feathers, dead animals) which is washed ashore and stranded by tides and storms. If stranded high enough on the shore, it can support a whole assemblage of organisms—its own temporary ecosystem with the rotting seaweed at the base of the food chain. **You might want to make it out of dark brown or black construction or crepe paper and add shells, feathers, and other things that would be washed ashore.**

Nearshore Water

Pelicans Over the Water: These huge birds have a wingspan of six and one half to seven and one half feet and are 45–54 inches tall from the tip of their beak to the tip of their tail. These birds fly above the water looking for fish, then make quick downward plunges—extending the neck and holding the wings far back as they hit the water. When not feeding, they fly just above the water, almost touching it with the tips of their wings. Marine pollution, including discarded fishing line and hooks and DDT, is a major threat to pelicans. **Make into a stuffed pillow.**

Surf Scoters Diving in the Waves Offshore: These are powerful diving birds, found on the West and East Coasts, that swim to a depth of 40 feet or more for food. They eat mussels, soft-shelled clams, snails, limpets, crabs, and some fish. They are 17–21 inches long from their beak to their tail. Gulls eat very young surf scoters. **Make into a stuffed pillow.**

Surfperch: These fish are found only in the North Pacific and the 18 different species are usually brightly colored. Many occur off sandy beaches in the surf. They are often caught by fishermen from the beach and some species are fished commercially. The young of these fish are born alive; no eggs are laid. The striped surfperch is very colorful with reddish orange and blue stripes along the body, and brilliant blue streaks and spots on the head and gill cover. The upper lip is black. The fish reaches a length of 15 inches. **Make into a stuffed pillow.**

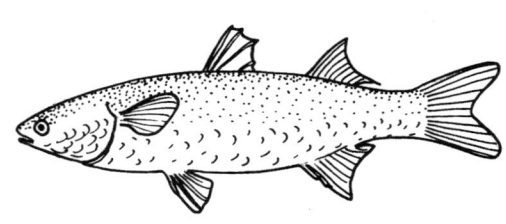

Striped Mullet: *Mugil cephalus* This is the most commonly observed fish in bays throughout the western Gulf of Mexico. This species swims in schools and frequently leaps from the water when threatened by a predator. Mullets leave the Gulf Coast bays in the fall to spawn in the open sea. They feed on detritus found on the ocean floor and cause a lot of sediment to cloud the water as they grub along looking for food. They are bluish-gray or greenish on the back and silvery on the sides and belly. A striped mullet can grow to a length of two and a half feet and can weigh over 15 pounds. **Make into a stuffed pillow.**

Plankton: Plankton are plants and animals that drift with the currents. Plankton can be any size (for example, jellyfish are plankton), but are usually very tiny. Phytoplankton are plants which supply over half of the world's oxygen. Zooplankton are animals. While some live their entire lives as plankton (like krill and copepods), others are the young of crabs, sea stars, beach hoppers and other animals which will one day live on a sandy beach. Many seashore animals eat plankton by filtering or straining the water. **You might want to show the plankton under a hand lens to show that it has been enlarged.**

Jellyfish: These animals, actually part of the plankton, are at the mercy of wind, waves, and currents and may be blown onshore. Although dead or dying once on shore, their stinging tentacles may still inflict painful stings. A common jellyfish on both coasts is *Chrysaora.* The species on the West Coast is brown and about one foot across the bell, with five foot long, reddish tentacles. The species on the Gulf Coast is pale yellow or pink, about 15 inches wide, and is called the sea nettle. *Pelagia*, another jellyfish found on West Coast beaches, has a bell two feet across with purple and white stripes and 10 foot long tentacles. A common and very dangerous relative of the jellyfish, found worldwide in warm water areas like the Gulf of Mexico, is the Portuguese man-of-war (*Physalia*). Its purple float, which looks like a partially inflated balloon, is attached to dozens of nearly invisible tentacles, armed with stinging cells, that stretch out for several yards. It captures and eats anchovies and other small fish. On the Gulf Coast, the most common jellyfish is the one-foot-wide, translucent white cabbage head (*Stomolophys*). It has no tentacles and is harmless to humans. **You might want to use inflated plastic bags or balloons for the bell and make tentacles out of ribbon or crepe paper. Some jellyfish are about one foot wide with five foot long tentacles.**

Sand Dollars: *Dendraster excentricus* on the West Coast and *Mellita quinquiesperforata* on the Gulf Coast. These animals live just offshore upright in the sand with one edge buried and the rest of the animal exposed. Young sand dollars ingest sand and store it in their gut as a "weight belt" to help hold them on the bottom. They are about three inches in diameter and light brown to dark purple when alive, but bleach to white when they die and are washed ashore. The Gulf Coast species has five oval holes through its test (its shell-like exoskeleton). These

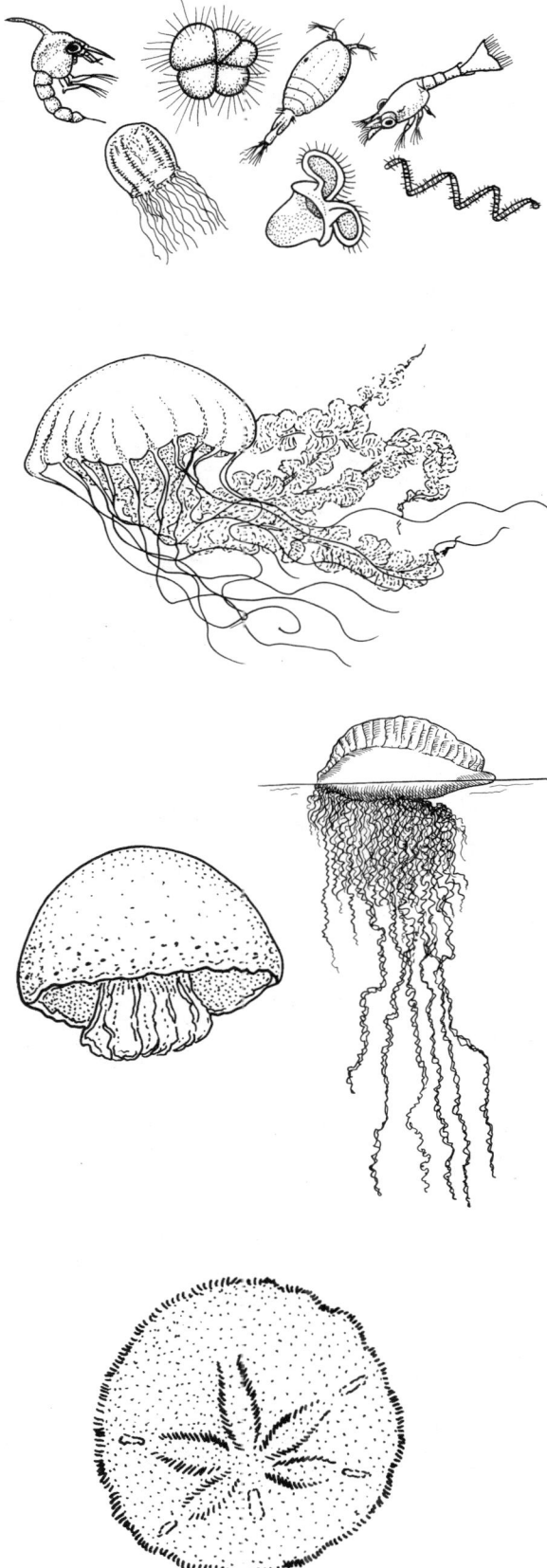

relatives of sea stars eat zooplankton and bits of algae found in the sand and are eaten by some fish and armored sea stars. **Make into a stuffed pillow.**

"Under the Sand"

Sand (Mole) Crabs: *Emerita* These animals, living on all coasts, are found in dense aggregations, buried in the sand with only their beady eyes and "hairy" antennae showing. They are about two inches long and bluish-gray or sand colored. As the backwash from each crashing wave recedes over them, they use their antennae to catch the drifting plankton as it floats by. They must dig very quickly to keep from being washed away by the next wave or eaten by hungry shorebirds or fish. **The illustration is life-size. Make into a stuffed pillow. Add small black eyes on stalks and split feathers for antennae. Show it buried in the sand with its eyes and antennae sticking up above the sand, or above the sand as if it were hit by a wave and about to dig in.**

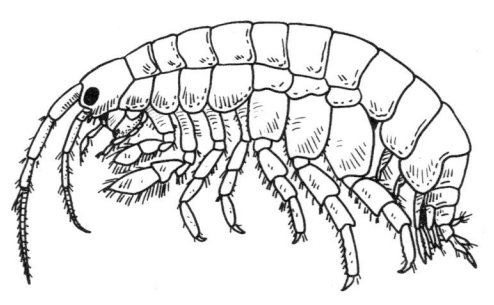

Beach Hoppers: *Orchestoidea* on the West Coast and *Ochestia* on the East and Gulf Coasts. These are small (about one inch long on the West Coast and one-quarter inch on the Gulf, not counting the antennae), shrimp-like animals with a body flattened side to side. They are crustaceans, related to lobsters and crabs. The West Coast species has a grayish white body and bright pinkish-orange antennae. The Gulf Coast species is olive to reddish brown. They are especially active at night and their primary food is the decaying seaweed they call home. During the day the hoppers are hidden away in burrows in the sand above the high tide line or underneath the wrack or driftwood. On a visit to the beach, you can usually see birds busily poking their bills into the kelp in search of beach hoppers. Other predators on the hoppers include pseudoscorpions, which capture their prey with their venomous pinchers, and rove beetles which capture them in their jaws and pierce their exoskeleton to suck out the fluids. **Life-size it is about one inch long. Enlarge it to about 20 inches long and make into a stuffed pillow.**

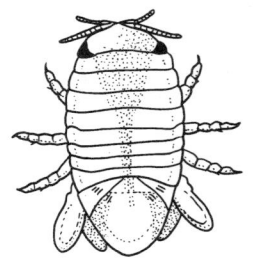

Isopod: *Ligia* These animals are the counterpart of terrestrial carrion beetles. They are such excellent scavengers that they can reduce a fish to a skeleton in no time. They occur in great numbers whenever a large animal carcass washes ashore. These scavengers are in turn eaten by birds and crabs. The isopod illustrated is about one and one-quarter inches long and grayish-blue to sand colored. **The illustration is about four times actual size. Make into a stuffed pillow. Don't forget the small black eyes and skinny antennae.**

Fiddler Crab: *Uca* These little crabs are found on many beaches around the world, including the Gulf and East Coasts and southern California beaches. The male crab has one enormous claw which it uses to signal females and fend off other males. The crabs excavate burrows in the sand and disappear very rapidly into the recesses of the burrow when disturbed. They eat small bits of plants and animals found in the sand, which they locate by sifting through a "clawful" of sand with their mouthparts. The crabs are eaten by shorebirds as they leave their burrows at low tide to wet their gills in the ocean. The crabs are dark brown during the day and beige at night. **Life-size the carapace is about three-quarters of an inch wide. Make into a stuffed pillow.**

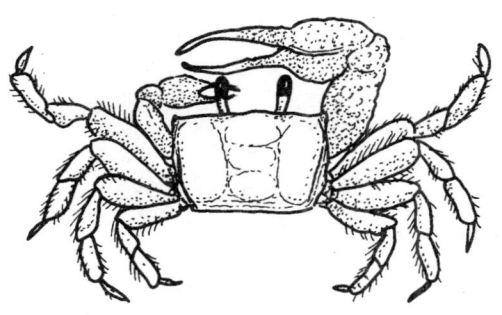

Bloodworms: *Euzonus mucronata* Dozens of bloodworms can be found in each shovelful of West Coast sand by digging from a few inches to a foot deep at about the mid-tide line. They are about two inches long and blood red with branched gills on both sides of nearly every segment of the worm. As they burrow through the sand they swallow many grains, much as an earthworm does in soil. Anything edible is digested—everything else passes right on through. **Footprints and holes in the sand show where birds have been feeding on these worms. You might use clay for the body and string for the gills.**

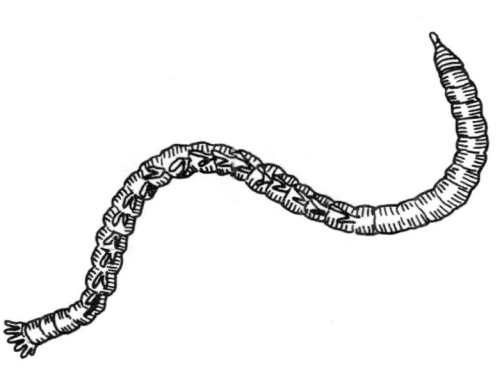

Bristle (or Red-Lined) Worms: *Nephtys* These worms are found on most coasts, one to two feet below the surface, often in the bloodworm zone where they are probably feeding on them or on other animals living in the sand. They are ferocious predators with hard, sharp jaws on the end of an extension of their throat (called a proboscis) which can shoot out from their mouth and grab their prey. The proboscis also helps them burrow through the sand. They are about six inches long and dark greenish-gray, with a red line down their back. **You might want to use clay and add strong pointed jaws and many bristles. Show some of these worms eating the bloodworms.**

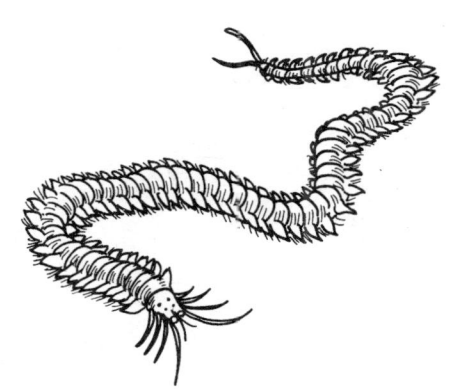

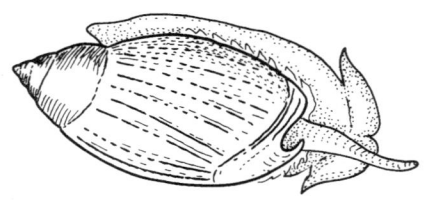

Olive Snail: *Olivella biplicata* on the West Coast and *Oliva sayana* on the Gulf and East Coasts. These are one of the few snails that make their living in sand, rather than on the sand. West Coast olive snails are about an inch and one-half long, and East and Gulf Coast olive snails are about one-half inch long, with a glossy, white and purple shell pointed at both ends so they can travel through the sand with less resistance. They have a large, wedge-shaped foot which they use to plough through the sand and a long siphon which they can extend above the sand to bring water to their gills. They are eaten by sea stars, octopus, moon snails, crabs, and fishes. The olive snail eats blades of drift kelp, and scavenges animals and small bits of food in the sand. **You might want to use clay (use a marble for a base) and don't forget to add the siphon and foot. Show the animal at low tide burrowing just under the sand (long slightly raised straight lines show where it is hidden). Also show it at high tide on the surface of the sand as it is searching for its prey.**

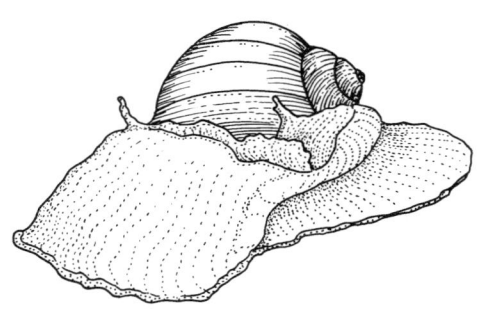

Moon Snails: *Polinices* spp. These are very large snails, up to four inches across, and are found on all coasts. Their shells are yellow to light brown with a beige to brown foot. They plow through the sand with their very large foot, with just the top one third of their shell showing above the sand. When their foot is fully expanded it is up to four times the size of the shell, but can actually be shrunk down enough to fit back into the shell completely with the trap door (operculum) closed tightly behind it. They prey on other mollusks, such as clams and snails by using their file-like tongue to drill a counter-sunk hole in the shell. They then insert their long snout into the hole and eat their prey. **Show the animal with about one third of its shell above the sand and its foot below, or show it completely in its shell with its trap door closed on the surface of the sand.**

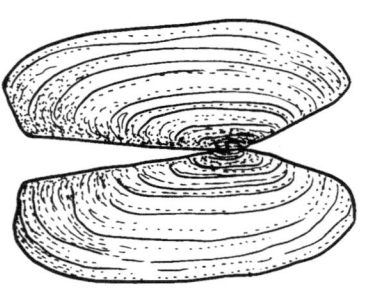

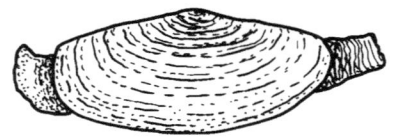

Razor Clams: *Siliqua patula* These West Coast clams can grow up to six and a half inches long. They have a brown shell, a white foot, and a brown-tipped siphon. They are very rapidly burrowing clams and can disappear from the surface between one wave and the next in about seven to ten seconds. They are able to burrow so fast because of their large, pointed foot which is up to 50 percent longer than their shell. The foot is thrust into the sand, the tip expands to form an anchor, then the muscle contracts and pulls the clam downward. They live on the lower part of the shore in shifting sand on surf-swept beaches. Like most other clams, they obtain food by using their siphon to suck in plankton-rich water which is then filtered and the plankton removed by the gills. People and starry flounders eat the razor clam. **Use paper plates and construction paper or clay. Show these clams about one foot down as if they were trying to escape a clam digger. Or show the clam near the surface with its siphon extended to feed on the plankton.**

Pismo Clams: *Tivela stultorum* The Pismo clam of California has a thick shell for protection against waves and predators because it cannot burrow as quickly as the razor clam. Their light brown shell has purplish-brown bands and may be up to seven inches long and four and one half inches wide. They live in a permanent burrow oriented with the narrow, hinged side of the shell facing the ocean. They have short siphons and need to be near the surface so they can filter feed. In fact, the tip of the shell can actually be seen just at the surface. These clams are now relatively rare because they have been over harvested by people. Sea otters also like to eat them. **Use paper plates and construction paper or clay. Show these clams with the siphon extended near the surface as they would feed at high tide, and also closed up tightly as if at low tide or when trying to escape a clam digger.**

Bean or Coquina Clam: *Donax* The bean clam is one of the most common animals on Gulf Coast beaches. This small (one inch) clam moves up and down the beach slope with high and low tides. This migration is cued by vibrations from the pounding waves. The clam burrows quickly in the sand with its large foot and streamlined shell. Many animals eat the bean clam including shorebirds, fish, crabs, and the moon snail. The bean clam is a filter feeder, bringing water in through its siphon and removing plankton from the water as it goes by the gills. **Use paper plates and construction paper or clay. Show the clam near the surface with its two short siphons extended to feed on plankton.**

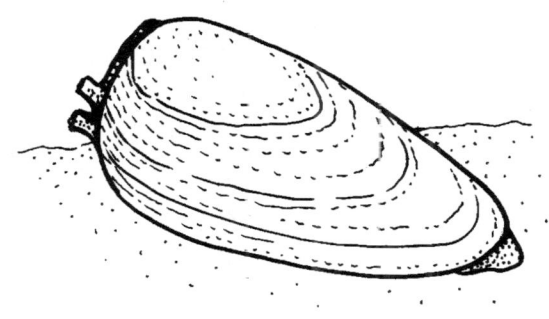

"Beach Wrack"

Beach Hoppers: *Orchestoidea* on the West Coast and *Ochestia* on the East and Gulf Coasts. These are small (about one inch long on the West Coast and one-quarter inch on the Gulf, not counting the antennae), shrimp-like animals with a body flattened side to side. They are crustaceans, related to lobsters and crabs. The West Coast

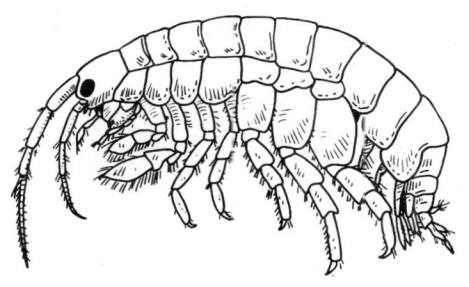

Activity 4 **85**

species has a grayish white body and bright pinkish-orange antennae. The Gulf Coast species is olive to reddish brown. They are especially active at night and their primary food is the decaying seaweed they call home. During the day the hoppers are hidden away in burrows in the sand above the high tide line or underneath the wrack or driftwood. On a visit to the beach, you can usually see birds busily poking their bills into the kelp in search of beach hoppers. Other predators on the hoppers include pseudoscorpions, which capture their prey with their venomous pinchers, and rove beetles which capture them in their jaws and pierce their exoskeleton to suck out the fluids. **Life-size it is about one inch long. Enlarge it to about 20 inches long and make into a stuffed pillow.**

Pseudoscorpions: *Garypus californicus* (other species of this genus are also found along the Florida coasts) These voracious predators resemble scorpions, hence their name, and are related to spiders and other arachnids. These are tiny, about one eighth of an inch long (when enlarged 20 times, they are about two and one half inches long). They have dark brown pinchers and head region, a yellowish body with brown-edged rectangles in each segment and striped brown and yellow legs. They live high up on the beach under debris, in rock crevices, and also within the kelp wrack where they find their food. They grab just-hatched kelp flies with their pinchers before they can fly away. They also seem to relish beach hoppers. The poison in their pinchers first immobilizes their prey and then much like spiders, they inject digestive juices with their mouth parts and suck out the digested prey. They are in turn eaten by rove beetles and birds. **You might like to use clay, toothpicks, pipe cleaners, and construction paper. Life-size it is about an eighth of an inch long. Enlarge it to about two and one half inches long.**

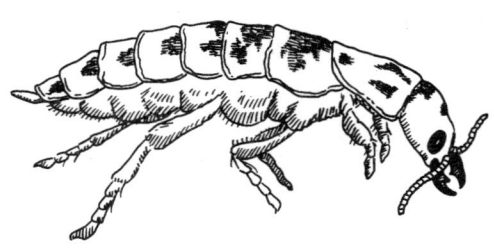

Rove Beetles: *Thinopinus pictus* These super predators of the California kelp wrack are only about three quarters of an inch long. When magnified 20 times, as in this display, they are about 15 inches long. Rove beetles are yellowish brown, much like the sand. These insects will eat anything that stumbles close enough for them to grab. They live in the sand and take advantage of the kelp when it is there. They have large jaws which they use like a knife to slice their prey. They mainly eat beach hoppers and kelp fly maggots and are eaten by birds pecking through the kelp. **Life-size it is less than an inch long. Enlarge it to about 15 inches long, and make into a stuffed pillow.**

Kelp Flies: *Fucellia* spp. These flies, which occur on all coasts, and are usually very annoying to humans, are about one half inch long, so when magnified 20 times are about ten inches long. They have hairy brown bodies with reddish legs. They complete their entire two week life cycle within the kelp wrack, so it is important that the kelp be high enough up on the shore that it doesn't get dragged out by the waves and tide. The maggots are found in the top four inches of the kelp and the adults are usually on top of the kelp, but may rest inside the wrack. Rove beetles and pseudoscorpions feed on the maggots and pseudoscorpions capture the young flies as they hatch out. Kelp flies eat the decaying kelp (they prefer giant kelp) and help break it down. **Life-size it is about one half inch long. Enlarge it to about ten inches long and make into a stuffed pillow.**

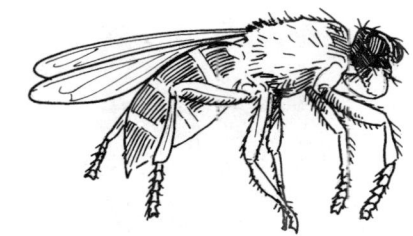

Giant Kelp: *Macrocystis pyrifera* Giant kelp is khaki brown and dominates in the offshore kelp forests of Central and Southern California. It grows to 150 feet long with blades about eight to nine inches long and three inches across, a one half inch wide stipe, and air bladders about one inch across and two and one half inches long. Giant kelp is the fastest growing plant on earth, growing up to two feet per day. Winter storms break the kelp loose from the rocks to which it is attached and wash it ashore where it forms the large mats of wrack. It is eaten by beach hoppers and kelp flies and acts as home to many other species. **The display will only show about a one-foot piece of the giant kelp because life-size kelp is so large.**

> **stipe**—roll brown paper into tubes about ten inches wide and tape together to a length of 20 feet.
> **air bladder**—stuff a large brown garbage bag with crumpled newspapers and tape the corners to round it out. Tape this to a paper tube five inches across and six inches long and then attach the tube to the stipe with tape. Make three of these air bladders and attach one to the stipe every eight feet.
> **blade**—a stuffed pillow 14 feet long and five feet wide at the widest point. Stuff it to a thickness of about two and one half inches. Make a total of three blades and tape each one to an air bladder.

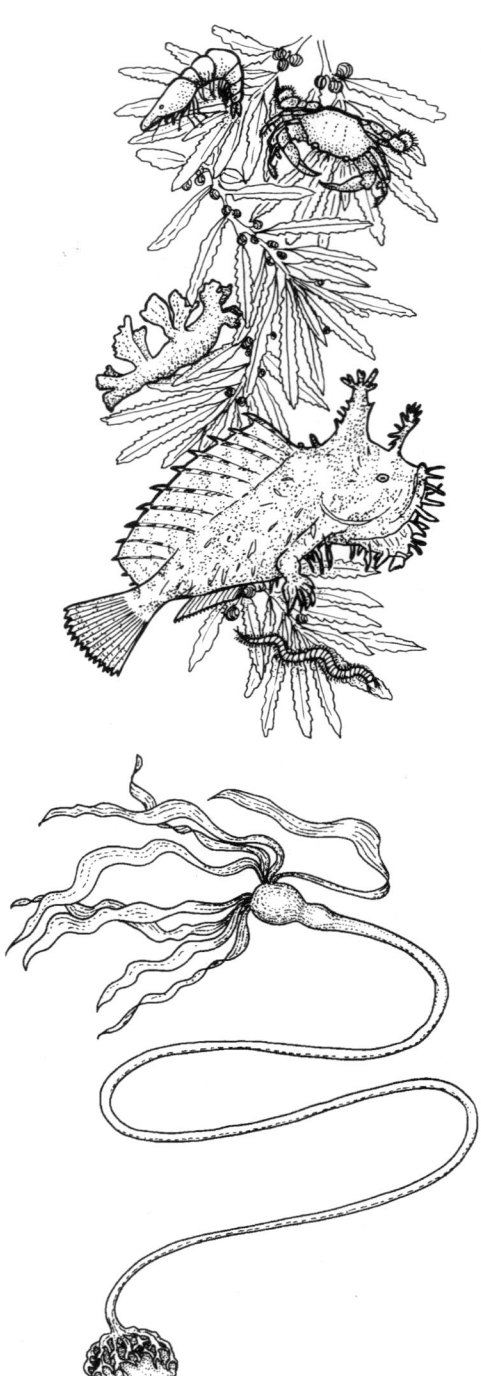

Gulfweed: *Sargassum* The Gulf Coast lacks the giant seaweeds that are common along the Pacific and Atlantic Coasts, but the floating, brown seaweed, *Sargassum*, is found on Gulf Coast (as well as Atlantic) beaches. It is transported by the same currents that bring the Portuguese man-of-war to Gulf beaches. It washes up on the beaches sporadically, bringing with it a fascinating community of specialized creatures, including worms, crabs, shrimp, and fish. It grows to about two feet in length, with small, pea-like (one-quarter inch) air bladders and is a light brown color.

> **stipe**—brown paper rolled into tubes about three inches wide and taped together to a length of 20 feet.
> **air bladder**—use greenish colored balloons blown up to about five inches.
> **blade**—a stuffed pillow six feet long and one foot wide.

Bull Kelp: *Nereocystis luetkeana* This is the predominant species of kelp forests in Northern California and further north. Bull kelp grows to about 100 feet long, with a stipe ranging from about three eighths of an inch over most of its length to up to three inches near the huge single air bladder which may be seven inches across. Today people make pickles, dolls, and baskets out of this kelp. Native Americans had many additional uses for it. The three-dimensional bull kelp will have to be a very young specimen because it would be impractical to make a large, older individual.

> **stipe**—roll paper into a funnel shape about ten inches across at the widest point where it joins the air bladder. Roll another piece of paper onto the narrow end of the first funnel and repeat until the tube is about 20 feet long. The last funnels should be about five inches across.
> **air bladder**—fill a large black plastic garbage bag with crumpled newspapers. Make it round by taping the corners.
> **blades**—tape many 20 foot long crepe paper streamers to the top of the air bladder or make stuffed pillow blades about six inches wide and two inches thick.

The Holdfast and Rocks: The entwining finger-like mass of the holdfast anchors the plant to rocks. It can be very large, up to three feet high and wide. Holdfasts often drag the rocks on which they were attached to shore with them. Many species can be found in a holdfast washed up on the beach including kelp crabs, sea urchins, octopus, clams, snails, and others. Boring clams can often be found in the rocks. **Twist brown crepe paper into ropes for the holdfast. Make ten ropes, each about two feet long. Glue one end of each rope to a rock (cardboard box) and gather and tie the other ends together to form the stipe.**

Barnacles: These volcano-shaped arthropods usually grow on the rocks to which the holdfast is attached. The holdfast then starts to grow over the shell, often causing the death of the barnacle. **Make a three foot high barnacle with a foot wide opening at the top.**

Bristle (or Red-Lined) Worms: *Nephtys* These worms are found on most coasts one to two feet below the surface, often in the bloodworm zone where they are probably feeding on them or on other animals living in the sand. They are ferocious predators with hard, sharp jaws on the end of an extension of their throat (called a proboscis) which can shoot out from their mouth and grab their prey. The proboscis also helps them burrow through the sand. They are about six inches long and dark greenish-gray, with a red line down their back. **Roll paper into a five inch wide tube and tape enough rolls together to make a six foot long worm. Don't forget really large bristles and black jaws.**

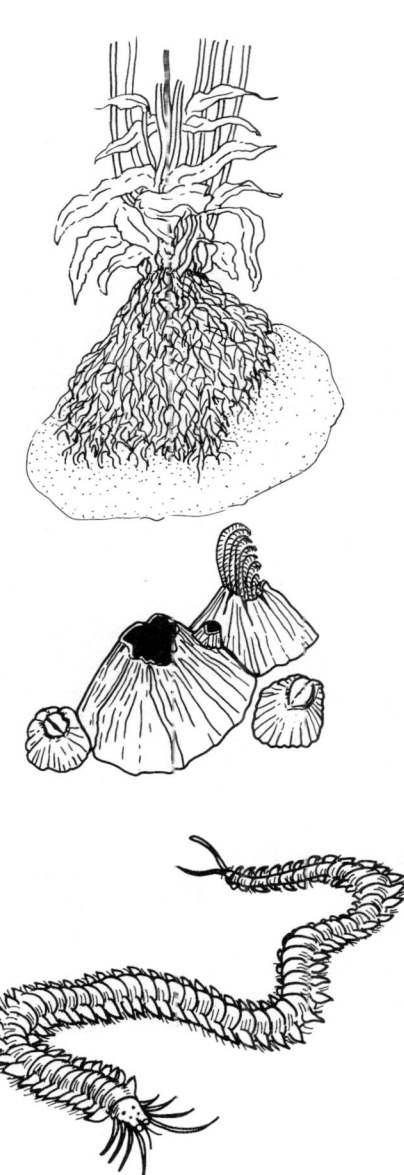

Activity 5: Oil on the Beach

Overview

People all over the world depend on oil. In the United States we use more oil per person than anywhere in the world for heating our homes; driving cars, trucks, buses, boats, and airplanes; lubricating machinery including bicycles; making plastics; and growing our food (petroleum-based fertilizers). The list goes on and on.

The more oil we use, the more we need to drill wells both on land and under the ocean, the more is transported, and the greater the probability that more is leaked, spilled, and dumped into the ocean. People can help prevent oil from polluting the ocean by using less, conserving energy, keeping cars well tuned, buying organically grown produce, and buying or using fewer plastic toys, bags, and other plastic products when other materials are available.

In this activity, students learn where oil comes from, the many ways people use oil, and how and why conservation of oil is important. They get "**Into** the Activities" with Partner Parade and a class Anticipatory Chart. In Session 2, students go "**Through** the Activities" as they investigate the effects of oil on the feathers of birds. In Session 3, the students help make a model beach in a tub and observe how it is affected by simulated tidal changes as oil spilled offshore washes onto the beach. In Session 4, students work in small groups to attempt to clean up an oil spill using a variety of methods.

Through experimentation, students discover that oil spills are almost impossible to clean up—the best defense is prevention. They discuss how oil spills can be prevented by reducing the use of oil and taking measures to make oil drilling and transport safer. Also reinforced by this activity is the concept that oil spilled at sea can travel with currents, tides, and waves to the sandy beach where it can harm the animals and plants that live there. Several "Going Further" activities are suggested for going "**Beyond** the Activities."

What You Need

For the class:
- a picture for each student from magazines or newspapers showing oil-based products (e.g., plastics) or showing oil being used in cars, trucks, motorcycles, tractors, factories, refineries, power plants, farm fields, etc.
- 6–10 sheets of chart paper (approximately 27" x 34")
- markers (several colors, wide tips)
- paper for sketches and Anticipatory Charts
- 1 cup of olive oil or other heavy vegetable oil (for the oil spill)
- 1 teaspoon of dry black tempera paint powder (to color the oil)
- 1 dropper bottle or squeeze bottle (for containing oil)
- 1 plastic dishpan
- a pencil or small cork to plug the hole made in the dishpan
- a pitcher or other container filled with enough water to fill the dishpan three quarters full
- a bucket or similar container to catch water
- a fist-sized rock
- 10–12 items to represent typical beach organisms, such as small rubber or plastic beach animals (crabs, etc.); drift algae, driftwood, plastic aquarium plants; crab molts, shells, etc.
- water-resistant glue (for gluing some of the "organisms" onto the rock)
- half a bucket of sand to form a sloping beach in the dishpan
- (*optional*) an empty quart and gallon container (see bottom sidebar on page 100)
- (*optional*) marine sanctuary posters (see "Resources")
- (*optional*) oil spill videos such as "When the Spill Hit Homer" (see "Resources")

Nearly all National Marine Sanctuaries in the United States provide free educational posters to teachers. See "Resources" for a list of addresses.

For Fouled Feathers in Session 2

For each group of 4 students:
- 1 cup of water
- the dropper bottle of prepared oil (see "Getting Ready" #3)
- 1 small bowl
- 4 bird feathers
- 2 hand lenses
- 2–3 sheets of newspaper to cover desks
- (*optional*) 1 tablespoon dishwashing detergent

For Cleaning the Oil Spill in Session 4

For each group of 6 students:
- ❏ a ziplock bag with one of each of the following clean-up items:
  - __ nylon stocking square (about 2" x 2")
  - __ cotton ball
  - __ sand (or kitty litter)
  - __ hay or straw (a small handful)
  - __ feather
  - __ fake fur (about 2" x 2")
- ❏ a plastic, aluminum, or paper bowl (plastic or aluminum bowls can be reused throughout this activity; paper bowls will also work, but you will need to use a new one each time)
- ❏ 10 drops of prepared oil (see "Getting Ready" #3)
- ❏ enough water to fill bowl two thirds full 1–2 times
- ❏ several paper towels
- ❏ 3–5 sheets of newspaper to cover desks
- ❏ 6 Oil on the Beach student sheets (masters on pages 106–108)
- ❏ 6 pencils

If your groups must be larger than six students, you will need some extra clean-up items. You could add spoons or 2" x 2" cardboard squares to the bags of clean-up items.

Getting Ready

1. A week or so before you plan to start this activity, have the students conduct interviews at home with parents, guardians, grandparents, siblings, and other family members or friends about their oil use using these questions:

   a. What are some ways that we use or depend on oil and oil-based products?
   b. Where do you think oil comes from?
   c. How do you think oil gets into the ocean?
   d. Where can we find out more about oil? (encyclopedia, library, internet, other friends or family)

   Students should take notes during the interviews and be prepared to share their findings with the class. Information from the interviews will also help prepare them for the Partner Parade discussions.

Many, if not most, children have no idea where oil comes from or that they use and depend on it in so many ways each day. The family interview gives them the opportunity to start thinking about the subject of oil and gives them some "prior knowledge" which they can then contribute to the class discussions.

2. Have students look with their families at home for magazine and newspaper pictures to bring to school. The pictures should be of oil-based products (e.g., plastics) or of oil being used in cars, trucks, motorcycles, factories, refineries, power plants, farm fields, etc. Start collecting any additional pictures that you can find on this subject.

Activity 5

3. Prepare the "oil" using the following recipe:

Oil Recipe

- *1 cup olive oil or other vegetable oil*
- *1 very scant teaspoon black powdered tempera paint*

Place in a dropper bottle or squeeze bottle and shake very well. Shake it again very well before every use. This is enough oil for the whole group.

You can test the mixture by putting a few drops in a cup of water—the drops should float at the surface. If they sink, add more oil.

The oil used in this activity is entirely biodegradable and safe for student use, yet looks and acts very much like crude oil. We must emphasize in the strongest possible terms that you should NOT use actual oil for these activities since it is a toxic substance and cannot be disposed of safely or legally through the garbage or down drains.

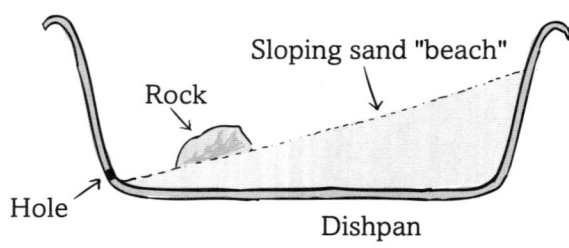

4. Pierce the dishpan on the side, very near the bottom corner using a nail or a drill. Small corks work the best to plug the hole, but if you use a nail to create a hole just a little smaller than a pencil, you can use a sharpened pencil to plug the hole.

5. Place enough sand in the pierced dishpan to simulate a sandy beach sloping up from the hole. Do not cover the hole with sand.

6. Glue one or two of the model beach organisms onto the rock and place it on the sand near the hole in the dishpan. Buy small, inexpensive plastic beach animals or use the beach drift from the Beach Buckets in Activity 1.

7. Start the class Anticipatory Chart. Draw a line down the middle of the chart paper to divide it in half lengthwise. At the top of one column write "What we already know about oil." At the top of the other column write "What we want to find out about oil."

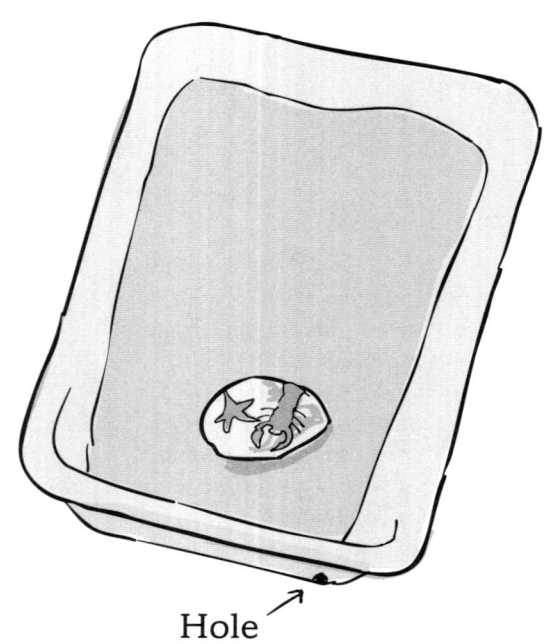

8. Write out the Key Concepts for this activity in large, bold letters on separate sheets of chart paper and set aside.

- **Oil spilled at sea can travel with currents, tides, and waves to the sandy beach where it can harm the plants and animals that live there.**

- **Oil spills are almost impossible to clean up. People can help to prevent them by reducing their use of oil.**

9. (*Optional*) Obtain videos that depict oil spills and marine sanctuary posters (see the "Resources" section).

Session 1: Partner Parade

1. Have the students recall the Partner Parade activity. Remind them that just as before, they need to cooperate, follow directions, and talk quietly with each of their partners. Pass out the pictures showing oil use that you and the students collected to aid their conversations.

2. Follow the steps on pages 30–32 to conduct Partner Parade.

3. Ask students the following Partner Parade discussion questions:

   - How do people use oil?
   - Where do you think oil comes from?
   - How does oil get into the ocean?
   - What are the effects of an oil spill?
   - How do you think you would clean up an oil spill?
   - How can people prevent oil from polluting the ocean?

4. Move along the two lines to help partners as needed. When you call time, have several students report what they discussed with their partners.

5. At the end of the activity, ask students to sit down with their final partner and think about some of the following questions. Then lead a class discussion.

   - Did it seem like the whole class was cooperating?
   - Did you learn something new?
   - Do you feel like you are becoming a better listener?
   - Did you like having the chance to talk to classmates that you don't usually talk to?

Anticipatory Chart on Oil

1. Have students continue to work with their final Partner Parade partner. Review with them how to create a class Anticipatory Chart. Pass out the paper and have students begin their own chart by copying the class chart onto a piece of paper.

Having students record their ideas and questions on their own charts provides valuable practice in organizing their thoughts in writing. If this type of recording is not appropriate for some of your students, then verbal discussions followed by a whole group sharing, with the teacher recording on the class chart, is a fine alternative.

The responses to the Partner Parade and the Anticipatory Chart can be used to assess your students' prior knowledge. If students seem generally familiar with the topics of where oil comes from, how we use it in our everyday lives, how we can conserve it, and the problem of oil spills, you can move directly into the Fouled Feathers activity and the activities that follow. If they do not seem to have much prior knowledge of these topics, you may have to proceed more slowly and provide more directed information.

2. Tell the class that through Partner Parade they have come up with some great ideas about oil and oil spills. Now it's time to get those ideas and their questions down on paper. Ask, "How will this chart help us later?" [It documents the wealth of our collective knowledge and gives us ideas for new projects and activities.]

3. Have them look at their pictures showing oil use from the Partner Parade. Tell them to discuss the two questions on the chart and write notes on their own charts.

4. When the class is ready, call them back together to share their best ideas with the whole group. Record the group's ideas on the class Anticipatory Chart. You can use pictures or icons representing everything the class can think of that uses or is made from oil. Display the chart and refer back to it throughout the activity.

Session 2: Brief Oil Talk

1. If it has not already been brought up in Partner Parade, you may want to **very briefly** tell students some information about oil use, drilling, transport, and spills (see in particular the second paragraph in "Behind the Scenes" for this activity, on page 115).

Using graphics to illustrate this brief introduction will give all students, especially English language learners, a better opportunity to learn and remember the content.

2. Illustrate your brief comments, as possible, with graphics, simple icons, and key words written on chart paper. Depending on your time limitations and level of student interest, you may want to encourage a few questions and brief discussion to lead into the Fouled Feathers activity.

Fouled Feathers

It is quite possible that some of your students have never seen crude oil, somewhat similar to used motor oil, and are not familiar with its properties. You may want to conduct a brief discussion about the oil's thickness, stickiness, and toxicity. You could also compare it to vegetable or other cooking oils with which your students may be more familiar.

1. Ask the students to imagine that they got oil all over their skin. What would it feel like? What would it do to their skin? How would they get it off? Say, "Now imagine you are a duck and have suddenly paddled into an oil spill!"

2. Tell them they are going to see what happens when birds get oil on their feathers. They will compare oiled feathers with those dipped in clean water.

3. Divide students into groups of four. Pass out the materials to each group. Have students cover their desks with newspaper. Tell them that they will each have a job to do in this investigation. Lead the students through the following steps.

4. Have one student in each group pour water into their small bowl until it is about half full.

5. Have another student dip two bird feathers into the bowl of plain water. This represents a bird that lands in the water to rest or catch food. Caution students to dip the feathers into the water **quickly** and then remove to dry. When they remove the feathers, they should place one on top of the other, and then set them on a table top to dry. (Leaving the feathers to soak too long may prevent the feathers from drying out properly.)

6. Have a third student shake the dropper bottle well then drop a single drop of oil onto the surface of the water in the bowl. Ask students to pretend that this is an oil spill from a tanker just offshore.

7. Have the fourth student quickly dip the remaining two clean, dry feathers into the bowl through the oil. Remove them. Is the oil visible? Place one on top of the other and set alongside the feathers that were dipped in plain water to dry.

8. Have each group look closely at the feathers. They can use hand lenses for more detailed examinations. Have them sketch each of the feathers including the barbs and shaft, and describe to their group what they observe. Assign one student in each group as a recorder to write down and illustrate what the group observes. What happened to the feathers? How did the feathers dipped into plain water compare to the ones dipped into oily water? Did they differ in how they dried? [In general, the feathers dipped into clean water dry quickly and separate from one another. The oiled feathers remain matted together.] Would matted feathers help or hurt the bird?

9. Explain to the students that when a bird has matted feathers, the feathers do not repel water. The cold ocean water gets under the feathers to the bird's skin, the bird cannot stay warm, and will freeze to death. Many oiled birds try to "clean" their feathers through preening and die from ingesting the oil.

Some teachers reinforce the division of labor on the student teams by numbering the students (1, 2, 3, 4) then providing instructions for Student #1, #2, etc.

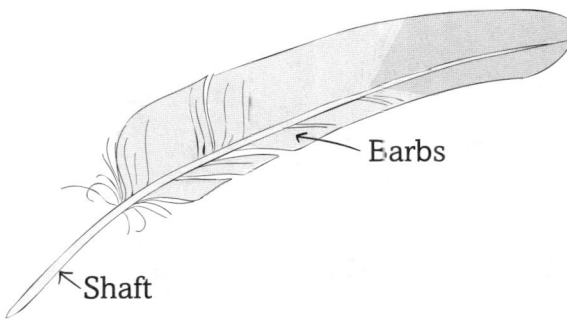

Several teachers have reported that students' interest about feathers and birds was so catalyzed by this observation they decided to do more activities related to the topic. You may want to have your students study feathers by looking at labeled diagrams, learning the names of feather parts, drawing different types of feathers, reading about their functions, etc.

10. (*Optional*) Now have each group wash the oiled feathers in the dishwashing detergent. (Dawn® was used on the *Exxon Valdez* spill to clean birds and other animals.) Again have them sketch the feather after it dries. Does it still look different from the feather dipped in plain water? In what ways? Explain that a bird whose feathers have been "cleaned" with detergent still cannot survive at sea. The problem is that the detergent also removes their natural oils, so the feathers appear fuzzy and messed up with all the barbs going in different directions. The birds must be kept warm in captivity until their natural oils are replenished or until they molt and grow new feathers. Washed birds are sometimes tested for buoyancy in a pool before being released.

Session 3: Oil on the Beach (Teacher Demonstration)

High Tide

1. Tell the students that they are going to create another beach model to find out more about the effects of oil on a sandy beach. Bring out the dishpan containing a layer of sand.

2. Divide students into groups of six and have them number off (1–6). Have Student #6 from each cooperative group come up to the front and choose one or two items from a pile of the beach debris (algae, crab molts, shells, plastic animals, etc.). Have them place the items one at a time on the beach model being created in the dishpan. Once all the items have been placed, carry the dishpan around the room so each group gets to see the beach that was created.

3. Plug the hole in the dishpan with a pencil or cork and fill it with water to the high tide line (until about three quarters of the sloping sand is covered). Call on Student #5 from each group to come up and see the high tide.

4. Ask the #5 students, "Do the organisms appear to be in the right place based on what we've learned about the sandy beach?" "Should we move some of the organisms to a different place on the shore?" Have them report back to their groups about what they saw. [The sand, debris, and organisms are now covered with water, except for those which were placed above the high tide line. Also, some

organisms, sand, and beach drift were moved by the incoming tide.]

5. Call on Student #4 from each group to watch as you remove the plug and the water drains into a bucket as the tide gradually changes from high to low. Have the students report back to their groups about what they saw. [The organisms are left strewn out on the beach as the tide recedes. Some sand is dragged out with the tide into the ocean bucket and some organisms were pulled towards the ocean.] Gently pour the water from the bucket back into the dishpan trying to disturb the sand as little as possible—it is now high tide again.

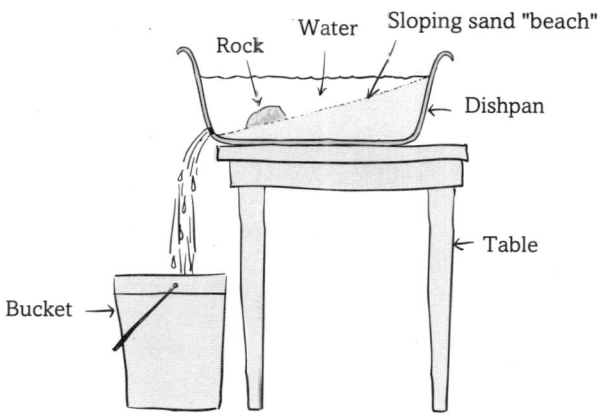

Oil Slick

1. Remind students that this whole activity is about oil on the beach. Given that, can they predict what might happen next?

2. Tell them that something terrible has indeed happened offshore of their beach. An oil tanker has collided with an underwater reef and oil is starting to leak out of the damaged hull. Call on Student #3 from each group to watch as you add about three tablespoons of oil to the surface of the water to simulate the offshore oil spill. Let students know it is high tide now in calm weather and the oil slick has not yet reached the beach.

3. Have the #3 students describe to the class the way the oil spreads out over the surface of the water to form a slick. Have the students report back to their groups about what it looked like as the oil slick formed.

4. Have the whole class file by to see the oil slick for themselves.

5. Have Student #2 from each group come up to observe what happens next. Remove the plug and again allow the water to drain into the bucket as the tide gradually changes from high to low. [Some of the oil will drain out to sea with the outgoing tide, but most of it will remain on the surface of the beach, coating the sand and the beach organisms.] Have students report back to their groups.

6. Have Student #1 from each group come up to watch as you replace the plug and pour the water from the bucket slowly back into the dishpan so that the oiled beach again approaches high tide. What happens to the oiled beach

If you are using fine sand, it may swirl up into the water at this point and make it difficult to see the organisms. This isn't a problem, but an opportunity to talk about what happens to the beach during a storm or with rough seas. You may want to tell students that a huge storm has just hit their beach.

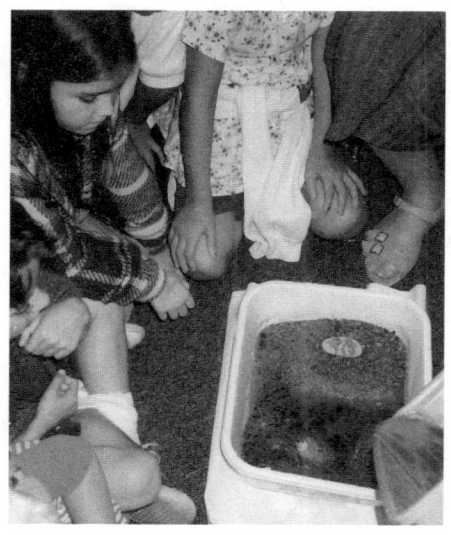

Activity 5

We have organized this powerful demonstration in this way to minimize crowd control problems around such a small viewing area. This method also emphasizes the importance of making good observations and communicating them clearly and completely to others. We encourage you to try it this way, but if you can't bear to have so few students observing each segment here are some options, suggested by teachers: video the demonstration and play it back for the whole class; do the demonstration twice, each time with half the class gathered around; have each group come up one group at a time to observe the results of each segment; gather the entire class around the demonstration area in small concentric rings, with the front row sitting, the next row kneeling and the last row standing—you could rotate students from the outer rows forward for each segment. Also, you may want to demonstrate another tidal cycle if you have time. The more times the tide changes, the more dramatic the results.

If three tablespoons of oil could cover this much water, can the students imagine how much water would be covered by the 11 million gallons of oil spilled in Prince William Sound, Alaska in 1989? Hold up empty quart and gallon containers for comparison. Then tell students these facts:
- *one quart of oil can produce a slick approximately two acres in size (an acre is almost as large as a football field)*
- *one gallon of oil can produce a slick about eight acres in size*

now? [The oil from offshore comes back in with the tide, and if the tide rises further than the first time, the mark of blackened sand also rises on the shore. This time, the oil is broken up into more, smaller globs, and is more evenly dispersed.] Have the students report back to their groups.

7. Remove the plug for a final low tide and have Student #6 from each group come up to watch how the oil covers the organisms on the beach. Have them dig down into the sand a little way to see if there is any oil below the surface. [The oil works its way deeper and deeper into the sand with each tidal cycle.] Have students look in the bucket to notice that the ocean stays polluted, and the beach looks worse and worse. Have the students report back to their groups.

8. Finally, carry the dishpan around the room so that everyone can have a look at the effects of oil on the beach.

9. Remind students that in real life on most coasts, the tide changes every six hours. The more times the tide changes, the more difficult it is to clean up the spill. The results students have before them represent a beach only 18 hours after a spill.

My Buddy Says

1. Your students by now are familiar with this activity structure. You may want to remind them about really listening to a classmate.

2. Conduct My Buddy Says, using three or four of the following prompts and questions:

- Pretend that the sandy beach organisms in our model beach were real. How do you think they would be affected by an oil spill washing up on their beach?

- Where did the oil seem to go at low tide?

- What happened to the oil at a very high tide?

- Do you think that the oil that got worked down into the sand would have any effect on the animals of the sandy beach?

- Do you think you could clean all the oil off the beach? How?

3. Spend some time discussing the last question with students. Write down their responses on chart paper or a chalkboard so they can be revisited after they actually try to clean up a spill in the next session.

Session 4: Cleaning the Oil Spill

1. Ask students to pretend there has been an oil spill out at sea. They know from the demonstration that once enough time has gone by for the tides to rise and fall, the oil will be impossible to clean up. Tell them their job is to try to clean up the spill before it hits the beach.

2. Divide the students into groups of six. Each group will receive their own small ocean where an oil spill has just occurred, and several clean-up items. Each item represents a method actually used to clean up oil spills.

3. Distribute the Oil on the Beach data sheets (masters on pages 106–108) to each student. Show and describe each clean-up item in the order on the data sheet. Point out the columns for predictions. Explain what it means to predict. Model the process of making a prediction for the first item on the list and recording the prediction on the data sheet by checking the appropriate box.

4. Ask all groups to have a brief discussion in which every student in the group makes a prediction about how well each of the items will clean up the oil. (The whole group doesn't have to agree, but they should discuss their ideas and reasoning with each other.) Tell students they'll get to write down why they predicted as they did on their data sheet.

5. Introduce and model the activity as necessary. Explain that they will work in their teams with a bowl of water that has a few drops of oil in it. Each student will choose one item from the bag. The student with the first item listed on the data sheet tries to clean up the oil from the water first. Then the student with the second item listed on the data sheet tries, and so on. Students should place the oiled clean-up items on the paper towels.

6. Have the groups cover their tables with newspaper. Distribute one bag of clean-up items to each group and have the students empty them out so they can look at each item.

7. Distribute the bowls and paper towels and have each group fill their bowl two thirds full with water and place it in the center of the group. Walk around the room and place 2 or 3 drops of oil into each bowl of water, remembering to shake the dropper bottle well.

8. Have each student choose one item from the bag and proceed as you described. Circulate to be sure students understand the task and are working together. If, after a student has tried their item, the group thinks most of the oil has been cleaned up, you can add 2–3 more drops of oil to their bowl for the next student to clean up. This gives each student the same opportunity to clean up the oil.

9. As each item is tried, each student should decide how well the item cleaned up the oil and check the appropriate box on their data sheet. (Again, the entire group doesn't have to agree, but they will probably want to discuss their results and talk about why their results may not agree.) Ask students to briefly describe their results on their data sheets.

Debriefing the Results

1. After each group has completed their oil clean up and recorded the results on their data sheets, lead a class discussion based on the questions below. Record conclusions of the discussion on chart paper or the chalkboard.

2. Ask, "What worked the best and what did not work well at all?" [The students may find that feathers and fur worked the best at cleaning the oil. This graphically demonstrates why oil spills are especially dangerous for shorebirds, seabirds, and sea otters. Their fur or feathers attract and soak up oil. The barbs of the birds' feathers stick together and the sea otters' pelt becomes sticky and matted. They are then no longer able to keep themselves waterproof and are therefore at risk of hypothermia and freezing. Also, both birds and mammals depend on preening to keep themselves meticulously clean. In the process of cleaning themselves they may become sick and weak from ingesting the toxic oil.]

3. Ask, "Which group thinks their water is now clean?" If a group thinks they really cleaned it up, ask, "Is the water clean enough to drink?" [No, so what does "clean water" really mean? How clean is clean? Should it be as clean as it was before the spill, or just cleaner than it was after the spill?]

4. Now raise the question—"Would any group say they really cleaned up their oil spill?" "Was any group 100 percent successful?" [Their responses may lead the class to conclude that the phrase "oil spill clean up" contradicts itself, because it is not really possible to clean up an oil spill completely.]

5. Ask, "Then what can we do to prevent oil spills from happening in the first place?" [engage in oil conservation, encourage use of alternative energy sources, tune up cars] Remind students that although oil spills by large vessels on the ocean are major disasters, much more oil makes its way to the ocean each year by leaking out of cars onto streets or being poured in small amounts down storm drains where it eventually drains to the ocean. This emphasizes the fact that individuals also have a great deal of responsibility for reducing oil pollution. As a society, we can also propose laws that make oil drilling and transportation safer.

6. Now ask, "What should we do with all the oil-soaked clean-up items?" Explain that this is the same question people ask when actual oil spills occur and the oil-soaked material is brought ashore. Some people say that these techniques simply move the oil spill from the water to the land.

7. Explain the ways that actual clean up procedures were simulated by the items used in this activity. For example, oil is strongly attracted to oil-based materials like nylon—the nylon floats on the surface and acts as a filter or sieve, collecting the oil and letting the water pass through. Sand and/or kitty litter absorb the oil, but because they are heavier than water, as they sink they carry the oil to the bottom with them. Cotton and hay are also used to absorb the oil. Feathers and fake fur represent the unlucky animals coming in contact with the sticky oil.

8. Hold up the Key Concepts for this activity one at a time, and have one or more students read them aloud. Post them near the class charts from this activity or sanctuary posters.

- **Oil spilled at sea can travel with currents, tides, and waves to the sandy beach where it can harm the plants and animals that live there.**

- **Oil spills are almost impossible to clean up. People can help to prevent them by reducing their use of oil.**

In real-life situations, often the oily clean-up material is burned, which just moves the pollution to the air. There are recycling centers which will take the used oil and oily water and materials used in a clean-up activity or the used oil from car oil changes. We can't just put motor or other industrial oil in landfills because it ultimately makes its way to the water and may also harm animals visiting the landfills in search of food. For this activity though, we don't have to worry because our oil is non-toxic and is made from biodegradable vegetable oil and tempera paint.

Going Further

1. Have students work in pairs to write their own Key Concepts for this series of environmentally-related activities. Students can take charge of their own learning by deciding for themselves what they think is important. These new Key Concepts can also become part of student portfolios used for assessment.

2. Students can create a mini-book which includes drawings and descriptions about what they learned (see pages 22–25 for instructions and templates). Have students title their books, "On Sandy Shores." Chapter titles can be: Chapter 1: The Sandy Beach; Chapter 2: The Oil Spill; and Chapter 3: Who Is Responsible?

3. Have students keep a tally of every time they do or use something that uses or is made from oil. Then discuss alternatives to each oil consuming activity. They can do this first at school in pairs, then at home.

4. Have students work in groups to make posters about conservation, such as walking or riding a bicycle to school or their parents taking the bus to work.

5. Visit a bird rescue center and find out how to volunteer during an oil spill.

6. Draw pictures of the marine sanctuaries and estuarine reserves around the United States. (See "Resources" for addresses for posters and information.)

7. Watch videos of oil spills and their aftermath such as the *Exxon Valdez* oil spill that occurred on March 24, 1989 in Prince William Sound in Alaska, or the Shetland Island spill in 1994. (See the "Resources" section.)

8. Have groups of students pick one of the following pantomime scenarios (or make up one of their own) to act out. Have the rest of the class try to guess what they are dramatizing. Alternatively, they can draw a mural depicting one of these scenarios.

- Sand crabs live just under the surface of the sand and stick out their feathery antennae in the waves to breathe and capture food. What if their antennae are covered with oil? Can they still eat?

A good connection to Activity 5 is provided in the Raindrops and Oil Drops activity from the GEMS Teacher's Guide Liquid Explorations. *In that activity, students have the opportunity to play with drops of water and oil to investigate questions about the shapes of the drops and their "mixability." This activity was used by many teachers in Alaska following the large oil spill there, giving students direct experience to help them better understand the news reports they heard.*

- Many shorebirds feed on sand crabs. What happens to the shorebirds if their sand crab food is covered with oil?

- Beach wrack is home and food for many organisms which in turn serve as food for shorebirds. What happens to this small community when it is coated with oil?

- Shorebirds feeding on the sandy beach may become covered in oil as they search for their prey and rest on the sand. What effect does the oil have on their ability to capture prey, escape predators, and stay warm?

9. Have students make posters, buttons, or bumper stickers to tell others about what they've learned about oil pollution and conservation.

Name _____

OIL ON THE BEACH

Prediction Data Sheet

Check the box which describes your prediction the best.

Name of clean-up item	PREDICT How well will it clean up the oil?		Why do you think this will happen?
	will clean up a little ☹	will clean up a lot ☺	
1. Nylon			
2. Cotton Ball			
3. Sand or Kitty Litter			
4. Hay			
5. Feather			
6. Fake Fur			

© 1996 by The Regents of the University of California, LHS-GEMS. *On Sandy Shores.* **May be duplicated for classroom use.**

Name _____

OIL ON THE BEACH

Results Data Sheet
Check the box which describes your results the best.

Name of clean-up item	TRY IT! How well did it clean up the oil?		Describe your results.
	cleaned up a little oil	*cleaned up a lot of oil*	
1. Nylon			
2. Cotton Ball			
3. Sand or Kitty Litter			
4. Hay			
5. Feather			
6. Fake Fur			

© 1995 by The Regents of the University of California, LHS-GEMS. *On Sandy Shores.* **May be duplicated for classroom use.**

Name _____

OIL ON THE BEACH

Data Sheet Questions

1. What worked well?

2. What did not work well?

3. Did your group clean up all the oil?

4. Think back to what you told your partner in the Partner Parade about how you would clean up an oil spill. What was your plan then?

5. Now, how would you clean up an oil spill?

Behind the Scenes

*The following information is provided as background, organized according to the five main activities in this guide. This section is **not** meant to be read out loud to or distributed directly to your students. It is intended to provide necessary and concise background for you in presenting the activities and responding to student questions. Please see the "Resources" section for books and other materials that will help you and your students delve more deeply into sandy beaches. Additional background information on sandy beach organisms can be found in the "Information for the Displays" section (on page 77) and in brief text on the masters of organisms that appear at the back of the book.*

Activity 1: Beach Bucket Scavenger Hunt

A sandy shore reveals evidence of nearly everything that has been to the beach or has been in the adjacent ocean. Look closely at sand and you might see pieces of rocks that have broken free from the rocky seashore, cliffs, and ocean floor. Rocks and minerals are also carried from tall and distant mountains to beaches through streams and rivers. There might be shells or shell fragments from animals that once lived on nearby reefs, bones from animals living in the ocean and on land, algae, coral fragments, glass, driftwood, plastics, feathers, and much more. Waves and wind push sediment and "beach drift" from the ocean onto beaches around the world. Marine debris (garbage that ends up in the ocean or at the seashore) is carried from land by the millions of visitors to the world's beaches and dumped from the world's fleet of private, commercial, and military boats and ships. As waves crash against the shoreline, all these objects are ground into sediments and rough edges are progressively smoothed and rounded into sand grains.

The things you find at the beach can be separated into many categories. You can find evidence of things that were once alive (or biotic materials), such as shells, bones, feathers, corals, egg casings, driftwood, and seaweeds. Biotic material can be further subdivided into evidence of plants or evidence of animals. You can also find evidence of things that were never alive (or abiotic materials). A few common types of abiotic materials are rocks, minerals, glass, and plastics. Evidence of people is another category, but these materials can be biotic (paper, pieces of lumber, chicken bones), or abiotic (plastic, glass, metal).

Beaches throughout the world are strewn with drift and debris, both natural and human-made. The human-made debris, mostly in the form of plastics, is often deadly to ocean and sandy beach inhabitants. It is important to recognize the different types of drift and debris, and to be able to distinguish between those that should be removed for the safety of people and animals from those that should not. For instance, drift and debris such as kelp and broken shells should be left on the beach because they form part of an important ecosystem. We can protect our beaches and keep them healthy through beach clean-up projects and prevention of littering in the first place.

Activity 2: Sand on Stage

Nearly all solid materials in the world, both living and non-living, will eventually be eroded into sand. Mountains, rocks, minerals, shells, corals, bones, metals, and glass are all worn down over time by wind, waves, rivers, earthquakes, and other forces into smaller and smaller particles. For this reason, sand is often said to be the Earth in miniature. The story of a grain of sand can be the story of the evolution of the crust of the earth. Thousands or millions of years may pass as a rocky outcropping on a mountain top is transformed into a grain of sand on a sandy beach which may finally fall into a submarine canyon where it again might be compressed into rock and be uplifted into a mountain. It is no wonder that sand, whether found on a beach, in a child's sandbox, or in Native American paintings, is often associated with soothing feelings such as drifting, flowing, and timelessness.

Beaches can form wherever water moves loose material onto a shore. Rivers, lakes, ponds, and oceans can all have beaches. These beaches can be made of sand, gravel, or cobbles—these terms refer only to the size of individual grains on the beach.

The sand on every beach has its own unique history. Detailed observations combined with some good detective work, however, can often allow us to make some reasonable hypotheses about where the sand originated, how old it is, and perhaps even from what part of the beach it was collected. Sand from the remains of plants or animals is referred to as biogenic, while sand from non-living sources is called abiogenic. A closer look at sand, through a hand lens or microscope also reveals the striking beauty of individual grains.

Some sand is produced right at the shore where waves crash on rocks, headlands, and reefs. For example, black or red sand beaches on the Hawaiian and the Galapagos islands are found directly next to or on top of lava flows of the same color. White sand beaches in Florida and in the Caribbean are primarily made of eroded coral reefs. Parrot fish, which eat coral polyps, grind up the corals with their sharp teeth, and can excrete up to 100 pounds of coral sand per year. Pink sand might be full of coralline algae fragments. Other sand comes from far inland. Mountains are weathered by freezing, wind, rain, and running water, and their fragments are carried down streams and rivers to the seashore. Quartz, a glass-like mineral, is the most common mineral on earth, and is nearly insoluble in water. It is often the most common component of these transported sands. In fact, most light colored sand beaches contain large amounts of quartz.

Sediments are classified by particle size, from mud to gravel. Particles are generally called sand when they are between .06–2 mm. Where particles are deposited depends on the speed of the water carrying them. In fast moving river or ocean water only the largest, heaviest sand grains settle out. On wave impacted outer coast beaches, only large sand grains or even gravel will be found. The smaller the particle, the slower the water must be moving for it to settle out. Mud grains are only found inside protected bays or far offshore on the deep ocean bottom where the water is barely moving.

On a normal coastal beach, no individual sand grain stays in the same place for long. Each wave picks up thousands of grains and deposits them somewhere else. If a prevailing wind causes waves to always strike the coast from the same angle, sand can be slowly transported great distances along the coast. The finest grains of sand can become airborne in the wind, and are often deposited high up on the beach in the dunes. Dune sand is usually noticeably finer and lighter than beach sand.

Sandy beaches surround the edges of nearly every coastline, but each is unique, and tells a different story about the history of the continents. Beaches are a shared resource, and are firmly embedded in the psyche of people from many cultures.

Activity 3: The Sights that Sand has Seen

Sandy beaches are the result of erosion. Every grain of sand has a history and is a tiny world in itself. It started its evolution as something other than a grain of sand, somewhere other than the beach where you see it today. To begin to trace its history we can look at the grain of sand under a microscope. White sand beaches might be made up of crushed coral or coralline algae. Black sand beaches are made up of crushed volcanic rock. There might be many different multi-colored minerals on the beach if the sand originally came from mineral-rich granite. Pieces of bone, shell, and feathers are also mixed in with the sand on many beaches.

Erosion can start long before a rock reaches the ocean. Wind, ice, and rain are powerful tools of erosion that break up rock formations high in the mountains. Wind can push boulders and stones loose, but it also gradually wears down rock surfaces by blowing particles such as sand, silt, and gravel into cliff sides. In essence these particles sandblast the rock into fine sediment. Rain often combines with the wind to wash out wind-loosened sediment. Rain water also can chemically dissolve many types of rocks. Some other erosion processes are seasonal. During the fall, water collects in rock fissures, and then freezes and expands during the winter and causes the fissure to get larger. This timeless seasonal cycle of ice forming in rock fissures, melting during spring and then freezing the following winter causes cracks to widen and lengthen and sections of rock to loosen and break off. Rivers and streams wash these rocks downstream toward the ocean, often breaking them up into smaller pieces along the way.

Once the pieces of rock reach the ocean, the strong, continuous force of ocean waves sorts the particles by size and further grinds them into smaller pieces. Waves are an important influence on life in the ocean. They can easily be observed from a sandy beach where they crash and pound in rhythmic swells throughout the year. Storm waves are especially powerful when they hit the shoreline and can cause serious erosion.

Waves in summer and winter are different in size and strength. Winter storms cause large, steep waves that crash onto the shore close together, pulling sand offshore with the power of their weight and force. Winter beaches are often eroded to become narrow and steep, sometimes reduced to cobbles with no sand at all. The sand is taken just offshore onto sandbars or out to sea. In summer, waves are less steep, shorter, and farther apart. As they roll in gently, the sand is deposited back on shore to form the beach again, now wider and less steep than in winter.

The rhythmic waves push a variety of objects other than sand onto the beach. The waves push objects such as kelp and other seaweeds, shells, human trash, and sometimes other organisms to the top of the high tide line. We call this line of kelp and other debris "beach wrack." Often beach wrack forms a visible line the length of the beach at the highest extent of the most recent high tide. Along with the kelp, a myriad of organisms living on the kelp stipes and fronds are carried into the beach wrack. Among these organisms might be snails, crabs, or limpets. A new community forms in the beach wrack as the kelp begins to decay. Worms, flies, and birds are attracted to the nutrient-filled mass. The beach wrack becomes a seasonal but quite visible ecosystem on the sandy beach.

The sand on the beach is in constant motion, due to the intense impact of regular wave action as well as the force of winter storms. Sand grains may be hit by as many as 8000 ocean waves a day! A single sand grain may move up and down the beach many times in a day in the wash of waves. Because the waves hit the beach at an angle, the sand is also moved along the beach. This is called the longshore current and it can move sand considerable distances. On the West and East Coasts movement is to the south. Beaches are one of the most unstable marine environments, better thought of as rivers of sand than anything permanent.

Activity 4: Build a Sandy Beach

We all have our "mind's eye" view of what we expect to see on a sandy shore. More than almost any other habitat, beaches conjure up just about as many different images as there are cultures around the world. What do you think of when the word beach is mentioned? Perhaps you see waves crashing, surfers riding the curls, vast expanses of sand, chilling fog, noisy cobbles grinding against each other, sunbathing, wind blowing, piles of kelp washing ashore, palm trees and sea turtles, cars and clam diggers, jellyfish glistening on the sand, shells strewn about after a storm, children and birds chasing the waves, etc.

We have many different images of beaches because there are many different kinds of beaches. Even the same beach may look entirely different from one season to the next or even day by day. There is one thing all beaches have in common however—the water and sand are in constant motion. Is it any wonder that most images of sandy beaches are quite barren of visible plants and animals? How could they make a living here? What is there to eat? How could they survive the crashing waves and scouring sand?

The answer to the riddle of life **on** a sandy shore is that most of the life is actually hidden **in** the sand or under the beach wrack. How might our image of a sandy shore change if we could actually see the myriad animals in this hidden world? Organisms occur in such numbers and such diversity that only a few can be mentioned here—sand (mole) crabs, olive and moon snails, beach hoppers, isopods, bristle worms, bloodworms, razor and Pismo clams, and along the Gulf Coast, the bean clam and turtles.

Another important component of many beaches is the offshore organisms that may get washed onto the beach by winter storms, high tides, and large waves. Depending upon where it is, beach wrack is made up of kelp, other seaweeds, various sea grasses, and anything else such as empty shells and evidence of people (plastic and glass) which is washed ashore and stranded by tides. If stranded high enough on the shore, it can support a whole assemblage of organisms—its own temporary ecosystem with the rotting plants at the base of the food pyramid. Most of the animals of the beach wrack are hidden underneath the seaweed (in California, mostly giant, feather boa, and bull kelps) to avoid the bird predators and the hot sun. Scientists have discovered much of the action inside this wrack by using miniature cameras like the ones surgeons use. Some of the organisms that take advantage of this transient resource include beach hoppers, pseudoscorpions, rove beetles, and kelp flies. Rocks—with attached holdfasts containing barnacles, worms, and many, many other species, including occasional octopuses—ripped from the offshore kelp forests may also be present. A Gulf Coast beach wrack would have turtle, shoal, and widgeon grasses and sargassum weed from the Sargasso Sea instead of kelp.

The vast expanse of beach and looming cliffs with which we are most familiar is host to another assemblage of organisms. Some of the organisms we associate with the beach, such as marine mammals, use it as a site for escaping from predators, birthing, and warming. Others, such as the birds, use it as a rich food resource. Some unlucky individuals, such as jellyfish and sand dollars, are found up on the beach as a result of waves pushing them ashore to their death. Many organisms are ultimately washed up onto the beach after they die offshore.

A variety of shorebirds, including sanderlings, willets, turnstones, and snowy plovers can be seen feeding on organisms living just under the sand, while scavenging gulls are looking for whatever they can find. The lucky beachcomber may see sea stars on the beach, pelicans over the water, and surf scoters diving in the waves close offshore. Plankton, sand dollars, surfperch, and halibut can be found in the nearshore water. Harbor and elephant seals may be seen hauled out on the beach. Beach wrack and grunions may be seen at the high tide line, the latter in Southern California. On the Gulf Coast loggerhead turtles, horseshoe crabs, ghost crabs, and laughing gulls reward visitors to the beach.

Activity 5: Oil on the Beach

People all over the world depend on oil. In the United States we use more oil per person than anywhere in the world for heating our homes; driving cars, trucks, buses, boats and airplanes; lubricating machinery including bicycles; making plastics; growing our food (petroleum-based fertilizers); and making petroleum jelly. The list goes on and on.

Oil is obtained by drilling deep wells, either on the land, or on the shallow continental shelf below the ocean's surface. Once the oil is removed from underground, it must be transported long distances and then refined. The more oil we use, the more drilling needs to be done, the more oil is transported, and the greater the probability that more is leaked, spilled, and dumped into the ocean.

Spilled oil is next to impossible to clean up. Oil which is not immediately recovered is at the mercy of currents, waves, and tidal changes that carry the oil to shore. Seabirds and sea otters become covered in oil and are no longer able to keep themselves waterproof and are then at risk of freezing. They are poisoned when they ingest the oil as they attempt to clean themselves by preening. As the oil reaches the beaches, intertidal life which filters the water for food, or feeds on suspended materials, is suffocated, poisoned, or starved. Shorebirds preying on sandy beach organisms are also covered with the oil and poisoned from preening or by eating contaminated food. They may also starve because they cannot find food.

Oil pollutes the ocean when there are major oil spills due to accidents at sea, but in addition, oil is constantly leaked and spilled in small amounts all the time. The greatest source of oil pollution in the ocean comes from "non-point source pollution" such as the small drops of oil that continually leak from cars onto our streets and then are carried by rain through sewers and storm drains to the ocean. Big spills make the news and anger the public, but our appetite for and excessive use of oil also "drives" the problem.

People can prevent oil from polluting the ocean by using less, conserving energy, driving less, buying organically grown produce, buying/using fewer plastic toys, bags, and other plastic products when other materials are available. Surprisingly, a huge percentage of oil pollution could be prevented simply by keeping our cars consistently well tuned.

In some nations and regions, these and related environmental concerns have also given rise to more large-scale solutions. In California, for example, marine sanctuaries now protect the coast from offshore oil drilling and transport in a continuous band starting from Bodega Bay in the north to Hearst Castle in the south. The three sanctuaries from north to south are Cordell Banks, Gulf of the Farallones, and Monterey Bay, the newest sanctuary. A fourth sanctuary, the Channel Islands, protects the islands off Southern California.

Resources

Sources for Materials

Rock/mineral, and sand kits can be ordered inexpensively from The Math/Science Nucleus, 3710 Yale Way, Fremont, CA 94538, (510) 490-MATH as well as from most large science and earth science supply houses. For example, both Ward's Natural Science Establishment, Inc., 5100 W. Henrietta Road, P.O. Box 92912, Rochester, NY 14692-9012, (800) 962-2660 and Frey Scientific, 905 Hickory Lane, P.O. Box 8101, Mansfield, OH 44901-8101, (800) 225-FREY carry rock and mineral kits.

Sand samples can also be obtained from members of the International Sand Collectors Society. For more information contact William Diefenbach, President of the ISCS at 43 Highview Ave., Old Greenwich, CT 06870-1703.

Another method of obtaining sand from around the world is through an Internet bulletin board service. Scroll to a heading called K12.Science.Ed and place your ad there.

The MARE Sandy Beach Slide Show with a script is available for purchase from the MARE program at Lawrence Hall of Science. (510) 642-5008

"Magiscopes" from Brock Optical are one highly recommended model because of their quality, durability and reasonable price. Young students can use them easily and they do not require electricity or mirrors. They can be ordered by calling (800) 780-9111.

Videotapes about oil spills such as *When the Spill Hit Homer*, are available from The Video Project, 5332 College Ave., Suite 101, Oakland, CA 94618 (800) 4-Planet. (See other video listings later in this section.)

To find out more about used motor oil, household hazardous wastes, and storm drain pollution prevention, call 1-800-CLEANUP. This will connect you to an Environmental Recycling Hotline made possible by the United States Postal Service, the Environmental Protection Agency, and other organizations and companies.

Books

Please be sure to see the many excellent books listed in the "Literature Connections" section on page 135.

Children

Beach Bird, Carol and Donald Carrick, Dial Press, New York, 1973.

A Beach for the Birds, Bruce McMillan, Houghton Mifflin, Boston, 1993.

A Coloring Book of Birds of California, John G. T. Anderson, Bellerophon Books, Santa Barbara, California, 1986.

Dune Fox, Marilynne K. Roach, Little, Brown, Boston, 1977.

Elephant Seal Island, Evelyn Shaw, Harper & Row, New York, 1978.

Elephant Seals, Sylvia A. Johnson, Lerner, Minneapolis, 1989.

Exploring the Seashore, William H. Amos, National Geographic Society, Washington, DC, 1984.

A Field Guide to Seashores Coloring Book, John C. Kricher, Houghton Mifflin, New York, 1989.

A First Look at Seals, Sea Lions, and Walruses, Millicent E. Selsam and Joyce Hunt, Walker, New York, 1988.

Kelp Forests, Judith Conner and Charles Baxter, Monterey Bay Aquarium Foundation, Monterey, California, 1989.

The Marine Biology Coloring Book, Thomas Niesen, HarperCollins, New York, 1982.

Monster Seaweeds: The Story of the Giant Kelp, Mary Daegling, Dillon Press, Minneapolis, 1986.

Night of Ghosts and Hermits: Nocturnal Life on the Seashore, Mary Stolz, Harcourt Brace Jovanovich, San Diego, 1985.

Ocean Life, David Cook, Crown, New York, 1983.

Oil Spill!, Melvin Berger, HarperCollins, New York, 1994.

Oil Spills, Madelyn Klein Anderson, Franklin Watts, New York, 1990.

Oil Spills: Damage, Recovery, and Prevention, Laurence Pringle, Morrow Junior Books, New York, 1993.

One Small Square: Seashore, Donald M. Silver, W. H. Freeman, New York, 1993.

Rocks and Minerals, R. F. Symes, Knopf, New York, 1988.

Sand and Man, Willma Willis, Children's Press, Chicago, 1973.

Sand Dunes, Jan Gumprecht Bannan, Carolrhoda Books, Minneapolis, 1989.

Sea Animals, Angela Royston, Aladdin Books, New York, 1992.

Seals & Sea Lions, Vicki León, Silver Burdett, Parsippany, New Jersey, 1995.

Seals, Sea Lions and Walruses, Dorothy Hinshaw Patent, Holiday House, New York, 1990.

Seashore, David Burnie, Dorling Kindersley, New York, 1994.

The Seashore, Elisabeth Cohat, Scholastic, New York, 1995.

Seashore, Steve Parker, Knopf, New York, 1989.

Seashore Life on Rocky Coasts, Judith Conner, Monterey Bay Aquarium Foundation, Monterey, California, 1993.

Seashore Surprises, Rose Wyler, Julian Messner, Englewood Cliffs, New Jersey, 1991.

Seashores, Joyce Pope, Troll, Mahwah, New Jersey, 1990.

Shell, Alex Arthur, Knopf, New York, 1989.

Shells, S. Peter Dance, Dorling Kindersley, New York, 1992.

Shore Life, Rena Kirkpatrick, Steck-Vaughn, Austin, Texas, 1991.

Shoreline, Barbara Taylor, Dorling Kindersley, New York, 1993.

Spill! The Story of the Exxon Valdez, Terry Carr, Franklin Watts, New York, 1991.

What Lives in a Shell?, Kathleen Weidner Zoehfeld, HarperCollins, New York, 1994.

Where the Waves Break: Life at the Edge of the Sea, Anita Malnig, Carolrhoda Books, Minneapolis, 1985.

The Wonderful World of Seals and Whales, Sandra Lee Crow, National Geographic Society, Washington, DC, 1984.

Adults

The Audubon Society Field Guide to North American Seashore Creatures, Norman A. Meinkoth, Knopf, New York, 1981.

Beachcomber's Guide to California Marine Life, Thomas Niesen, Gulf Publishing Co., Houston, Texas, 1994.

Beachcomber's Guide to the Gulf Coast Marine Life, Thomas Niesen, Gulf Publishing Co., Houston, Texas, 1989.

Beachcomber's Guide to the Gulf Coast Marine Life: Florida, Alabama, Mississippi, Louisiana, and Texas, Nick Fotheringham and Susan Brunenmeister, Gulf Publishing Co., Houston, Texas, 1989.

Between Pacific Tides, Edward F. Ricketts, Jack Calvin, and Joel W. Hedgpeth, Stanford University Press, Stanford, California, 1939.

A Field Guide to Atlantic Coast Fishes of North America, Richard Robins, G. Carleton Ray, Houghton Mifflin, Boston, 1986.

A Field Guide to Atlantic Seashores, Kenneth Gosner, Houghton Mifflin, Boston, 1978.

A Field Guide to Pacific Coast Fishes of North America, William N. Eschmeyer, et. al., Houghton Mifflin, Boston, 1983.

Fishes of the Gulf of Mexico: Texas, Louisiana, and Adjacent Waters, H. Dickson Hoese and Richard H. Moore, Texas A&M University Press, College Station, Texas, 1977.

An Instant Guide to Seashore Life, Cecilia Fitzsimons, Bonanza Books, New York, 1989.

Intertidal Invertebrates of California, Robert H. Morris, Donald P. Abbott, and Eugene C. Haderlie, Stanford University Press, Stanford, California, 1980.

Origami Sea Life, John Montroll and Robert J. Lang, Dover, New York, 1990.

Sand, Raymond Siever, Scientific American Library, New York, 1988.

Seashells of the World, R. Tucker Abbott, Golden Press, New York, 1985.

Seashore Identifier, Bob Lollo, Mallard Press, New York, 1992.

Seashores: A Guide to Animals and Plants Along the Beaches, Herbert S. Zim and Lester Ingle, Golden Press, New York, 1989.

The Seaside Naturalist: A Guide to Nature Study at the Seashore, Deborah Coulombe, Prentice Hall, New York, 1984.

Shells of the World, A. P. H. Oliver, Henry Holt, New York, 1975.

Shore Ecology of the Gulf of Mexico, Joseph C. Britton and Brian Morton, University of Texas Press, Austin, Texas, 1989.

Shorebirds of North America, Alan Richards, W.H. Smith, New York, 1991.

Waves and Beaches, Willard Bascom, Anchor Books, Garden City, New York, 1964.

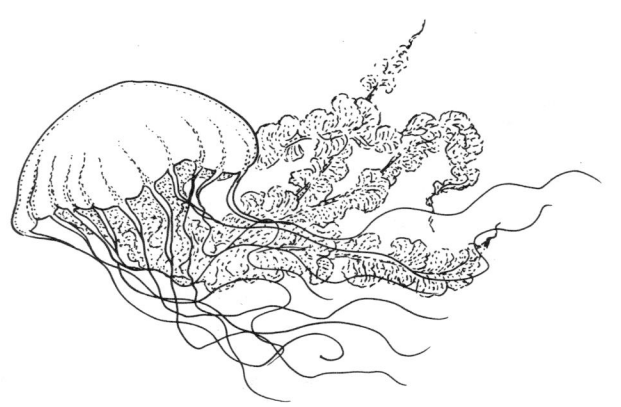

Magazine Articles

"Beaches," *Scientific American,* August 1960.

"Collecting and Examining Beach Sand: Getting Started," *Microscopy Today,* 96(5): 18–20, June 1996.

"Sand," *Scientific American,* April 1960.

"Sands of the World," *Scientific American,* 275(2): 62–67, July 1996.

Music

Daughters of Water, Sons of the Sea
by Jesse Boggs
Schneider Educational Products, Inc.
San Francisco. 1991

This cassette is full of delightful songs about the ocean and some of the creatures in it.

Penguin Parade
by Banana Slug String Band
Music for Little People
Redway, California. 1996

In the style of the Banana Slug String Band, this cassette is full of fun and entertaining nature songs.

Slugs at Sea
by Banana Slug String Band
Music for Little People
Redway, California. 1991

This cassette contains many fun and entertaining songs all about the ocean. The most appropriate song for *On Sandy Shores* is "Life on the Shore" where the lyrics say if you live on the shore "you've got to move with the tide…run real fast or burrow and hide."

Videos

Ancient Sea Turtles: The Last Voyage
Steve Cowan
Sea Turtle Restoration Project
300 Broadway, Suite 28
San Francisco, CA 94133
(415) 788-3666
20 minutes

This video tape provides an overview of the extraordinary natural history of sea turtles and vividly exposes the major threats to these giant reptiles. Biologists and environmentalists describe the international efforts to save one of the oldest living links with the past.

Jack, the Seal and the Sea
a Reading Rainbow video production
Contact your local public television station, or
Great Plains National
Box 80669
Lincoln, NE 68501
(800) 228-4630
29 minutes

The book, upon which this Reading Rainbow episode is based, tells the story of a fisherman who, after finding and helping an ailing seal, can no longer ignore the polluted state of the world's oceans. In the video, host LeVar Burton goes on a Discovery Voyage in the San Francisco Bay to learn more about the preservation of our water and ways we can preserve the oceans. He also looks at a variety of marine life. Also in the video, viewers get a first-hand look at the clean-up effort after a disastrous oil spill in Alaska.

Life on Earth
Warner Home Video
30952 San Clemente Street
Building D, Suite #4
Hayward, CA 94544
(800) 775-4300
Two videos, each is 232 minutes

Life on Earth, the result of a three-year, 1.3-million-mile odyssey to all seven continents, tells how a few life forms came to be as they are, not as isolated oddities but as elements in a long and continuous story that began billions of years ago.

New England Aquarium Videos (various titles)
New England Aquarium Teacher Resource Center
Attn: Joel Rubin
Central Wharf
Boston, MA 02110-3399
(617) 973-6590
various lengths

The Teacher Resource Center maintains a large collection of circulating videos, slide shows, software, filmstrips, posters, and small kits available to teachers nationwide. Included are about 10 video titles on a wide variety of topics. Call or write for a list of titles.

Oceans Alive!
Environmental Media & Marine Grafics
P.O. Box 1016
Chapel Hill, NC 27514
(800) 368-3382
50 minutes (each part has 10 five-minute programs)
available in English or Spanish

Oceans Alive! illustrates the relationships among marine life and supports the teaching of life science. Filmed entirely in the wild in many locations, this series encourages students to ask questions and share experiences. The series is divided into four main parts, each with 10 programs ranging over a wide and diverse spectrum of organisms, habitats, and environmental issues. It is recommended for ages 10 to adult.

Sand Through a Microscope, second edition
Warren A. Hatch Productions
1330 SW Third Avenue, #703
Portland, OR 97201-6636
52 minutes

Shows a large variety of sands from around the world. The video ends with a question time when the viewer is asked to guess the types of sand shown.

Scientists and the Alaska Oil Spill
Exxon Company, USA
Public Affairs Department
P.O. Box 2180
Houston, TX 77252
(713) 656-8758
22 minutes

The 1989 oil spill in Alaska's Prince William Sound led to an unprecedented response from the scientific community. This video presents Exxon's viewpoints about the science behind the cleanup efforts.

Sea World Videos (various titles)
Sea World
Education Department
1720 South Shores Road
San Diego, CA 92109-7995
(619) 226-3834
40 minutes—except *Meet the Challenge: Marine Conservation* (28 minutes)

Sea World's education department has a wide array of educational materials available to teachers including videos, teacher's guides, posters, information booklets, and even a live TV program. Video topics include marine conservation issues, baby animals, sharks, polar animals, dolphin research, and coral reefs. Call or write for details.

Seashores
Hollywood Select Video Inc.
10010 Canoga Avenue, B5
Chatsworth, CA 91311
(818) 773-0299
25 minutes

This video explores the inhabitants of the Atlantic and Pacific coasts. The Atlantic seacoast has a varied and exciting panorama from the Bay of Fundy with its gigantic tides and the rockbound shores to the marshes of the Chesapeake and the islands of Florida's Keys. The Pacific shore is diverse with its sandy beaches and its spectacular shoreline flowers plus its tidepools and fascinating creatures that inhabit them. A detailed view of both is presented in this colorful video.

Trashing the Oceans
NOAA Marine Debris Information Office
c/o Center for Marine Conservation
580 Market Street, Suite 550
San Francisco, CA 94104
(415) 391-6204
7:21 minutes

Trashing the Oceans describes the threats of marine debris using graphic video footage.

Trials of Life
Time Life Video
777 Duke Street
Alexandria, VA 22314
(800) 621-7026
60 minutes

In this video, anthropologist Sir David Attenborough has captured the life-and-death struggle in the "realest" world of all.

All the tools of the hunter and the hunted are on display: camouflage, mimicry, booby traps, even chemical warfare. Includes footage of orcas attacking sea lions.

When the Spill Hit Homer
The Video Project
5332 College Avenue, Suite 101
Oakland, CA 94618
(800) 4-PLANET
26:30 minutes

This video portrays the devastating human impact of the *Exxon Valdez* oil spill. It provides a firsthand account from the perspectives of the residents of Prince William Sound and nearby Alaskan Native villages, which rely on the sea for their subsistence.

World Alive
Sea Studios
810 Cannery Row
Monterey, CA 93940
(408) 649-5152
25 minutes

The wonder of life, the splendor of birth and growth, the grace of motion, the drama of survival, the beauty of courtship and renewal, and the activities and interactions of the myriad creatures of the planet are profiled in this video.

World of the Sea Otter
Marine Mammal Fund
Fort Mason Center, Bldg. E
San Francisco, CA 94123
(800) 3-DOLFIN or (415) 775-4636
30 minutes

You'll get to know this fascinating marine mammal, as well as the harbor seal and the California sea lion from a surface and underwater perspective.

Posters

California Kelp Forest
Center for Marine Conservation
1725 DeSales Street N.W., Suite 600
Washington, DC 20036
(202) 429-5609

Don't Teach Your Trash to Swim
Center for Marine Conservation
580 Market Street, Suite 550
San Francisco, CA 94104
(415) 391-6204

I Help Make the Beach See Worthy/Annual Beach Clean-up
California Coastal Commission
45 Fremont Street, Suite 2000
San Francisco, CA 94105-2219
(415) 904-5206

If You Take It Out, Matey, Bring It Back
Center for Marine Conservation
580 Market Street, Suite 550
San Francisco, CA 94104
(415) 391-6204

Los Pajaros de los Esteros
Gulf of the Farallones National Marine Sanctuary
GGNRA, Fort Mason
San Francisco, CA 94123
(415) 556-3509

Mamiferos Marinos de Mexico
Pieter Folkens
940 Adams Street, Suite F
Benicia, CA 94510
(707) 746-1049

Marine Mammals of the Gulf of the Farallones
Gulf of the Farallones National Marine Sanctuary
GGNRA, Fort Mason
San Francisco, CA 94123
(415) 556-3509

Mollusks and Crustaceans of the Coastal United States
National Marine Fisheries Service
501 W. Ocean Boulevard, Suite 4200
Long Beach, CA 90802-4213
(310) 980-4000

Oceans in Peril
National Audubon Society
National Education Office
Route 1, Box 171
Sharon, CT 06069
(203) 364-0048

Olympic Coast National Marine Sanctuary Dedication
Olympic Coast National Marine Sanctuary
138 W. First Street
Ft. Angelos, WA 98362
(206) 457-6622

Pinnipedia
Pieter Folkens
940 Adams Street, Suite F
Benicia, CA 94510
(707) 746-1049

Pinnipeds of North America
Center for Marine Conservation
1725 DeSales Street N.W., Suite 600
Washington, DC 20036
(202) 429-5609

Save Our Schools
F.I.S.H. Habitat Education Program
45 S.E. 82nd Drive, Suite 100
Gladstone, OR 97027-2522
(503) 650-5400

Save Our Seas Curriculum Poster
California Coastal Commission
45 Fremont Street, Suite 2000
San Francisco, CA 94105-2219
(415) 904-5206

Sea Turtles of the World
Center for Marine Conservation
1725 DeSales Street N.W., Suite 600
Washington, DC 20036
(202) 429-5609
available in English or Spanish

Surf and Shore Birds of Monterey Bay California
SHG Enterprises
P.O. Box 777
Los Altos, CA 94023
(415) 941-2662

Wetlands: Water, Wildlife, Plants and People
NSTA Publications
1840 Wilson Boulevard
Arlington, VA 22201-3000
(703) 243-7100

The U.S. Government Printing Office has several posters showing oceans and ocean life. For a complete list of titles and ordering information, write to
U.S. Government Printing Office
Superintendent of Documents
Washington, DC 20402

Many marine sanctuaries and estuarine reserves provide educational posters for teachers. Contact any of the following for more information. These estuaries and marine sanctuaries can also be a great source for local information.

National Estuary Program Contacts

1
Puget Sound, WA
Puget Sound Water Quality Authority
(206) 407-7300

2
Tillamook Bay, OR
Tillamook Bay National Estuary Program
(503) 842-9922

> For information on estuaries **1** and **2**, you may also contact:
> U.S. EPA, Seattle, WA
> Surface Water Branch
> (206) 553-4183

3
San Francisco Estuary, CA
San Francisco Estuary Project
San Francisco Bay Regional Water Quality Control Board
(510) 286-0625

4
Santa Monica Bay, CA
Santa Monica Bay Restoration Project
(213) 266-7515

> For information on estuaries **3** and **4**, you may also contact:
> U.S. EPA, San Francisco, CA
> Watershed Protection Branch
> (415) 744-1953

5
Corpus Christi Bay, TX
Corpus Christi Bay National Estuary Program
(512) 985-6767

6
Galveston Bay, TX
Galveston Bay National Estuary Program
(713) 332-9937

7
Barataria-Terrebonne Estuarine Complex, LA
Barataria-Terrebonne National Estuary Program
(504) 447-0868
(800) 259-0869

> For information on estuaries **5–7**, you may also contact:
> U.S. EPA, Dallas, TX
> Water Quality Branch
> (214) 655-7135

8
Tampa Bay, FL
Tampa Bay Estuary
National Estuary Program
(813) 893-2765

9
Sarasota Bay, FL
Sarasota Bay National Estuary Program
(813) 361-6133

10
Indian River Lagoon, FL
Indian River Lagoon National Estuary Program
(407) 984-4950

11
Albemarie-Pamilco Sounds, NC
Albemarie-Pamlico Estuarine Study
NC Department of Environment, Health, and Natural Resources
(919) 733-0314

> For information on estuaries **8–11**, you may also contact:
> U.S. EPA, Atlanta, GA
> Wetlands, Oceans, and Watershed Branch
> (404) 347-1740

12
Delaware Inland Bays, DE
Delaware Inland Bays Estuary Program
Delaware Department of Natural Resources and Environmental Control
(302) 739-4590

13
Delaware Estuary, DE, PA, and NJ
Delaware Estuary Program
U.S. EPA, Philadelphia, PA
(215) 597-9977

> For information on estuaries **12** and **13**, you may also contact:
> U.S. EPA, Philadelphia, PA
> Environmental Assessment Branch
> (215) 597-1181

14
New York-New Jersey Harbor, NY and NJ
New York Department of Environmental Conservation, Albany, NY
(518) 485-7786
New Jersey Department of Environmental Protection and Energy
(609) 292-1895

15
Long Island Sound, NY and CT
Long Island Sound Office
(203) 977-1541

16
Peconic Bay, NY
Peconic Bay Program
Suffolk County Department of Health Services
(516) 852-2080

> For information on estuaries **13–16**, you may also contact:
> U.S. EPA, New York, NY
> Marine & Wetlands Protection Branch
> (212) 264-5170

17
Narragansett Bay, RI
Narragansett Bay Project
Rhode Island Department of Environmental Management
(401) 277-3165

18
Buzzards Bay, MA
Buzzards Bay Project
(508) 748-3600

19
Massachusetts Bays, MA
Massachusetts Bays Program
(617) 727-9530

20
Casco Bay, ME
Casco Bay Estuary Project
(207) 828-1043

> For information on estuaries **15** and **17–20**, you may also contact:
> U.S. EPA, Boston, MA
> Water Quality Branch
> (617) 565-3531

21
San Juan Bay, PR
PR Environmental Quality Board
(809) 751-5548
Puerto Rico Department of Natural Resources and Environment
(809) 724-5516

For information on estuary **21**, you may also contact:
U.S. EPA, Caribbean Field Office
Santorce, PR
(809) 729-6921
U.S. EPA, New York, NY
Marine & Wetlands Protection Branch
(212) 264-5170

National Marine Sanctuaries

Channel Islands
National Marine Sanctuary
113 Harbor Way
Santa Barbara, CA 93109
(805) 966-7107   fax (805) 568-1582

Cordell Bank
National Marine Sanctuary
Fort Mason, Building 201
San Francisco, CA 94123
(415) 556-3509   fax (415) 556-1419

Fagatele Bay
National Marine Sanctuary
P.O. Box 4318
Pago Pago, American Samoa 96799
(684) 633-5155   fax (684) 633-7355

Florida Keys
National Marine Sanctuary
9499 Overseas Highway
Marathon, FL 33050
(305) 743-2437   fax (305) 743-2357

*Key Largo
National Marine Sanctuary
P.O. Box 1083
Key Largo, FL 33037
(305) 451-1644   fax (305) 451-3193

*Looe Key
National Marine Sanctuary
Rt. 1, Box 782
Big Pine Key, FL 33043
(305) 872-4039   fax (305) 872-3860

*Part of Florida Keys National Marine Sanctuary

Flower Garden Banks
National Marine Sanctuary
1716 Briarcrest Drive, Suite 702
Bryant, TX 77802
(409) 847-9296   fax (409) 845-7525

Gray's Reef
National Marine Sanctuary
P.O. Box 13687
Savannah, GA 31416
(912) 598-2345   fax (912) 598-2367

Gulf of the Farallones
National Marine Sanctuary
Fort Mason, Building 201
San Francisco, CA 94123
(415) 556-3509   fax (415) 556-1419

Hawaiian Islands Humpback Whale
National Marine Sanctuary
1305 East-West Highway
SSMC4, 12th Floor
Silver Springs, MD 20910
(301) 713-3141

Monterey Bay
National Marine Sanctuary
299 Foam Street, Suite D
Monterey, CA 93940
(408) 647-4201   fax (408) 647-4250

Stellwagen Bank
National Marine Sanctuary
14 Union Street
Plymouth, MA 02360
(617) 982-8942

Monitor (named after a sunken ship)
National Marine Sanctuary
NOAA
Building 1519
Fort Eustis, VA 23604-5544
(804) 878-2973   fax (804) 878-4619

Proposed Sanctuaries:
Sanctuaries and Reserves Division
National Oceanic and Atmospheric
Administration
1305 East-West Highway
SSMC4, 12th Floor
Silver Springs, MD 20910
(301) 713-3125

Curriculum Resources

Adopt-A-Beach School Education Program Curriculum
California Coastal Commission
45 Fremont Street, Suite 2000
San Francisco, CA 94105-2219
(415) 904-5206

Alaska Oil Spill Curriculum Grades K–3
Prince William Sound Science Center
Box 705
Cordova, AK 99574
(907) 424-5800

Año Nuevo Education Packet
Año Nuevo Interpretive Association
95 Kelly Avenue
Half Moon Bay, CA 94019
(415) 879-2025

A Child's Place in the Environment
Konocti Unified School District
c/o Olga Clymire
Lake County Office of Education
1152 South Main Street
Lakeport, CA 95453
(707) 263-7249

Critters: K–6 Life Science Activities
AIMS Education Foundation
P.O. Box 8120
Fresno, CA 93747
(209) 255-4094

Earth Island Institute Sea Turtle Restoration Project Curriculum and Videos
Earth Island Institute
300 Broadway, Suite 28
San Francisco, CA 94133-3312
(415) 788-3666

MARE Curriculum Guides
The MARE program offers teacher's guides by habitat, including: the rocky shore, sandy beach, wetlands, and kelp forest. Other titles are available.
Marine Activities, Resources & Education (MARE)
Lawrence Hall of Science
University of California
Berkeley, CA 94720-5200
(510) 642-5008

MARE Teacher's Guide to Marine Science Field Trips
Marine Activities, Resources & Education (MARE)
Lawrence Hall of Science
University of California
Berkeley, CA 94720-5200
(510) 642-5008

Marine Mammal Activity and Curriculum Guide
Marine Mammal Center
Marin Headlands
GGNRA
Sausalito, CA 94965
(415) 289-7330

Marine Science Project: FOR SEA Grade Two
Marine Science Center
17771 Fjord Drive N.E.
Pculsbo, WA 98370
(206) 779-5549

NatureScope: "Birds, Birds, Birds!" and "Diving Into Oceans"
National Wildlife Federation
1412 16th Street N.W.
Washington, DC 20036-2266
(703) 797-6800

NOAA's Marine Debris Teachers and Educators Packet
Marine Debris and Entanglement Slide Show
Trashing the Ocean Video and Curriculum
Center for Marine Conservation
580 Market Street, Suite 550
San Francisco, CA 94104
(415) 391-6204

Plastic Eliminators: Protecting California Shorelines
CASEC
University of California
Santa Barbara, CA 93106
(805) 893-2739

Project MER, Elementary Curriculum
Learning Resource Services—Publication Sales
Office of the Alameda County Superintendent of Schools
313 W. Winton Avenue
Hayward, CA 94544
(510) 887-0152

Seals, Spouts and Sandpipers
Manomet Bird Observatory
P.O. Box 936
Manomet, MA 02345
(617) 224-6521

"Tortugas Marinas:" Sea Turtles Curriculum and Coloring Book (Bilingual)
Center for Environmental Education
624 9th Street N.W.
Washington, DC 20001

Whales in the Classroom, Volume 1: Oceanography
Singing Rock Press
5831 74th Avenue North
Brooklyn Park, MN 55443
(612) 566-4540

Zoobooks Exploring Ocean Ecosystems
Wildlife Education
9820 Willow Creek Road, Suite 300
San Diego, CA 92131
(800) 477-5034

Other

Wavelets
These are handouts on different ocean topics. Each one contains background information on the topic, and a game, puzzle, or activity. Single copies are free. For a list of these and other marine publications, write to
Sea Grant Communications
Virginia Institute of Marine Science
Gloucester Point, VA 23062
(804) 642-7000

The **Monterey Bay Aquarium** has printed educational materials, slide sets, and a video. For more information, write to
Monterey Bay Aquarium
Education Department
886 Cannery Row
Monterey, CA 93940
(408) 648-4941

Aquatic Project WILD has topics which cover both fresh and salt water environments in broad categories such as diversity and ecological principles. It can be obtained only through your state fish and wildlife or fish and game agency.

The Rocky Shore and *The Salt Marsh* are guides to conducting successful field trips. For more information, write to
Seacoast Science Center
P.O. Box 674
Rye, NH 03870
(603) 436-8043

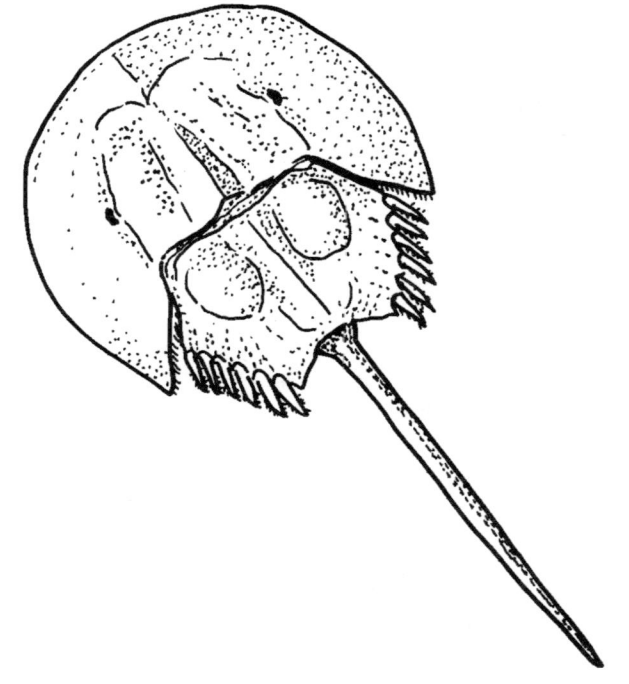

Assessment Suggestions

Selected Student Outcomes

1. Students deepen their understanding of the history, formation, composition, and characteristics of sand.

2. Students are introduced to the role of erosion in creating sand, and gain knowledge about how sand is transported and beaches are formed.

3. Students demonstrate an improved ability to sort and classify items that could come from a sandy beach and to evaluate whether these items represent evidence of plants, animals, humans, and/or are biotic or abiotic.

4. Students improve in their ability to work cooperatively with others, to use appropriate language and vocabulary in a variety of learning formats, and to communicate and refine their communication based on new experience.

5. Students increase their knowledge of the ways that the sandy beach, beach wrack, and nearby waters provide homes to many organisms, and students demonstrate a detailed familiarity with some of these organisms.

6. Students gain an enhanced sense of personal and social responsibility for prevention of oil spills and preservation of the natural environment.

Built-In Assessment Activities

In Activity 1, Session 2, students sort and classify a number of items, based first on their own categories and then as to whether the items indicate evidence of plants, animals, humans, and/or are biotic or abiotic. As students sort and then share their ideas and have the classifications recorded with simple drawings, the teacher can observe improvements in their understanding and ability. Students could be asked to make Venn diagrams or display in other ways which items go in which categories. This activity can also help teachers evaluate growth in student ability to make reasonable inferences from evidence. (Outcomes 3, 4, 6)

In Activity 1, Session 3, students use words and pictures to make a mini-book about visiting a sandy beach, with

Note: There are numerous activities in this unit that lend themselves to assessment. The Anticipatory Chart provides an excellent way to gain information on what students already know, for example, about sand or oil spills. All of the "activity structures," such as My Buddy Says and Partner Parade, lend themselves to teacher observation of student participation, use of language, and level of knowledge.

chapters on plants and animals, people at the beach, and the best thing about beaches. Mini-books are an excellent assessment mode and in this case can help the teacher become aware of what students already know about the sandy beach. Students are also asked to discuss how they decided to include things in their book and how the book reflects what they've learned. Observing participation in the discussion can help teachers assess students' ideas about their own learning. (Outcomes 1, 2, 3, 4)

In Activity 2, students record observations on the Sand on Stage student sheet and also fill out an Expert Group student sheet. In addition to observing students as they do the sand-related activities, both of these written records can provide good information on how well students are grasping the main ideas. The Expert Group student sheet provides both written and pictorial representations of students' understanding of how sand is formed geologically and how the characteristics of sand can reflect the specific conditions of a particular beach environment. (Outcomes 1, 2)

In Activity 3, Session 2, students design postcards with picture and text to reflect the main parts of the story "Sandy's Journey to the Sea." Teacher review of this work can help assess how well students have understood and followed the story, and how well they are able to generalize from the story, their hands-on experience with sand, and other geological knowledge they may have. In addition, teacher observation of their group work on the postcards can note progress in working together, use of language, and communication. The Postcard Game Show activity in Session 3 provides additional teacher opportunities to assess student understanding of the story. (Outcomes 1, 2, 4)

A Going Further for Activity 3 suggests that students create their own, original "postcard" story about any item or organism that may be on a sandy beach. Students are encouraged to tell a story of its travels or life cycle from the first person perspective. This provides information on student understanding of the sequence of events and other information on beach debris, etc. explored so far in the unit. If a student chooses an organism that will provide some pre-assessment information on what she knows about that organism before the class learns about beach organisms in the next activity. (Outcomes 1, 2, 3, 4)

Activity 4, in which students create three displays of a sandy beach, contains numerous opportunities for assessment of student understanding. Student drawings and three-dimensional models reflect their increasing knowledge of and research into specific organisms. Session 5, which includes class presentations, making a key for the classroom displays, playing Who Am I? and Twenty Questions, presents numerous opportunities for teachers to observe the level of student knowledge and the ability to recall, apply, and communicate that knowledge. (Outcomes 4, 5)

A Going Further for Activity 5 suggests that students create a mini-book which includes drawings and descriptions about what they learned about oil spills and their impact on the sandy beach. This mini-book can provide information on what the students gained from the activities as well as their sense of personal and social environmental responsibility. (Outcome 6)

Going Furthers for Activities 4 and 5 suggest that students work in pairs to write their own Key Concepts. Both of these activities are rich in learning. Students become more conscious of and connected to their own learning when they are given the chance to express what they think is important. Their own Key Concepts can also become part of student portfolios used for assessment. Insight into student perceptions can also provide very helpful information to the teacher concerning possible future adjustments in content and method of presentation. (Outcomes 5, 6)

Additional Assessment Ideas

Covering the Oil Spill. Have students pretend they are journalists covering a big oil spill on a sandy beach. They are working on a feature article. Their article should describe the unique features and natural history of their beach. They could even "interview" some of the plants, animals, and people affected by the spill. The article might conclude by discussing the pros and cons of proposals that have been made to prevent oil spills in the future. (Outcomes 1, 2, 5, 6)

Comparing Habitats. Students could visit and observe nearby habitats or locales, at school and in the community (playground, sidewalk, vacant lot, stream, under a tree, etc.). At each location they could engage in "scavenger hunts" for items left there. They could collect, sort, and classify what they find, looking for evidence of plants, animals, and people, just as they did in the Beach Buckets activity. They could then write up their notes, comparing what they found in different habitats. This assessment encourages students to apply what they learned in the unit in a new context. The teacher can evaluate their writing for the accuracy of its observation and classification, and for the ability to make appropriate inferences from the evidence presented. (Outcome 3)

Reflecting on Building a Sandy Beach. Encourage students to write about their experiences building the sandy beach displays. What were their favorite organisms? Why? Did their group cooperate well? What are the most important things they learned? If they had a chance to make another display, how would they do it? (Outcomes 4, 5)

Environmental Essay. Have students write a short essay on the saying: "Take only pictures and leave only footprints." Encourage them to build on their experiences in the unit to explain why they think people should protect the natural environment. (Outcomes 1, 3, 5, 6)

Literature Connections

Books selected as literature connections for *On Sandy Shores* include those that focus on sand, erosion, waves, currents, organisms that live on or near the beach, and oil spills. Some books extend into areas such as conservation and ecology. For example, *Miss Rumphius* and *My Grandpa and the Sea* carry a strong conservation message. *The Magic School Bus on the Ocean Floor* gives students a look at the entire ocean ecosystem.

In the listings below, the grade level estimates reflect both interest level and reading level. Many of the books can be enjoyed by a wide age range—older students can read them on their own, or they can be read out loud to younger students. Some books, like *Pagoo*, intended for older readers can be browsed by younger students looking at the pictures. Others, like the wordless *Follow Me!*, intended for a young audience, can be used successfully—even at the third or fourth grade level—to encourage language development in English-language learners.

Please be sure to see the many excellent resource and reference books for students and teachers listed in the "Resources" section on page 118. You may also want to refer to the GEMS literature connections handbook, *Once Upon A GEMS Guide: Connecting Young People's Literature to Great Explorations in Math and Science,* which lists books according to science themes and mathematics strands, as well as by GEMS guide. We welcome your suggestions for other books to connect to *On Sandy Shores* and will consider them for inclusion when this guide or the literature handbook is revised.

At the Beach
by Huy Voun Lee
Henry Holt, New York. 1994
Grades: K–3

With help from delightful paper cut pictures, the story is told of a mother who draws Chinese characters in the sand for her young son. She explains how the shape of the characters is related to their meaning. As the characters are described, borders and background scenes help illustrate the meaning as well as show the life and activities that occur on a beach. Included is a list of all the characters and their pronunciation. This book provides a nice cultural connection for *On Sandy Shores*.

Brown Pelican at the Pond
by Edward O'Reilly; illustrated by Florence Strange
Manzanita Press, San Rafael, California. 1979
Grades: K–2

Written by a child, this simple story tells of a boy and his friends, who on a visit to a pond, find an injured pelican, take it to a vet, then nurse it back to health. The boy then returns it to the pond "because he belonged with other pelicans." Can be the start of a classroom discussion on understanding the needs of animals.

Call it Courage
by Armstrong Sperry
Macmillan, New York. 1940
Grades: 3–5

Based on a Polynesian legend, this chapter book for older students tells the story of a young boy who overcomes his fear of the sea and proves his courage to himself and his tribe. The story illustrates his culture's connection to the ocean. In Planet Ocean Brainstorm, students discuss ways people use and depend on the ocean. The whole story or selected passages could be read aloud to early elementary students. Newbery medal winner.

The Castle Builder
by Dennis Nolan
Macmillan, New York. 1987
Grades: Preschool–3

A young boy builds a fantastic castle in the sand near the ocean. In his imagination, he enters the castle and has quite an adventure. The story is told skillfully and is enhanced by the changing perspective of the illustrations. The story ends with a demonstration of one of the key concepts from Activity 3—waves and currents constantly move sand.

Follow Me!
by Nancy Tafuri
Greenwillow Books, New York. 1990
Grades: Preschool–2

This is a very gentle story of a young sea lion who follows a crab traveling along the rocks. It can support or spawn discussions of animals and their habitats. Another excellent use of this book is for sheltered instruction. Since the book is wordless, the students themselves can write the story—in the language of their choice.

Houses from the Sea
by Alice E. Goudey; illustrated by Adrienne Adams
Charles Scribner's Sons, New York. 1959
Grades: K–4

This is an informative story of a brother and sister who spend a day at the beach admiring shells. They find shells in a variety of shapes and colors, and compare each shell to objects that mimic their shape—butterfly wings, castle turrets, spiral staircases, tops, and more. Information is given about the mollusks that live in shells and about how shells are made.

The Magic of Sea Shells
by Fredlee; illustrated by Sandra Romashko
Windward Publishing, Miami, Florida. 1985
Grades: 2–4

This tale is about vacationing children who learn about shells from another child who is native to the islands where the shells are found. The book is basically a handbook showing large color photographs of shells, identified by common and scientific name, with size indicated for each. The shells are interesting and quite beautiful, and include many examples which children may recognize.

The Magic School Bus on the Ocean Floor
by Joanna Cole; illustrated by Bruce Degen
Scholastic, New York. 1992
Grades: 1–4

In her own predictable style, Ms. Frizzle takes her class on a field trip to the ocean (though the students expected a trip to the beach). The focus of the book is the open ocean and sand is only briefly mentioned, yet the book could help to put the sandy shore into the big picture—the whole ocean ecosystem. It can also be a useful resource book when building organisms in Activity 4.

Miss Rumphius
by Barbara Cooney
Puffin Books, New York. 1982
Grades: K–4

A young girl tells the story of her aging aunt, Alice Rumphius who had two wishes in life—to travel to faraway places and to live beside the sea. Those wishes have come true, but now Miss Rumphius must fulfill a charge from her grandfather: "You must do something to make the world more beautiful." Miss Rumphius is unsure how to carry out her grandfather's advice. Finally she does this by sowing lupine seeds throughout her town. This book reminds us that we all have the responsibility to take care of our planet and leave it a better place for future generations—an idea which may surface during Activity 5, Oil on the Beach.

My Grandpa and the Sea
by Katherine Orr
Carolrhoda Books, Minneapolis. 1990
Grades: K–4

Grandpa is a careful Caribbean fisherman, using his old dugout canoe and taking only what the sea can give. There comes a day when he can no longer compete with the power boats and their big nets. He casts about trying other work, but is unsatisfied. Knowing that seamoss, a local delicacy, is getting scarce, Grandpa successfully farms it. Although Grandpa does not join the organized religion of the rest of the family, there is a spiritual, conservationist message in his actions.

Nate the Great and the Boring Beach Bag
by Marjorie Weinman Sharmat; illustrated by Marc Simont
Coward-McCann, New York. 1987
Grades: 2–3

In this easy-reader mystery, Nate the great detective helps a friend search for his lost beach bag. Through a series of clues and some logical thinking, Nate solves the mystery. Could be useful to help students learn about evidence for the Beach Explorations in Session 2 of Activity 1.

Pagoo
by Holling Clancy Holling
Houghton Mifflin, Boston. 1957
Grades: 3–8

This is the classic story of Pagoo, a hermit crab, as he grows and learns about life in the sea. Although *On Sandy Shores* does not feature hermit crabs, this book could be useful. Selected passages could be read aloud to help students learn more about some of the organisms mentioned in Activity 4. Or students could browse through the book and pick up plenty of information from the illustrations.

Prince William
by Gloria Rand; illustrated by Ted Rand
Holt, New York. 1992
Grades: 1–3

Denny rescues a baby seal caught in an oil spill in Prince William Sound, Alaska. She takes the seal—whom she names Prince William—to an emergency animal rescue facility, where he, with hundreds of other animals, is cared for and cleaned of oil. Denny follows his progress for weeks, until Prince William is ready to return to the sea. The story is based upon actual events and brings home the suffering experienced by wildlife. The reader can see, in both text and illustrations, the ecological impact of oil spills, and the effort involved in attempting to restore the damage. An author's note at the end of the book tells of the Alaskan schoolchildren whose volunteer efforts helped save the lives of many seals.

Sally and the Limpet
by Simon James
Macmillan, New York. 1990
Grades: Preschool–2

This is a funny, touching, story about a young girl who gets a limpet stuck on her finger and the things she (and the limpet) must endure for about the next 24 hours. Although the story begins and ends in ocean water, it is sprinkled throughout with dry humor. Students will enjoy the many improbable situations that befall Sally and the limpet, and they'll learn a bit about limpet biology too.

Sea Squares
by Joy N. Hulme; illustrated by Carol Schwartz
Hyperion, New York. 1991
Grades: 2–4

More than a mere counting book, this book introduces squaring numbers in a fun and playful way. From one one-ton whale with one waterspout to ten squirmy squids pulling ten tentacles, students will enjoy following along with the rhyming text. Pictures in the border give a clue about what the next organism will be. Provides a nice math connection to *On Sandy Shores*.

The Seal Mother
by Mordicai Gerstein
Dial, New York. 1986
Grades: K–3

Many Scottish folktales tell of the selkies, seals who can remove their skins and appear to be people, and there are many tales of fisher folk who fall in love with selkies. Gerstein has woven this legend into an original tale of a selkie mother whose human son helps her return to her sea home. This is a beautifully illustrated fairy tale and a good read-aloud. There are points of discussion here too—children may want to talk about what the selkie mother means when she says of seals, "They are the animals most like humans." The John Sayles film *The Secret of Roan Innish* is another beautiful variation on the same theme.

The Seashore Book
by Charlotte Zolotow; illustrated by Wendell Minor
HarperCollins, New York. 1992
Grades: Preschool–3

Rich full-page paintings help tell the story of a visit to the beach—a visit that takes place only in the minds of a mother and her son. With beautifully descriptive language, the mother describes for the boy, who has never seen the sea, what a day at the seashore is like. An excellent book to evoke the sights, sounds, and emotions of a visit to a beach. It could be a read aloud, for example, at the end of Activity 1.

Sukey and the Mermaid
by Robert D. San Souci; illustrated by Brian Pinkney
Four Winds Press, New York. 1992
Grades: 1–4

Based on an African-American folktale from South Carolina, this is the story of Sukey, befriended by Mama Jo the mermaid, and sheltered from her stepfather's ill-treatment in Mama Jo's sea home. Much of the story, which has a happy ending, takes place along the sandy beach that fringes Sukey's island home. Illustrated in beautifully executed, colorful scratchboard, this book would work well as a self-reader or a read aloud.

The Summer Sands
by Sherry Garland; illustrated by Robert J. Lee
Harcourt Brace, San Diego. 1995
Grades: 1–4

Children vacationing on the beach discover and observe the plants and animals found on the dunes. A late summer storm erodes the dunes and the children are dismayed by the destruction. The mid-winter gift of recycled Christmas trees from dedicated volunteers helps, over time, to restore the dunes. An author's note tells of actual events along the Gulf Coast upon which the story is based. This book connects very well to Activity 3 and "Sandy's Journey to the Sea."

Tracks in the Sand
by Loreen Leedy
Doubleday, New York. 1993
Grades: Preschool–3

This book shows sand being used in a way we don't often consider—as an incubator and a nest. With full-page illustrations and clear text, it describes the life cycle of loggerhead turtles, beginning with the female leaving the sea to bury her eggs in the sand. An afterword provides more in-depth biological information. Connects nicely to both Activities 1 and 4.

The Turtle Watchers
by Pamela Powell
Viking, New York. 1992
Grades: 4–6

This tells the story of three sisters' efforts to protect the eggs (and eventually the hatchling turtles) laid by a leatherback turtle on the Caribbean island of St. Lucia. To accomplish their goal, the girls must learn about the life cycle of the turtles and fend off a greedy turtle hunter and natural predators. Notable for its strong ecological and conservation messages.

The Village by the Sea
by Paula Fox
Orchard Books, New York. 1988
Grades: 4–6

When her father must go to the hospital and her mother is occupied with hospital visits, ten-year-old Emma is sent to live with her aunt and uncle in their house on a bay. Emma soon discovers that her aunt is very difficult to live with and seeks solace on the peaceful bay. Though the beach appears lonely and deserted, Emma knows the beach is not empty. She thinks, "…it was teeming with tiny living creatures, some as soft as custard, others hard as stone, hidden in shells and sand and seaweed." Emma and a neighbor girl spend time on the beach happily making a miniature village from biotic and abiotic beach debris—an activity which proves therapeutic for Emma. A great chapter book for older students. The last several chapters are liberally sprinkled with descriptions of the beach debris used to make the village.

When the Tide is Low
by Sheila Cole; illustrated by Virginia Wright-Frierson
Lothrop, Lee & Shepard Books, New York. 1985
Grades: Preschool–3

One fine summer day a little girl asks her mother if they may go to the beach. Her mother explains that they'll go when the tide is low. They then have a nice conversation about all the things they will see when the tide is low. As the girl swings, her mother draws a nice analogy to explain the tides. The book contains colorful watercolor illustrations of several organisms and an illustrated glossary.

Why the Tides Ebb and Flow
by Joan Chase Bowden; illustrated by Marc Brown
Houghton Mifflin, Boston. 1979
Grades: K–3

This is a folktale of irresistible charm, whose flowing language, humorous situations, and repeated rhymes make it a favorite read-aloud in many classrooms. In this tale that explains the tides, a very stubborn old woman has been promised a rock to shelter her from the weather. She chooses the very rock that Sky Spirit *doesn't* want to give her—the rock that plugs the hole in the bottom of the sea. Her humorous persistence finally wins her all she wants and more.

A Woman Who Cared
by Patsy Becvar
Nystrom, Chicago. 1992
Grades: K–3

As a young girl and her father watch people working to clean up an oil spill on a beach, the girl tells the story of Rachel Carson and her work to save the environment. *A Woman Who Cared* is a simply worded introduction, packaged with a variety of kits, including different combinations of the following products: an audiocassette, a 7" x 10" book, a large 14" x 20" book for a large group, and a teacher's guide. You may call the publisher at (800) 621-8086 for kit information and prices. A good way to spark classroom discussion of ways to protect our beaches and natural environment.

Summary Outlines

Activity 1: Beach Bucket Scavenger Hunt

Getting Ready
1. Gather pictures/photos of sandy beaches/organisms.
2. Collect items for beach buckets.
3. Assemble beach buckets, adding sand and placing marine debris/beach drift on or in sand.
4. Have chart paper, markers, and masking tape at front of room.
5. Divide chart paper into three columns each one headed by simple drawings of plant, animal, or human. On another piece of chart paper, draw a large question mark as heading.
6. (*Optional*) Hang the posters/calendar pictures of beach scenes/animals.
7. Write out Key Concepts on chart paper: **Objects found on the sandy beach can be grouped into: evidence of plant life, evidence of animal life, evidence of humans, and non-living material. /Sand is made up of tiny bits of everything that is found on the beach.**

Session 1: Planet Ocean Brainstorm

1. Ask students to brainstorm ways people use/depend on the ocean. Hold up globe, show Americas, then turn to show Pacific Ocean. What does this view tell about the world? [Most of the earth is covered by oceans.]
2. As appropriate, discuss: Most of our planet is covered by ocean; people get food and water from the ocean; over half our oxygen comes from plants in the ocean; the ocean plays a major role in moderating climate.
3. Tell students they'll be learning more about the ocean and the place where the water meets the land. What's that place called? [beach, shore, shoreline]

My Buddy Says
1. Ask, "Has anyone been to a beach?" "What kinds of things are at a beach?" Remind students a beach could also be next to a river or creek.
2. Tell students they'll participate in an activity called My Buddy Says. They'll be learning more about beaches from each other. Discuss what it means to really listen.
3. Form student pairs and assign students to be either a #1 or a #2. Pass out a picture of a beach or beach organism to each student. Ask students to look at pictures closely.
4. Ask a question from list below, and give Buddy #1 30–60 seconds to talk about their response with Buddy #2 (who listens only).
5. Ask several Buddy #2's what their Buddy #1 said about the question. List responses on board using words or pictures.
6. Switch roles. Pose a question for Buddy #2 to answer. If time allows, repeat process so each buddy responds to at least two questions.

7. Use the following prompts and questions for My Buddy Says: (1) Close your eyes and imagine you are sitting on a beach. Look down the beach. Now open your eyes and describe what the beach looked like. (2) Where are some beaches you have visited? (3) What are some things you like best about beaches? (4) If you walked along a sandy beach looking very carefully, what types of things do you think you might find?

8. Discuss the last question with the class. You may want to record/categorize responses: evidence of plants, animals, people, non-living things.

9. Ask students to think about several of the following questions then have a class discussion: (1) When you were speaking, how did you know if your buddy was listening? (2) Did you learn anything new? (3) What did it feel like to talk while your buddy only listened? (4) What did it feel like to listen without answering back? (5) What helped you to remember what your buddy said? What could help you remember more? (6) Did anyone notice that the teacher hasn't taught anything yet? You've been teaching each other!

10. Tell students this activity will help them be better listeners when they work together on the next activity. Collect the pictures of beaches/organisms.

Session 2: Beach Explorations

Explore-a-Beach

1. Students have the chance to explore a "beach" in their classroom. Show the beach buckets and ask them to handle items carefully.
2. Divide class into groups of four to six. They can feel the sand and pick up pieces of drift and debris, but keep sand in tub to keep classroom clean.
3. Pass out tubs and have them begin. Circulate, asking questions to focus observations.

Sorting and Classifying

1. After observation, encourage students to sort into categories of their choice.
2. Give groups time to share and describe their categories.
3. Explain that at a sandy shore, we may not at first see many living plants/animals, but if we look closely, we find **evidence** of them.
4. Have students re-sort items into four groups: evidence of plant life, animal life, humans, and unknown items (or items about which they can't agree).
5. Display chart paper with three columns headed by simple drawings, and the second chart paper with question mark for unknown items.
6. Have groups share again. Record, with labeled drawings, the items groups share. Explain that everything in first two categories is evidence of life (biotic). Evidence of humans could be biotic or abiotic. Can anyone identify the unknown items?

7. (*Optional*) Point out classroom posters of animals and plants from which biotic material came.
8. Ask if there are things left in their beach buckets that were never alive. These are called non-living (abiotic) materials. Ask if there are items that go in more than one category? Things found at the beach are called "beach drift." Things left by humans are called "marine debris."
9. Ask students what might eventually happen to all of this beach drift and marine debris if it were left on a real beach? Many of the items would be pounded by wind, waves, tides and each other, and ground into sand. Sand can be either biotic or abiotic—usually a combination of both.
10. Hold up Key Concepts for one or more students to read aloud.

Session 3: Make a Mini-Book

1. Tell students they'll create a book about visiting a beach. Pass out paper for the version they'll be making.
2. Encourage students to write their book, placing text and illustrations on alternate pages.
3. Provide time to write and draw.
4. When done, give students time to share their books with their group.
5. Ask students to think about some of these questions and hold a class discussion: How did you decide what to include in your book? Was there anything special you did to help you remember what you learned in this activity? Are you proud of your book? Could you improve it? Do you think this book will help you remember what you learned? Does your book reflect the most important things you learned?

Activity 2: Sand on Stage

Getting Ready
1. Obtain rock and mineral kits.
2. Acquire sand.
3. Organize sand samples.
4. Decide if all groups will blow on trays of sand to simulate wind, or if this will be a class demonstration. If all groups will simulate the wind, place $1/2$ cup of sand on tray for each group. If this will be a teacher demonstration, prepare just one tray.
5. (*Optional*) Make a Sand Display by gluing a small amount of sand from each sample to a paper plate or construction paper. Label each sample with its location.
6. Obtain hand lenses (or low magnification microscopes).
7. Duplicate Sand on Stage and Expert Group student sheets for each student.
8. Start class Anticipatory Chart with column heads: "What we already know about sand" and "What we want to find out about sand."
9. (*Optional*) Place masking tape on floor for Partner Parade.
10. Write out Key Concepts on chart paper: **Sand grains can be made of**

animals, plants, rocks, or minerals. /Sand grains come in many different shapes, sizes, and colors. /Differences between sand grains can be clues about where the sand came from and how it got to the beach.

Session 1: Partner Parade

1. Have students recall My Buddy Says. Partner Parade is a similar activity.
2. Ask students to recall what a good listener should do. In Partner Parade, both partners will be able to discuss each question or topic.
3. Pass out picture of sand or beach to each student. Have students stand shoulder to shoulder to form two parallel lines, each person facing a partner.
4. Tell students you will be asking a question or giving them an idea to talk about with their partner. They will have about a minute to talk. They can discuss their pictures.
5. Pose first question then ask subsequent questions as partners change: (1) When was the last time you visited a sandy beach? Where was it? (2) What do you think of when you hear the word "sand?" (3) Describe all the different places you might find sand. (4) What color is sand? (5) Where do you think sand comes from? What is it made of? (6) How do you think sand gets to the beach?
6. Move along the two lines to help partners get started. When you call time, have a few students report something their partner told them.
7. Before the next question, say the "parade" needs to move along. Have one of the lines move one step to the left so everyone is facing a new person (person at the end of line goes to beginning of line).
8. Have each student greet new partner, then ask next question.
9. Repeat steps 6 and 7 until all questions asked.
10. Ask students to sit down with final partner and consider some of these questions then discuss as a class: Did it seem like the whole class was cooperating? Did you remember to listen well to each of your partners? What did you learn that was new? Which questions were the easiest and hardest to answer? Did you feel comfortable doing this activity? Why?

Anticipatory Chart on Sand
1. Students work with final partner. Show them start of class Anticipatory Chart. Distribute paper to each pair and have them create their own chart.
2. Pass out a few more pictures of different beaches to each pair to give them ideas. Tell them to discuss what they know and want to know about sand and write notes on their own chart.
3. Bring class back together to share ideas and questions. Record the group's ideas on class Anticipatory Chart. If same idea comes up more than once, put a star next to it each time. Display chart and refer back to it during activity. Collect pictures of sand, beaches, and organisms.

Session 2: Comparing Sands

Observing Samples
1. Divide students into groups of six. Tell the groups they'll observe sand from different places.
2. Give each group the bag containing six small bags of sand. Have each of the six students take out one small bag of sand. They should not open the bag but should make observations by looking or feeling through the bag **gently,** being careful not to puncture the bag. Ask, "How big are the sand grains?" "Can you tell what they're made of?" "What colors do you see?" "What do the sand grains look like?"
3. Have each group compare their six samples.
4. Bring class back together for short discussion. What did they discover about their sand? How were samples the same? different?
5. Ask students to imagine a clam living burrowed in the beach sand. How might its shell end up as sand? How might a rock on a mountain top become sand? How about coral on a coral reef? Why might there be so many different colors of sand?
6. (*Optional*) Show students the Sand Display and ask them to look at how different sand can be. Ask students to collect sand for the display.

Making Sand Slides
1. Students get to make a "sand slide" from their sample. Pass out index cards and glue to each group. If their sand sample is light colored, they take a dark index card; if their sand sample is dark, they take a light colored card.
2. Have students label their card with where sand came from and their own name.
3. Demonstrate how to make a sand slide, by sprinkling a small pinch of sand above a nickel-sized circle of white glue spread near the edge of an index card.
4. Have students make sand slides. Collect or have students keep them for next session. Collect the sample bags of sand.

Session 3: Observing and Recording

1. Regroup students into Comparing Sands groups of six. Give each student a Sand on Stage student sheet and their sand slide. Give each group the large bag containing the six small bags of sand. Ask each student to get the same small bag they used to make their sand slide. Have pencils, crayons/markers, magnets, hand lenses, and rock/mineral kits available for each group. With younger students, go through student sheet step by step. Older students can work independently.
2. Have each group compare responses on student sheets. Why might some have different answers? What do these differences tell about different types of sand?

Sand in the Wind

1. Explain that sand is almost always in motion—sand grains on a beach one day might be entirely replaced by others in a few weeks. One way that sand moves is by the wind.

2. Hand out trays of sand to each group and give each student a chance to **gently** blow on it for about five seconds. What happens? At a real beach, the wind blows almost all the time. What effect does this have on beach and dune sand? [The "wind" separates or sorts the grains by size—the smaller ones are blown the farthest.]

3. Have students look at their own sand slide. If all grains are roughly the same size, they may have come from a windy beach. If the sample is "mixed" in size, then it may have come from a beach with little wind. Can they guess about whether or not their sand came from a windy place?

4. Have groups clean up materials. They'll need Sand on Stage student sheet, sand slide, and small bag of sand for next session.

Session 4: The Experts Meet

1. Ask students from each group with same type of sand to meet in "expert groups." Have them compare responses on student sheets and discuss discrepancies.

2. Ask them to consider where their sand may have come from before it was on the beach.

3. Have each student complete Expert Group student sheets together in their groups.

4. Ask them to imagine the beach where their sand came from and draw a picture of it.

5. Students can present drawings and evidence to the class. Collect student sheets, artwork, sand slides, and bags of sand. Post student art next to sand sample it illustrates.

6. Discuss why sand is important to people and items made/derived from sand.

7. Hold up Key Concepts for one or more students to read aloud.

Activity 3: The Sights that Sand has Seen

Getting Ready

1. Have students bring postcards from home and share them before activity.

2. Make the skeleton for the Story Chart. Write the name of each story part at the top of one sheet of chart paper until all six parts are on their own sheet.

3. Write out Key Concepts on chart paper: **Erosion is the gradual wearing away of objects by water, wind, waves, or glaciers. /Sand is created by erosion, and can be transported long distances by streams, rivers, and ocean currents. /Waves and currents constantly move sand on and offshore and along the coastline to form beaches which change with the seasons.**

Session 1: My Buddy Says/Story Chart

My Buddy Says
1. Remind students of My Buddy Says; review what it means to really listen.
2. Conduct My Buddy Says, using questions such as: (1) Where does sand come from? (2) If sand could talk, what might it tell you? (3) If sand had eyes, what are some things that it might see? (4) What is the most interesting, best, coolest thing you have learned about sand? (5) What do you still want to know about sand? (6) We are going to read a story called "Sandy's Journey to the Sea." What do you think it is going to be about?
3. Briefly discuss the last question with your students.
4. Ask students to consider some of these questions then have a class discussion: When you were speaking, how did you know your buddy was listening? Did you learn anything new? How much of what your buddy said did you remember? What helped you to remember what your buddy said? What could help you remember more? Did you do better this time at remembering what your buddy said than you did the first time we did this activity? Did anyone notice that the teacher hasn't taught anything yet? You've been teaching each other!
5. Tell students that this activity will help them to be better listeners and to recall details of the story they are about to hear.

Journey of a Sand Grain: Creating a Story Chart
1. Gather the class into a listening circle for a story about a sand grain named Sandy. The story is divided into chapters or parts. They should listen carefully so they can summarize what happens to Sandy on her journey.
2. Turn to the story on page 55. Read aloud Part 1: The High Mountains in Winter. Post first sheet of Story Chart. Ask students the most important things in this part and record them.
3. Repeat the process for each part. Very briefly outline main concepts of each part on Story Chart.
4. At end of story, ask students to quickly review Story Chart. Do they have any questions, clarifications, or additions?

Session 2: A Postcard Story

1. Ask students if they've ever been on an exciting trip, and mention postcards, asking, "Have you ever written or received a postcard?" "When do people send them?" "What types of messages or pictures are on them?"
2. If needed, describe how postcards have photo/picture on one side and brief letter on the other.
3. Students are to imagine they are Sandy and write a postcard home describing one part of their journey. Divide class into groups of six. Give each student a blank 4" x 6" index card. Explain that each card will be a scene from Sandy's journey. Distribute a seventh card to each group to be a title card. Review six parts of the story.

4. Pass out crayons, markers, or colored pencils to each group. Assign each of the six students in each group a part of the story to illustrate. Have students draw where they are in their journey, and include Sandy in each picture.

5. Pass out the ball-point pens or pencils to each group. On the back of each card, have students write a postcard message from Sandy.

6. When first person in each group finishes, ask them to make title card that says "Sandy's Journey to the Sea."

7. Have students make a postcard storybook by lining up all seven postcards in a row sequentially and taping the short edges together, alternating the tape on the front and back so it opens/closes like an accordion.

8. Have each student describe their postcard to the rest of their group.

9. Hold up Key Concepts for one or more students to read aloud.

Session 3: Postcard Game Show

1. Have students work in Postcard groups of six, with their own postcard storybooks available. Have class number off so each student has a different number from 1 to 6. Points will be awarded in game; keep score on chalkboard.

2. Tell students they're going to play Postcard Game Show. You'll ask a question about Sandy's journey and each group will discuss the question for about a minute and decide on an answer. Everyone in group should know the answer.

3. Explain that you'll pick a group, then a number. The student with that number in that group stands up. You again ask the question and the student answers it. If she gives a "complete" answer, her group gets five points. If she gives a partial answer, call another number from her team and give that person a chance to complete the first person's answer. Each group gets three tries to complete the answer and get five points.

4. If three students from the group fail to give the complete answer, have students in that group take their best guess about which part of the story is involved. Read that part aloud and have students raise hands if they hear the answer. If they give a complete answer now, the group is awarded three points.

5. Ask if there are questions about rules and clarify as needed. Begin the Postcard Game Show by asking Question #1. Give 30–60 seconds for all the groups to discuss the answer. Then select a group and a number and ask the appropriate student to stand up. Repeat the question, ask the student to give the answer, and proceed as described.

6. Repeat the process using a new question each time. Make sure each group is asked to answer an equal number of questions.

7. After the game show, tell the students that soon they will be learning about many of the plants and animals that live on the sandy shores. Ask questions to prepare them for the next activity, such as, "What were some of the plants and animals that Sandy saw on her journey?" "How did those plants and animals use the sandy beach?" "Can you think of any other ways organisms use the beach?"

Activity 4: Build a Sandy Beach

Getting Ready
1. Decide how you want to conduct the simulated classroom field trip. Gather resources with sandy beach images.
2. Consider how and when you will divide the class into teams for three displays.
3. Decide on strategy for how to create and where to place the displays. Create and place the displays.
4. Write out Key Concepts on chart paper: **Sandy beaches—and the beach wrack that washes ashore on them—provide homes to many kinds of organisms. /Most of the animals living at the sandy beach are hidden from view under the sand to escape the pounding surf and hungry birds.**

Session 1: Partner Parade

1. Recall Partner Parade from Activity 2: Sand on Stage.
2. Follow steps for Partner Parade, as described on pages 30–32. Move along the two lines to assist as needed. When you call time, have several students report on what they discussed with their partners.
3. Ask students the following Partner Parade questions: What would you like to do on a field trip to the beach? What animals or plants might we see there? What sandy beach animals do you think live on top of the sand? What sandy beach animals do you think live under the sand? Besides plants and animals, what else could we see at the sandy beach?
4. Have students sit down with their final partner for the simulated class field trip.

Simulated Classroom Field Trip
1. Show pictures or slides of beaches with little narrative, or video with the sound turned off. As they watch, students may talk with their partner about the different scenes as if they were really on a field trip.
2. At the end of the images, have them talk to their partner about everything they can remember that they saw on their field trip.
3. Brainstorm and record a class list of all the animals, plants, and physical features that students saw on their field trip.
4. Cluster or group together those organisms which have something in common. Discuss the attributes of each of the clusters.
5. Show the pictures, slides, or video again, adding information about the habitat and organisms.

Introducing the Sandy Beach Displays
1. Explain that the class will become more familiar with beach animals and plants when each student chooses one to draw in its habitat. They will make a three-dimensional model of an organism. Then they will place these organisms in one of three different views or displays of a sandy beach.

2. Tell students the displays will show the same sandy beach from three different views: "Above the Sand," "Under the Sand," and "Beach Wrack."

3. Tell students each group will become experts on organisms living in their view of the beach. They will also have a chance to share what they learned with the other groups. Emphasize that making the organisms and arranging them in the displays will take place over at least several days.

Session 2: Drawing Organisms and Habitats

Coloring Sandy Beach Organisms
1. Divide the class into three groups. Give each group appropriate collection of illustrations. Have students choose one to color.
2. Place construction paper, markers or crayons, glue, and scissors on each group's table.
3. Have students look at drawing, read description, color organism, then cut out organism and glue it onto construction paper.

Drawing the Habitat
1. Ask students to draw in a habitat scene around their organism, including physical aspects of the beach. The habitat scenes should be labeled with the name of the organism.
2. Remind students to follow directions given on the illustration. If students want more clues about their habitat scene, encourage them to look through the illustrations or other resource materials on hand.
3. Students may also to choose to draw the animal that eats their organism.
4. Ask several students to briefly describe their organism and its habitat. Ask, "What are some of the ways your organism is suited to its environment?" Explain that animals often change or adjust to better survive in a particular environment. This is called *adaptation*.
5. Tell students that in next session they'll get to build a three-dimensional model of their organism using many interesting materials.

Session 3: Making the Organisms

Introducing Tasks and Methods
1. Remind students about the three beach view displays. Use the information under "Three Sandy Beach Displays" on page 64 and in the "Information for the Displays" on page 77 to orient them to the task of making three-dimensional organisms for the displays.
2. Ask older students especially to consider size/scale differences between organisms.
3. Show students the variety of art materials and ask them to think about how they might use it to build a three-dimensional model of their organism.

4. If the students already have ideas, they should go ahead and experiment using any of the materials available. They can make two or three individuals of their organism, and if there is time, they can design and make another organism.

5. You may want to model some techniques for making three-dimensional organisms (see page 71 and "Information for the Displays" section).

6. Ask students if they have any questions.

Creating Three-Dimensional Organisms

1. Set the student groups to work making three-dimensional organisms.

2. Circulate around the room responding to questions about the organisms and helping students design their three-dimensional models.

3. Keep in mind the specific attributes of each of the displays, so you can assist students in creating the appropriate organisms.

4. Depending on your schedule and time constraints, you may want to extend this creative part of the activity for several class sessions.

Session 4: Arranging the Displays

Placing the Organisms

1. Tell students that they now have the chance to arrange the three-dimensional organisms in the displays.

2. After all groups arrange their organisms, each group will give a brief report on their display and a few things they learned from it, so groups should decide on two students to make that report.

3. Have each group work together to place their organisms in appropriate spots within their group's display of the sandy beach.

4. Help groups of students work together and discuss placement of their organisms cooperatively.

5. Further questions about a particular organism may arise. Encourage students to refer to resource books. Or you could consult the more detailed scientific summaries in the "Information for the Displays" section on page 77.

6. Encourage students to remember any unanswered questions that arose about an organism or its placement, so they can find out more later and/or summarize some of their reasoning in the class presentations.

Session 5: Class Presentations

Group Reports and Reaction

1. Have group representatives make presentations to the class.

2. After each report, allow about five minutes for the rest of the class to ask questions, having other members of the reporting group respond.

3. After the final group's report, ask students for additional questions they still may have.

Making a Key
1. Have a student randomly choose one of the drawings of an organism with its habitat that the class made earlier and hold it up in front of the class, covering the name of the animal.
2. Students take turns answering questions about that organism such as: "What is my name?" "What do I eat?" "What adaptations do I have to live on sandy shores?" "In what ways am I connected to other sandy beach organisms?" and "Can you find me in the sandy beach displays?"
3. As each organism is selected, the picture could be taped up near the appropriate display, or used to create a border for the "Above the Sand" bulletin board. These pictures can then serve as the key for the displays.

Who Am I?
1. Give students clues about animals featured in the three-dimensional models. See page 74 for sample clues.
2. Call on one student to give the answer; have all keep track of their correct responses. The student who guesses correctly can be next to select an organism and make up clues.

Playing Twenty Questions
1. Have students play Twenty Questions. One student selects an organism, but doesn't tell anyone except the teacher. Class asks questions phrased for yes/no answers until organism is identified.
2. Hold up Key Concepts for one or more students to read aloud.

Activity 5: Oil on the Beach

Getting Ready
1. A week or so before you start this activity, have students conduct family interviews about oil use. See suggested questions on page 93. Students should take notes during interviews and be prepared to share their findings with the class.
2. Have students look with families at home for magazine/newspaper pictures to bring to school. The pictures should be of oil-based products or of oil being used. Start collecting additional pictures.
3. Prepare the "oil" using recipe on page 94.
4. Pierce dishpan on the side, very near the bottom corner using nail or drill. Small corks work best to plug the hole, but if you use a nail to create a hole just a little smaller than a pencil, you can use a sharpened pencil to plug the hole.
5. Place enough sand in pierced dishpan to simulate a sandy beach sloping up from the hole. Do not cover hole with sand.
6. Glue one or two of the model beach organisms onto the rock and place it on sand near the hole in dishpan.
7. Start the class Anticipatory Chart.
8. Write out Key Concepts on chart paper: **Oil spilled at sea can travel with currents, tides, and waves to the sandy beach where it can harm the plants and animals that live there. /Oil spills are almost impossible**

to clean up. People can help to prevent them by reducing the use of oil.
9. (*Optional*) Obtain marine sanctuary posters/oil spill videos.

Session 1: Partner Parade

1. Have the students recall Partner Parade. Hand out pictures showing oil use.
2. Begin Partner Parade.
3. Ask students the following Partner Parade discussion questions: How do people use oil? Where do you think oil comes from? How does oil get into the ocean? What are the effects of an oil spill? How do you think you would clean up an oil spill? How can people prevent oil from polluting the ocean?
4. Move along the lines to help partners as needed. When you call time, have students report what they discussed with their partners.
5. At the end of the activity, ask the students to sit down with final partner, think about these questions, then have class discuss: Did it seem like the whole class was cooperating? Did you learn something new? Do you feel like you are becoming a better listener? Did you like having the chance to talk to classmates that you don't usually talk to?

Anticipatory Chart on Oil
1. Have students continue to work with final Partner Parade partner. Review how to create an Anticipatory Chart. Pass out paper and have them create their own chart on what we know and want to know about oil by copying the class chart.
2. Have them look at their pictures of oil use as they add to their charts.
3. Bring class back together to share ideas. Record group's ideas on class Anticipatory Chart. Display chart and refer to it during the activity.

Session 2: Brief Oil Talk

1. If it has not already been brought up in Partner Parade, you may want to **very briefly** tell students some information about oil use, drilling, transport, and spills.
2. Illustrate your brief comments, as possible, with graphics, simple icons, and key words written on chart paper.

Fouled Feathers
1. Ask students to imagine they got oil all over their skin. What would it feel like? What would it do to their skin? How would they get it off? Say, "Now imagine you are a duck and have suddenly paddled into an oil spill!"
2. Tell them they are going to see what happens when birds get oil on their feathers, and compare oiled feathers with those dipped in clean water.
3. Divide students into groups of four. Pass out materials to each group. Have students cover desks with newspaper. Tell them they will each

have a job to do in this investigation. Lead them through the following steps.

4. Have one student in each group pour water into their small bowl until it is about half full.

5. Have another student dip two bird feathers into the bowl of plain water. This represents a bird that lands in the water to rest or catch food. Caution students to dip the feathers into the water **quickly** and then remove to dry. When they remove the feathers, they should place one on top of the other, and then set them on a table top to dry.

6. Have a third student shake dropper bottle then drop a single drop of oil onto the surface of the water in the bowl. Ask students to pretend this is an oil spill from a tanker just offshore.

7. Have the fourth student quickly dip the remaining two clean, dry feathers into the bowl through the oil. Remove them. Is the oil visible? Place one on top of the other and set alongside the feathers that were dipped in plain water to dry.

8. Have each group look closely at the feathers. They could use hand lenses. Have them sketch each of the feathers including barbs and shaft, and describe observations to their group.

9. Assign one student in each group as recorder to write and draw group's observations. What happened to the feathers? How did the feathers dipped into plain water compare to the ones dipped into oily water? Did they differ in how they dried? Would matted feathers help or hurt the bird?

10. Explain that when a bird has matted feathers, the feathers do not repel water. The cold ocean water gets under the feathers to the bird's skin, the bird cannot stay warm, and will freeze to death. Many oiled birds try to "clean" their feathers through preening and die from ingesting the oil.

11. (*Optional*) Have each group wash the oiled feathers in the dish detergent.

Session 3: Oil on the Beach (Teacher Demonstration)

High Tide

1. Tell students they will create another beach model to find out more about the effects of oil on a sandy beach.

2. Divide students into groups of six and have them number off (1–6). Have Student #6 from each cooperative group choose one or two items from pile of beach debris, and place items one at a time on beach model in dishpan. Once all items are placed, carry dishpan around for all to see.

3. Plug hole with pencil or cork and fill dishpan with water to high tide line (until about three quarters of the sloping sand is covered). Call on Student #5 from each group to observe high tide.

4. Ask the #5 students, "Do the organisms appear to be in the right place based on what we've learned about the sandy beach?" "Should we move some of the organisms to a different place on the shore?" Have them report to their groups.

5. Call on Student #4 from each group to watch as you remove plug so water drains into bucket as tide gradually changes. Have students report to their groups. Gently pour water from bucket back into dishpan trying to disturb the sand as little as possible—it is now high tide again.

Oil Slick

1. Remind students this activity is about oil on the beach. Can they predict what might happen next?
2. Yes, offshore their beach, an oil tanker has collided with an underwater reef and oil is starting to leak out of the damaged hull. Call on Student #3 from each group to watch as you add about three tablespoons of oil to surface of water to simulate an oil spill. It is high tide in calm weather and oil slick has not yet reached beach.
3. Have the #3 students describe to the class the way the oil spreads out over water's surface to form a slick. Have students report back to their groups about what the oil slick looked like.
4. Have class file by to see the oil slick for themselves.
5. Have Student #2 from each group observe what happens next. Remove plug and allow water to drain into bucket as tide changes from high to low. Have students report back to their groups.
6. Have Student #1 from each group watch as you replace plug and pour water from the bucket slowly back into the dishpan so the oiled beach again approaches high tide. What happens to the oiled beach now? Have students report back to their groups.
7. Remove plug for final low tide and have Student #6 from each group watch how oil covers organisms on beach. Have them dig down into the sand to see if there is any oil below the surface, look in the bucket, and report back to their groups.
8. Carry dishpan around room so all can see effects of oil on the beach.
9. Remind students that the tide changes every six hours. The more times the tide changes, the more difficult it is to clean up the spill. This beach model represent a beach only 18 hours after a spill.

My Buddy Says

1. Remind students about really listening to a classmate.
2. Conduct My Buddy Says, using these prompts/questions: (1) Pretend that the sandy beach organisms on our beach model were real. How do you think they would be affected by an oil spill washing up on their beach? (2) Where did the oil seem to go at low tide? (3) What happened to the oil at a very high tide? (4) Do you think that the oil that got worked down into the sand would have any effect on the animals of the sandy beach? (5) Do you think you could clean all the oil off the beach? How?
3. Spend some time discussing the last question with students. Write down their responses to revisit after they try to clean up a spill in next session.

Session 4: Cleaning the Oil Spill

1. Ask students to pretend there's been an oil spill at sea. Their job: try to clean up the spill before it hits the beach.
2. Divide students into groups of six. Each group will receive their own small ocean where an oil spill has just occurred, and several clean-up items that represent methods actually used.
3. Distribute the Oil on the Beach data sheets to each student. Show and describe each clean-up item. Model how to predict and fill in sheet.
4. Ask groups to discuss so every student makes a prediction about how well each of the items will clean up the oil. (The group doesn't have to agree, but should discuss their reasoning with each other.) Tell students they'll get to explain their predictions on their data sheets.
5. Introduce and model the activity as necessary. Students will work in teams with a bowl of water that has a few drops of oil in it. In order, each student chooses one item from bag, tries to clean up the oil with it, and places oiled item on the paper towels.
6. Have groups cover tables with newspaper. Distribute one bag of clean-up items to each group. Have students empty them out to see all items.
7. Distribute bowls and paper towels and have each group fill their bowl two thirds full with water and place it in the center of the group. Walk around, placing 2 or 3 drops of oil into each bowl of water, remembering to shake dropper bottle well.
8. Have each student choose one item from bag and begin. If, after each person has tried their item, students think they've cleaned up most of the oil, you can add 2–3 more drops of oil to the bowl for the next student to clean up.
9. As each item is tried, each student should check the appropriate box on data sheet. Ask students to briefly describe results on their data sheet.

Debriefing the Results
1. After each group has completed oil clean up and recorded results, lead a class discussion based on the questions below. Record conclusions of the discussion.
2. Ask, "What worked the best and what did not work well at all?"
3. Ask, "Which group thinks their water is now clean?" "Is the water clean enough to drink?"
4. Ask, "Would any group say they really cleaned up their oil spill?" "Was any group 100 percent successful?"
5. Ask, "Then what can we do to prevent oil spills from happening in the first place?" Remind students that although oil spills are major disasters, much more oil gets to the ocean each year by leaking from cars or being poured down storm drains where it eventually drains to oceans.
6. Ask, "What should we do with all the oil-soaked clean-up items?" This is what people ask when actual oil spills occur and oil-soaked material is brought ashore. Some people say this only moves the oil spill from water to land.

7. Explain ways that actual clean up procedures were simulated by items used in this activity.

8. Hold up Key Concepts for one or more students to read aloud.

On Sandy Shores
(with all due apologies to William Wordsworth)

On sandy shores
On sandy shores
That's where I love to roam
On sandy shores
Life of all kinds
Makes its home sweet home.

On sandy shores
The habitats
Tell many different stories
On sandy shores
The beach wrack teems
With life in all its glories.

Why does the sand crab move that way?
Why did the tide just slide away?
Why do those birds have such big bills?
Why do there have to be oil spills?
Is seaweed really good for you?
Are sharks afraid of humans too?

All this and more
My mind explores
When inward eye
Sees sandy shores—
And then my heart with pleasure flows
To feel the sand between my toes.

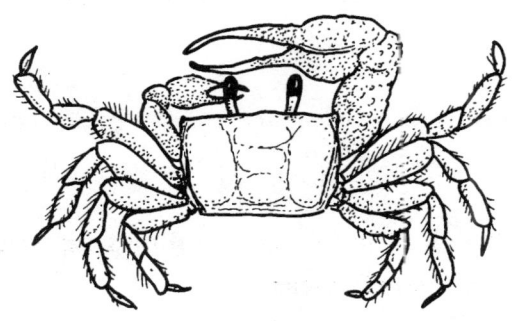

by Lincoln Bergman

Name _____

SAND ON STAGE!

1. Look closely at your sand with a magnifier. List or use crayons to show all the different colors you see.

2. Draw a picture of some of your sand grains. Draw them BIG!

3. Circle the pictures that have shapes like your sand.

    not rounded   a little rounded   very rounded

  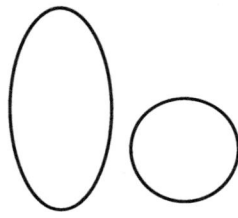

4. Gently rub a magnet on the outside of your bag of sand. Are any of the grains in your sand attracted to the magnet?

If so, what color are the magnetic sand grains?

5. Which of the following things can you find in your sand?
- ○ small rocks
- ○ pieces of glass
- ○ pieces of plants
- ○ other things. They are:
- ○ pieces of shells
- ○ pieces of wood
- ○ pieces of plastic

6. Look at the rock kit. Does your sand have pieces of rock that match some in the kit? List the kinds of rocks that may be in your sand.

7. Which sand in your group is the lightest in color?

Which is the darkest?

Put them in order from lightest to darkest.

8. Compare your sand slide to the size chart below. Imagine that the black dots are grains of sands. Color the group of dots that are about the size of your sand grains. If your sand is not like any of these use the empty circle to draw how yours looks.

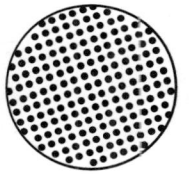  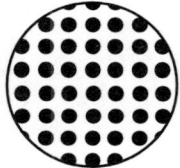  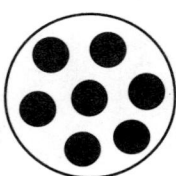 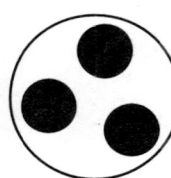 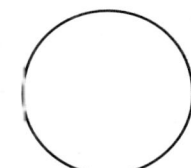

Are your grains all about the same size or many different sizes?

9. Which sand in your cooperative group has the biggest grains?

Which has the smallest grains?

Put them in order from smallest to biggest.

© 1996 by The Regents of the University of California, LHS-GEMS. *On Sandy Shores.* **May be duplicated for classroom use.**

Name _____

EXPERT GROUP STUDENT SHEET

1. Where do you think your sand was collected from?

2. What do you think your sand is made of?

3. How do you think your sand got to the beach?

4. On the back of this sheet, draw a series of pictures to show the story of how your sand became sand. Be sure to include crashing waves, freezing mountain tops, rushing rivers, or exploding volcanoes, or anything else you think helped to form your sand.

© 1996 by The Regents of the University of California, LHS-GEMS. *On Sandy Shores.* **May be duplicated for classroom use.**

- **Part 1:** Draw a picture of where your sand came from (a clam, a mountain, a coral reef, or ?...) before it arrived on the beach.

- **Part 2:** Here's what happened next.

- **Part 3:** Look what happened next!

- My grain of sand now looks like this.

© 1996 by The Regents of the University of California, LHS-GEMS. *On Sandy Shores.* **May be duplicated for classroom use.**

Name _____

OIL ON THE BEACH

Prediction Data Sheet

Check the box which describes your prediction the best.

Name of clean-up item	PREDICT How well will it clean up the oil?		Why do you think this will happen?
	will clean up a little ☹	will clean up a lot 😀	
1. Nylon			
2. Cotton Ball			
3. Sand or Kitty Litter			
4. Hay			
5. Feather			
6. Fake Fur			

© 1996 by The Regents of the University of California, LHS-GEMS. *On Sandy Shores.* **May be duplicated for classroom use.**

Name _____

OIL ON THE BEACH

Results Data Sheet
Check the box which describes your results the best.

Name of clean-up item	TRY IT! How well did it clean up the oil?		Describe your results.
	cleaned up a little oil ☹	cleaned up a lot of oil 😀	
1. Nylon			
2. Cotton Ball			
3. Sand or Kitty Litter			
4. Hay			
5. Feather			
6. Fake Fur			

© 1996 by The Regents of the University of California, LHS-GEMS. *On Sandy Shores.* **May be duplicated for classroom use.**

Name _____

OIL ON THE BEACH

Data Sheet Questions

1. What worked well?

2. What did not work well?

3. Did your group clean up all the oil?

4. Think back to what you told your partner in the Partner Parade about how you would clean up an oil spill. What was your plan then?

5. Now, how would you clean up an oil spill?

Above the Sand

On the Beach

Sanderlings

I run along the beach and look like I am chasing the waves.
I eat beach hoppers and small sand crabs.
I use my bill to pick food off the surface of the sand and just under it.
I am seven inches tall with a one-inch-long bill.
I am pale gray in color.
Peregrine falcons eat me.

Above the Sand

On the Beach

Herring Gulls
I have a white body, a gray back, and gray wings with black tips.
I am two feet tall and my open wings are almost five feet across.
I rest on the beach at high tide.
I look for food at low tide.
I am a scavenger and will eat almost anything.
Peregrine falcons try to eat me when I am small.

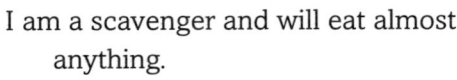

Laughing Gulls
I have a white body, a gray back, and gray wings with black tips.
I am 16 inches tall and my open wings are over three feet across.
I have a black head in the summer.
I rest on the beach at high tide.
I look for food at low tide.
I am a scavenger and will eat almost anything.
Peregrine falcons try to eat me when I am small.

Above the Sand

On the Beach

Willets

I am very noisy when I fly along the beach.
I have a black wing with a white stripe you can see when I fly.
I am 15 inches tall and my bill is two-and-one-half inches long.
I poke my bill into the sand to find worms, sand crabs, and clams.
I pick through the beach wrack to find beach hoppers and crabs.
Peregrine falcons eat me.

Above the Sand
On the Beach

Loggerhead Turtles
My shell is called a carapace.
I have a reddish-brown back and yellow belly.
People catch me in shrimp nets and sharks eat me when I grow up.
Out in the water, I eat jellyfish and the Portuguese man-of-war, but nearshore
    I like to eat crabs, clams, and urchins.
I lay my eggs on the beach.

Above the Sand
On the Beach

Horseshoe Crabs

I am not really a crab although I look like one.
I have a long stiff tail which I use to keep my balance.
I am brown like the sand.
I am a scavenger and will eat clams, worms, and bits of algae.
I come ashore to mate and lay eggs in the spring.

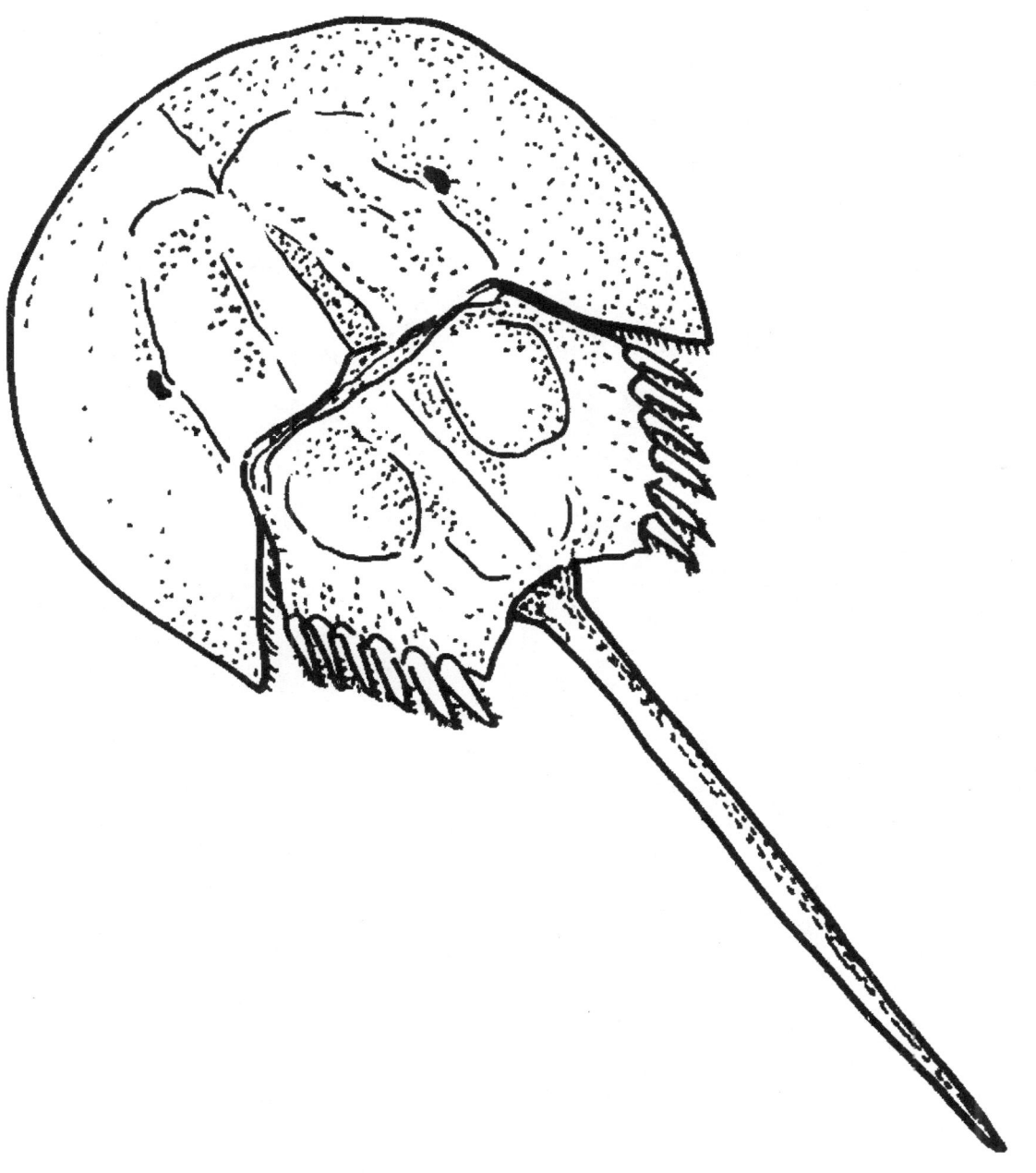

Above the Sand
On the Beach

Trash

I come in many different forms—plastic toys, bottles, bags, paper, or fishing line.
Currents and waves wash me onto the beach.
Animals may eat me because they think I am food.
Sometimes people do beach clean-ups to get me off the beach.
I look ugly on the beach and may harm the animals there.

Above the Sand
On the Beach

Elephant Seals

I am a marine mammal.
I am brown and have a huge nose and loud roar.
I am a great swimmer and dive very deeply.
I eat fish and squid—white sharks and killer whales eat me when I am small.
I can stay on the beach for three months at a time without eating.

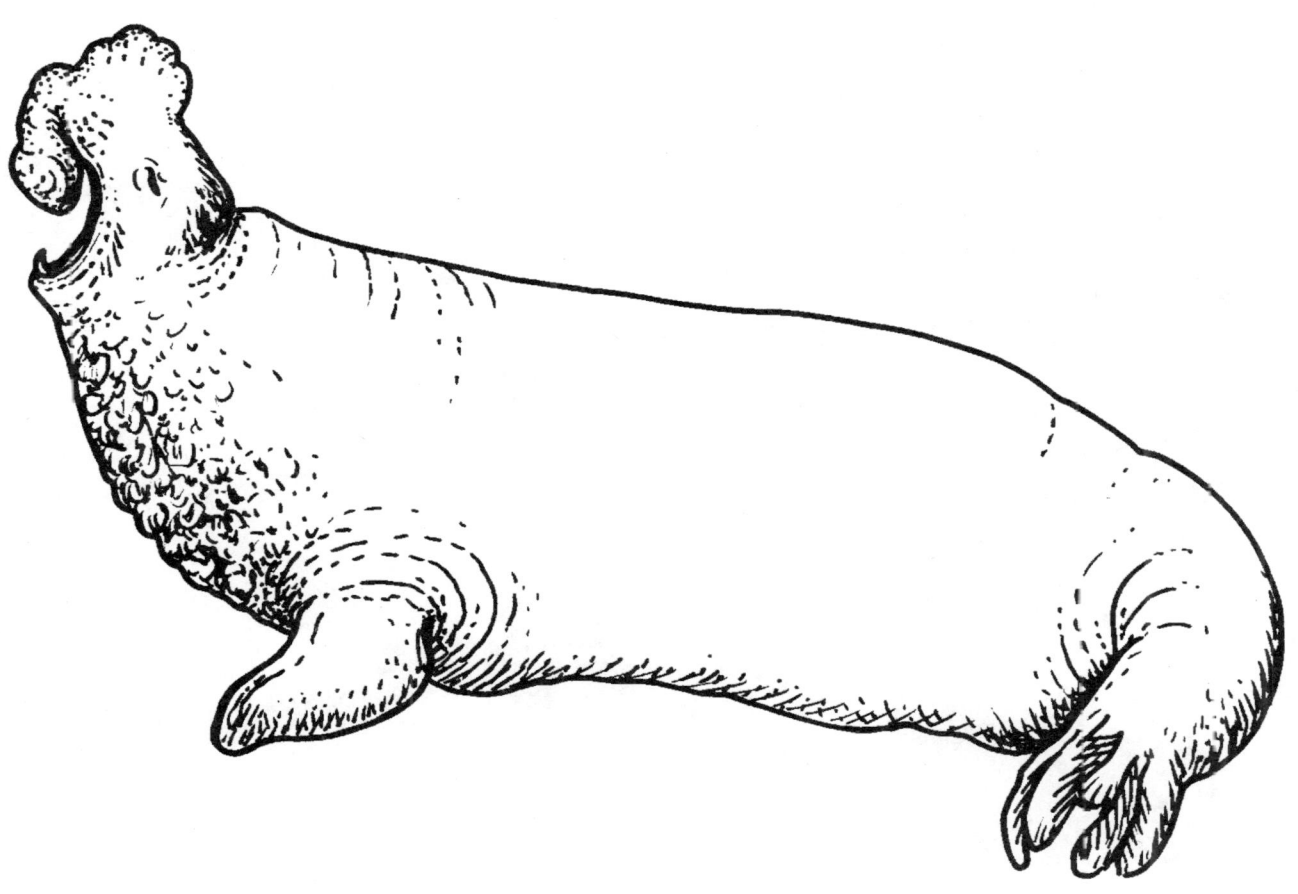

Above the Sand

On the Beach

Harbor Seals

I am a marine mammal.
I am silver gray with black spots.
I eat fish and squid.
White sharks and killer whales eat me.
I spend about seven hours a day on the beach where I rest and get warm.

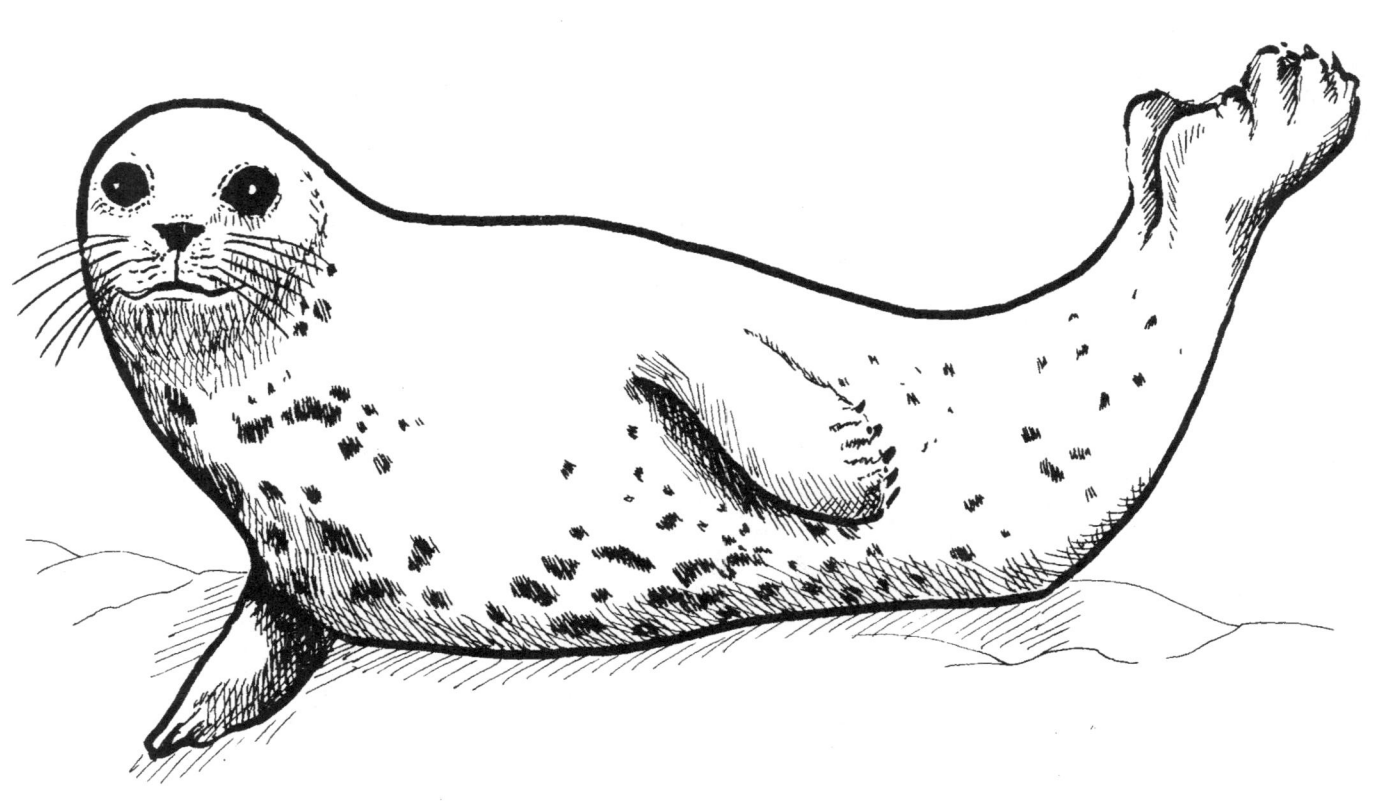

Above the Sand
On the Beach

Armored Sea Star

I live under the water and get washed onto the beach by storms.
I am pink in color and my arms have many spines.
I am about six inches across.
I eat olive snails and sand dollars whole and spit the shells out my mouth.
I also eat dead animals.

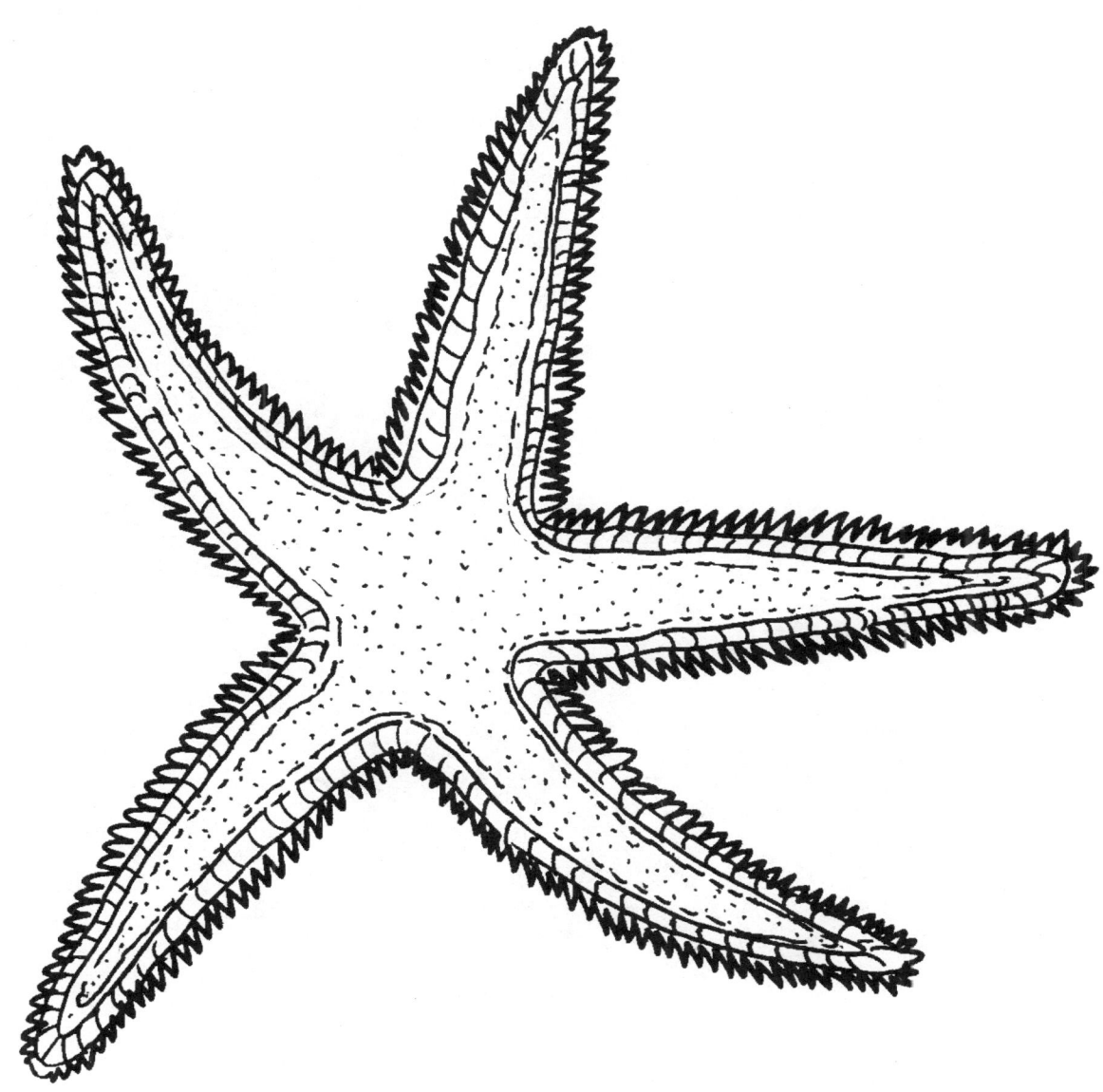

Above the Sand

At the High Tide Line

Beach Wrack

I am made of kelp and things like feathers and empty shells.
I was washed ashore and got stranded by the high tide.
Many animals make a home in me while I am on the beach.
Birds search through me for their hidden food.
Beach hoppers and kelp flies eat my kelp.

Above the Sand

Nearshore Water

Pelicans over the Water

I am a big silvery brown bird with a white and yellow head.
I have a long yellow bill and a big black throat pouch.
When I get hungry, I fly over the ocean looking for fish.
I dive into the water to catch my dinner.
When I'm not looking for fish, I fly so close to the water that my wings almost touch it.
I am in most danger from marine pollution like pesticides, fishing line, and hooks.

Above the Sand

Nearshore Water

Surf Scoters

If I am a boy, I am black with a white patch on my forehead and the back of my neck and a bright orange, black, and white bill.

If I am a girl, I am dark brown with light brown patches on the sides of my head and a black bill.

I paddle on the surface of the ocean where the waves break.

I swim under water with my wings.

I can swim down to 40 feet to find my food.

I eat mussels, clams, snails, limpets, crabs, and some fish.

Above the Sand

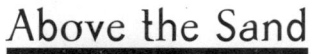

Surfperch

I have red-orange and blue stripes along my sides and bright blue streaks and spots on my head.
I live in the ocean where the surf breaks.
I am about one foot long.
I am caught by people fishing from the beach.
I eat all sorts of little animals like shrimp.

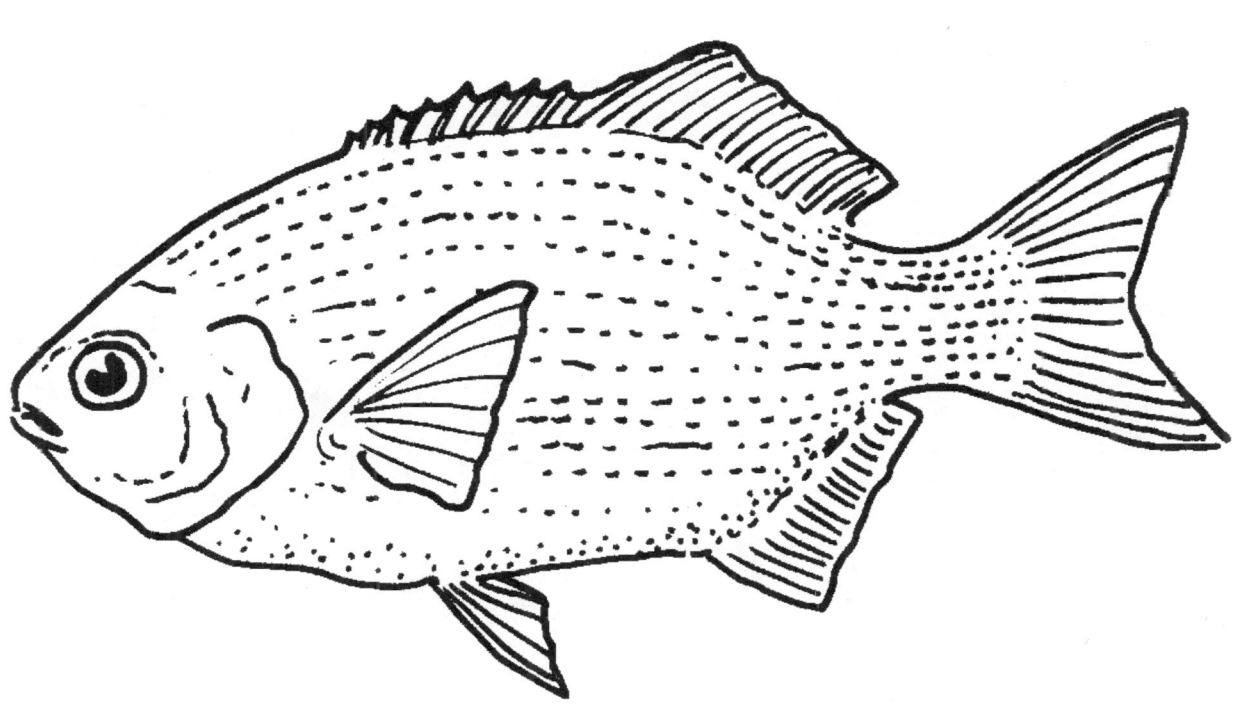

Above the Sand

Nearshore Water

Striped Mullet

I have a bluish-gray or green back and silvery sides and belly.

I live in the bays of the Gulf of Mexico.

I grub in the mud on the bottom of the ocean to find little bits of plants and animals to eat.

I am about two and a half feet long.

I swim in schools and leap from the water when predators, such as larger fish or dolphins, come near.

Above the Sand

Nearshore Water

Plankton

I can be almost invisible so that predators don't see me.
Some of us are tiny animals and some are plants.
I am not a strong swimmer.
I get pushed around by the currents and waves.
There are many animals at the seashore that eat me as they filter the water.
I am a very important part of the ocean food chain.

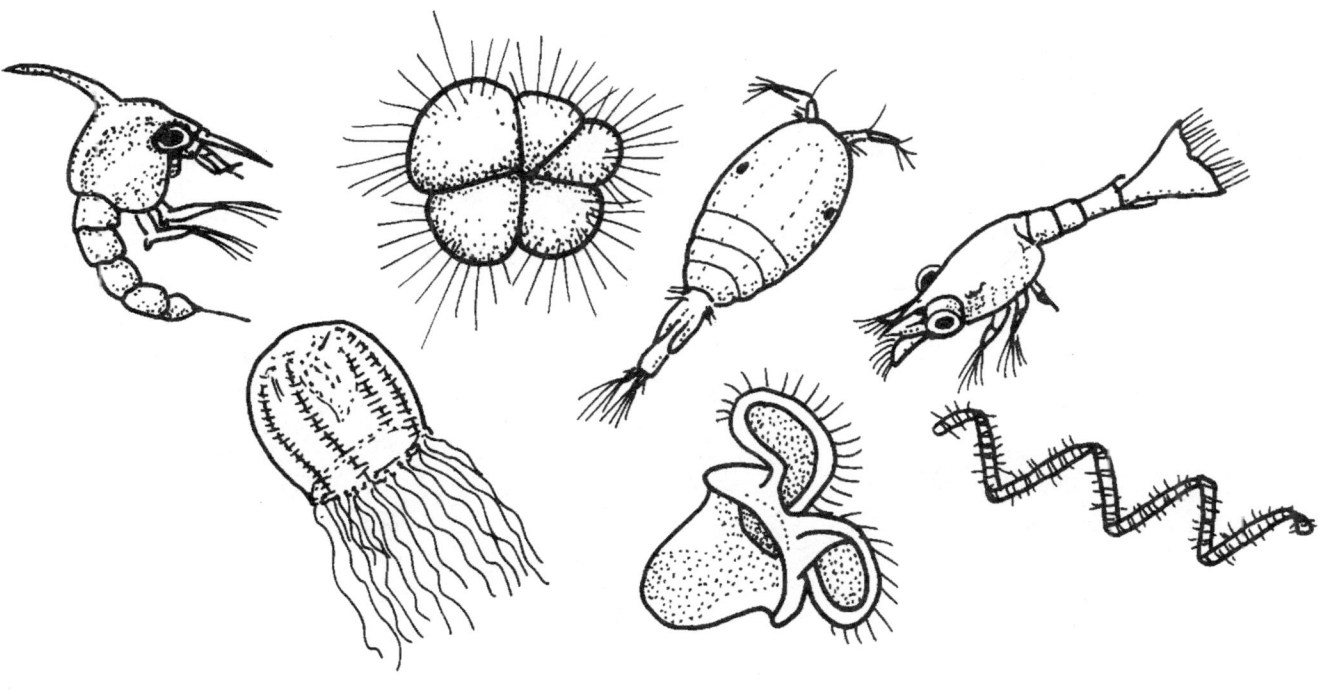

179

Above the Sand

Nearshore Water

Jellyfish
I am part of the plankton and I eat small fish.
I get washed onto the beach by big storms.
I can sting you even if I am on the beach.
Sea turtles eat me.
Some jellyfish are brown, some are pale pink or white, and others have
    purple and white stripes.

Portuguese man-of-war
I look like a small, pale purple balloon that has lost some air.
I have many very long tentacles which I use to sting and capture fish.
I can sting you even if I am on the beach.
Sea turtles eat me.
I look like a jellyfish but I am really a colony of several different kinds of
    individuals, each with a different job.

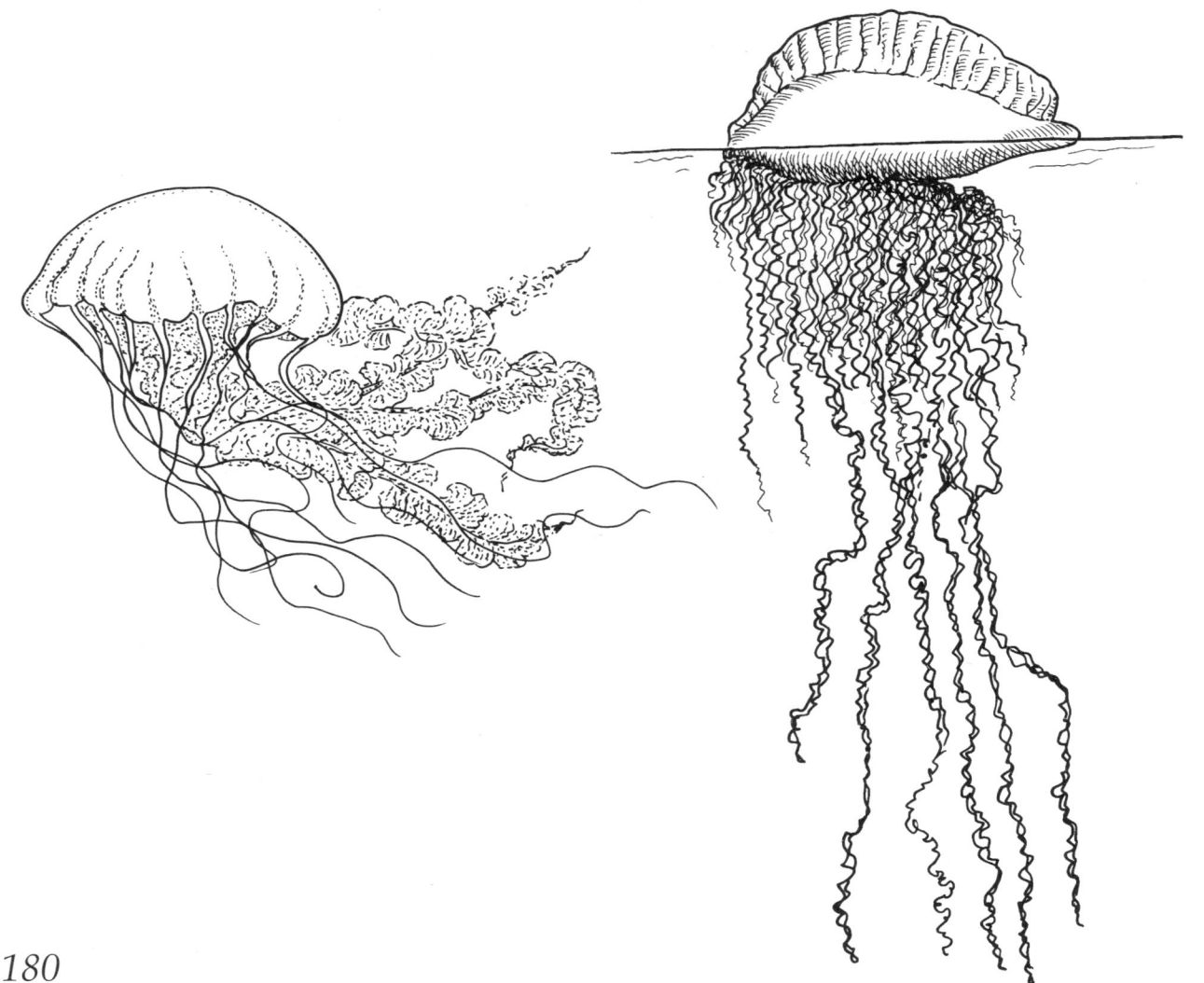

Above the Sand

Nearshore Water

Sand Dollars

I am light brown to dark purple.
I live under the water balancing on one edge of my shell.
Big storms may wash me up onto the beach where I die.
I am white when I die.
I eat plankton and fish and armored sea stars eat me.

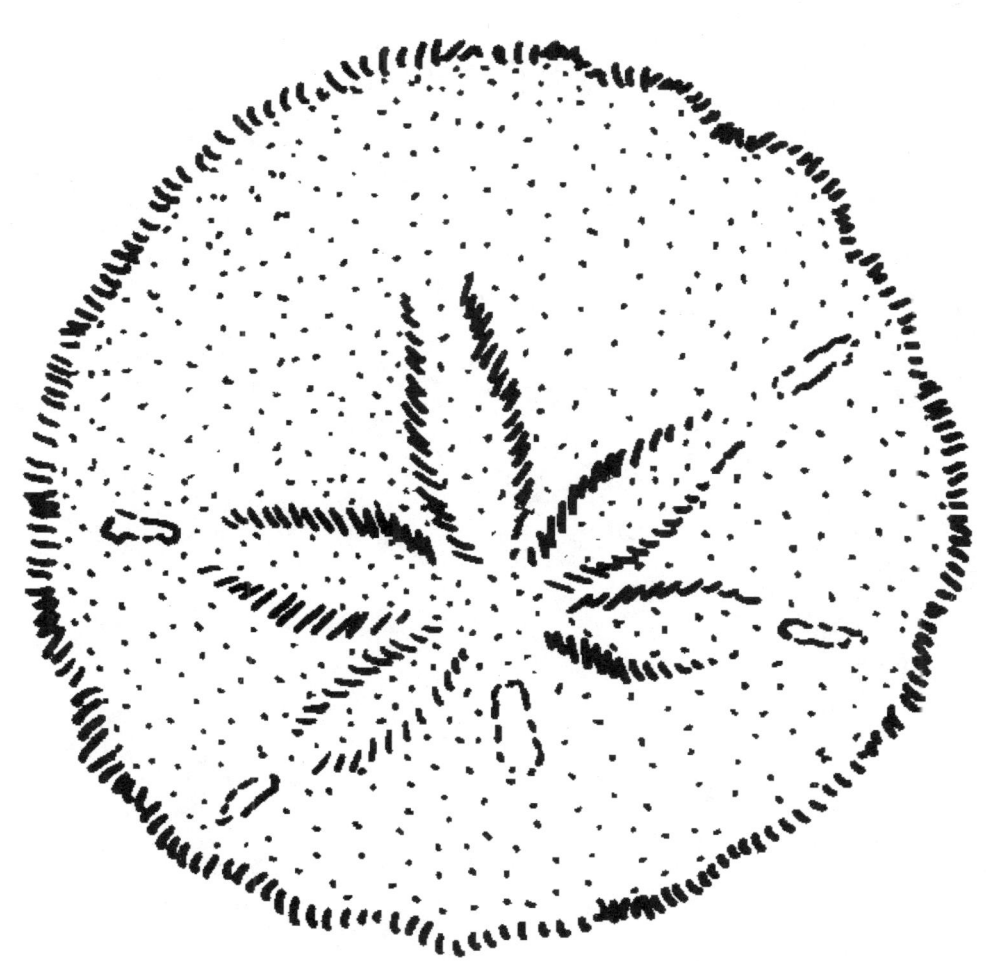

Under the Sand

Sand (Mole) Crabs
I burrow into the sand tail first.
My antennae and eyes stick out of the sand.
I stay where the waves break.
I catch plankton on my hairy antenna.
Birds eat me.
I am blue-gray or the color of sand.

Under the Sand

Beach Hoppers (West Coast)
I have a gray body and bright orange and pink antennae.
I live in burrows in the sand by the beach wrack.
I have long back legs to help me jump high.
I eat kelp.
Birds and rove beetles eat me.

Beach Hoppers (East and Gulf Coast)
I have an olive green or reddish brown body.
I live underneath driftwood or seaweed on the beach.
I eat algae.
Birds and ghost crabs eat me.

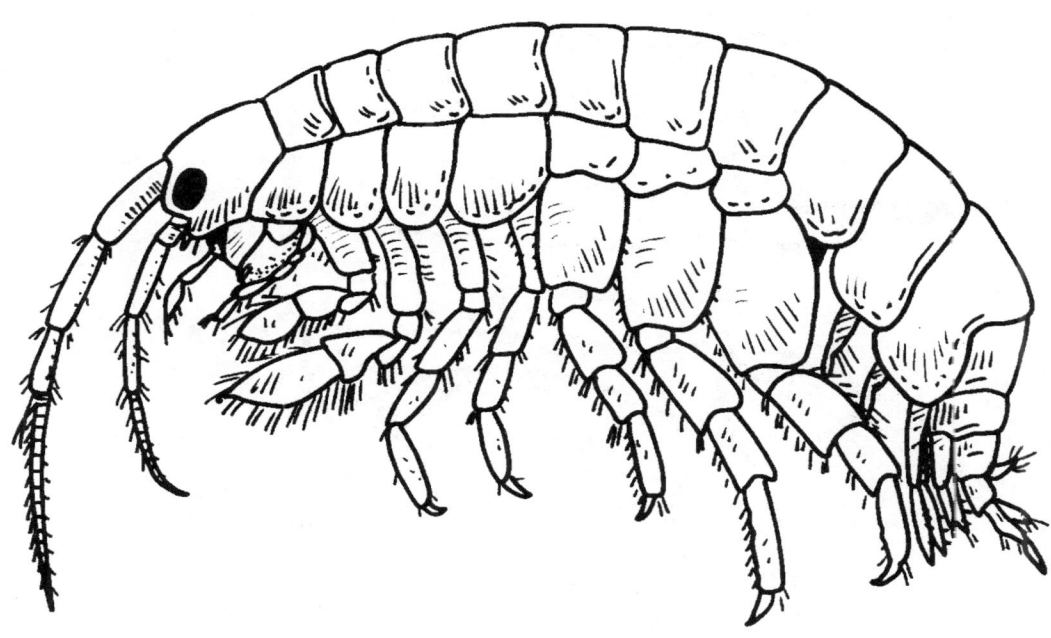

Under the Sand

Isopod
I am a scavenger on dead animals.
I am blue-gray or sand colored.
Birds eat me.
I may nip your toes.

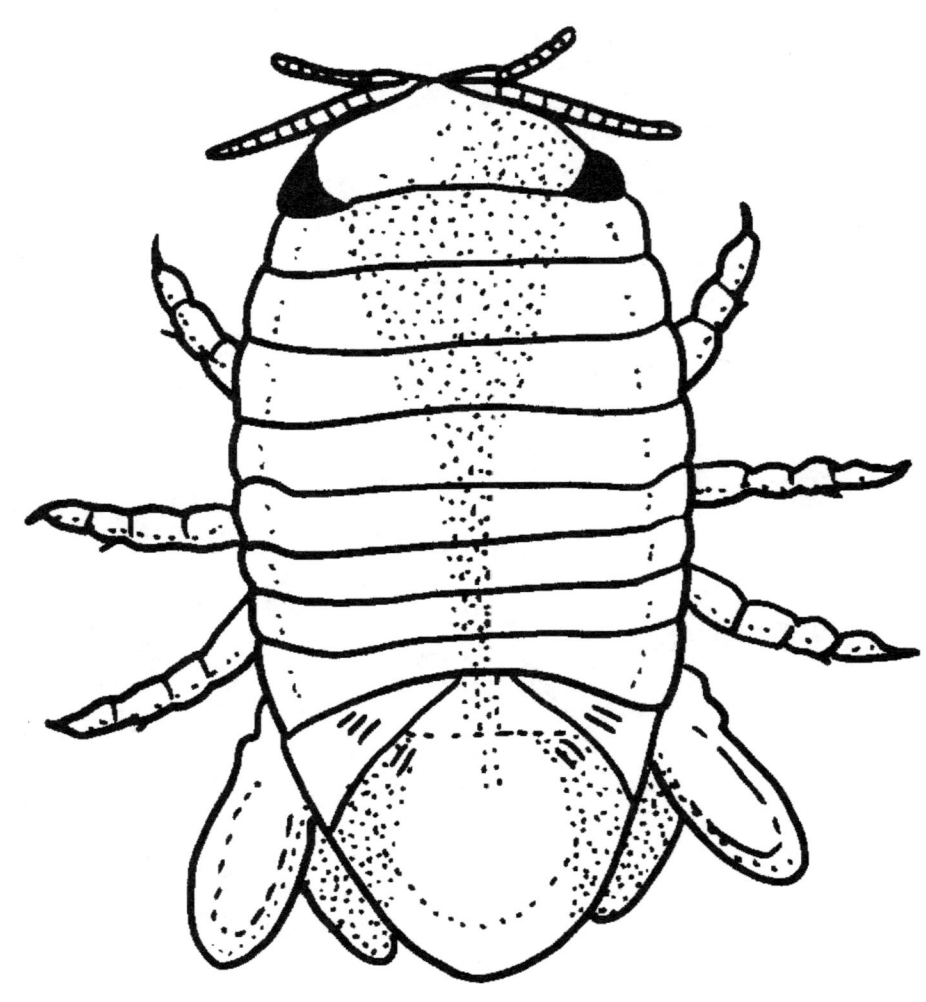

Under the Sand

Fiddler Crab

If I am a boy crab, I have one very large claw and one smaller claw.

If I am a girl crab, both of my claws are the same size.

I eat small bits of plants and animals which I find in the sand.

I dig burrows in the sand to hide from the hot sun and from birds that want to eat me.

I am dark brown during the day and light colored at night.

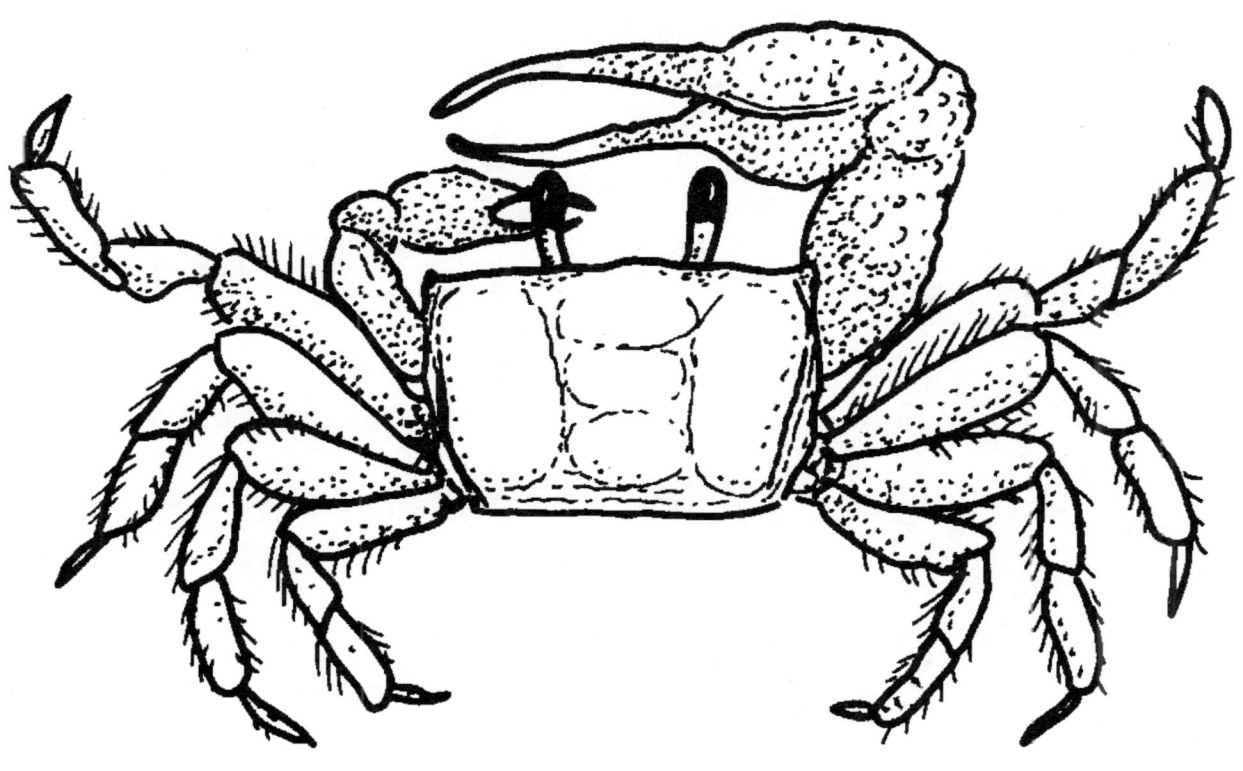

Under the Sand

Bloodworms
I am colored bright red.
I have red gills on the sides of my body.
Birds and bristle worms eat me.
Footprints and holes in the sand show where birds found me.
I swallow sand to get the tiny bits of food as I burrow.

Under the Sand

Bristle (or Red-lined) Worms

I have sharp black jaws to catch other worms.
I have many bristles on my sides to help me burrow.
I am a dark green color.
Birds eat me.
I burrow through the sand looking for food.

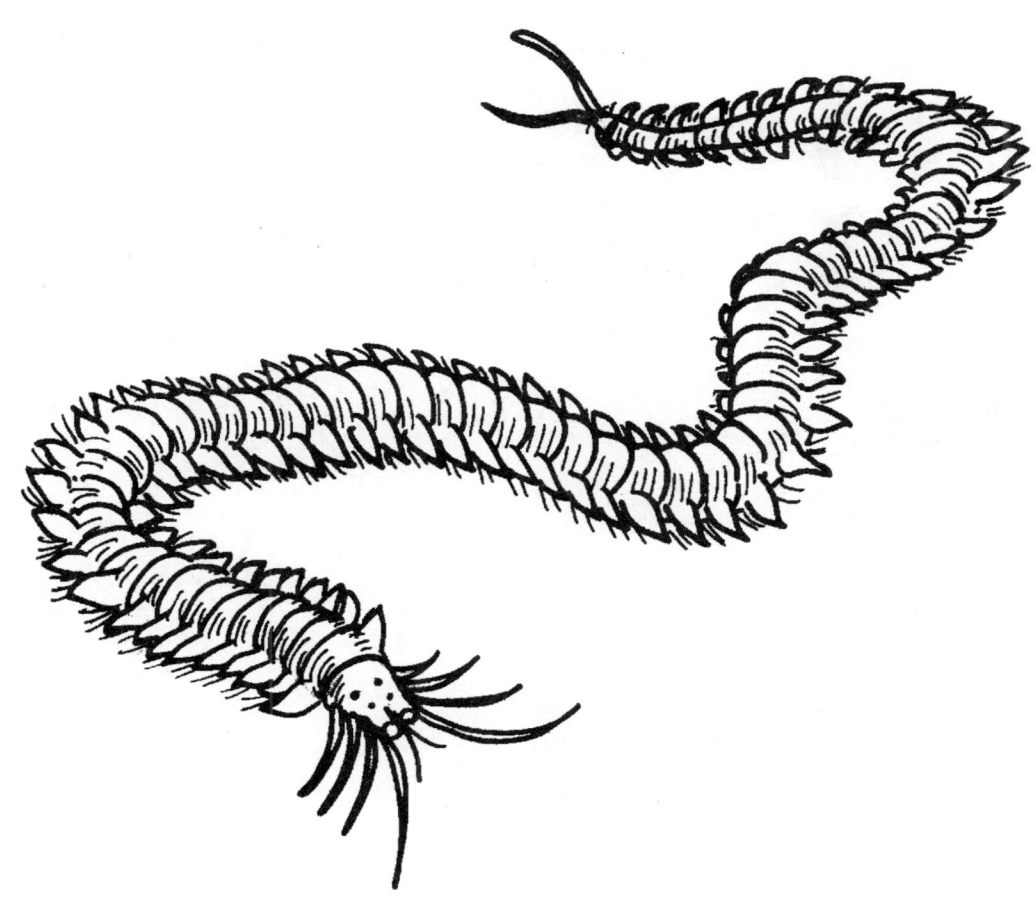

Under the Sand

Olive Snail

I have a white and purple shell.
I have a white siphon and foot.
I use my foot to burrow at low tide just under the sand.
I come to the surface at high tide to feed.
I am a scavenger.
Sea stars and moon snails eat me.

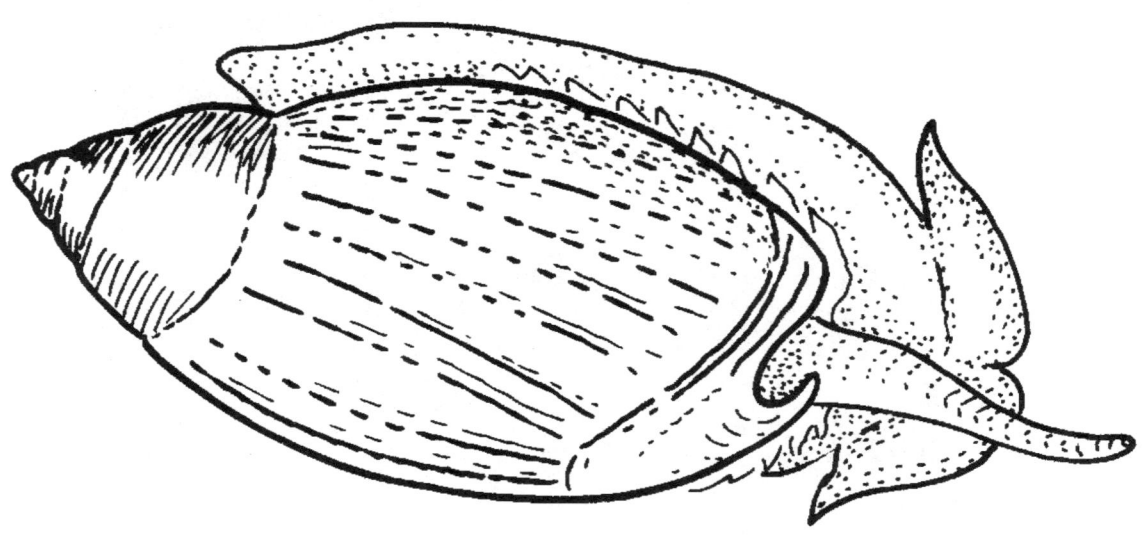

Under the Sand

Moon Snails

I have a light brown shell and beige foot.
I drill holes in clams to eat them.
I plow through the sand to look for clams.
Only the top of my shell shows above the sand.
Bat rays eat me.
Native Americans used to eat me.

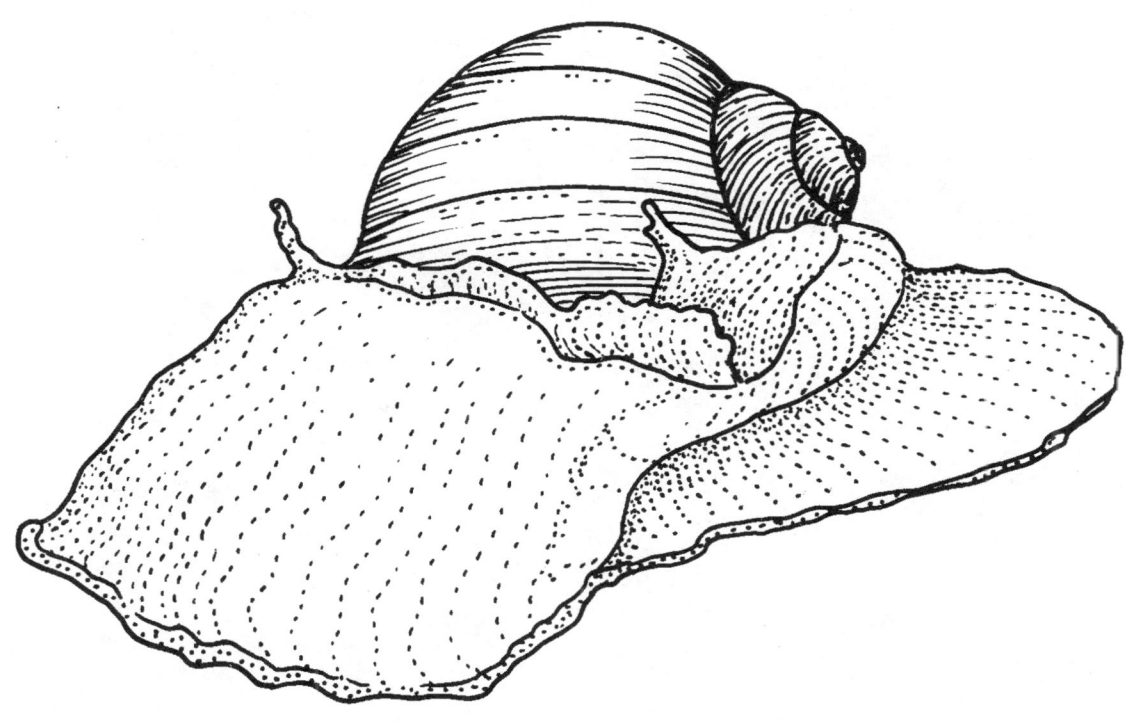

Under the Sand

Razor Clams
I have a brown shell and white foot.
My siphon has a brown tip.
I filter plankton from the water for food.
I burrow into the sand very quickly.
People like to eat me.

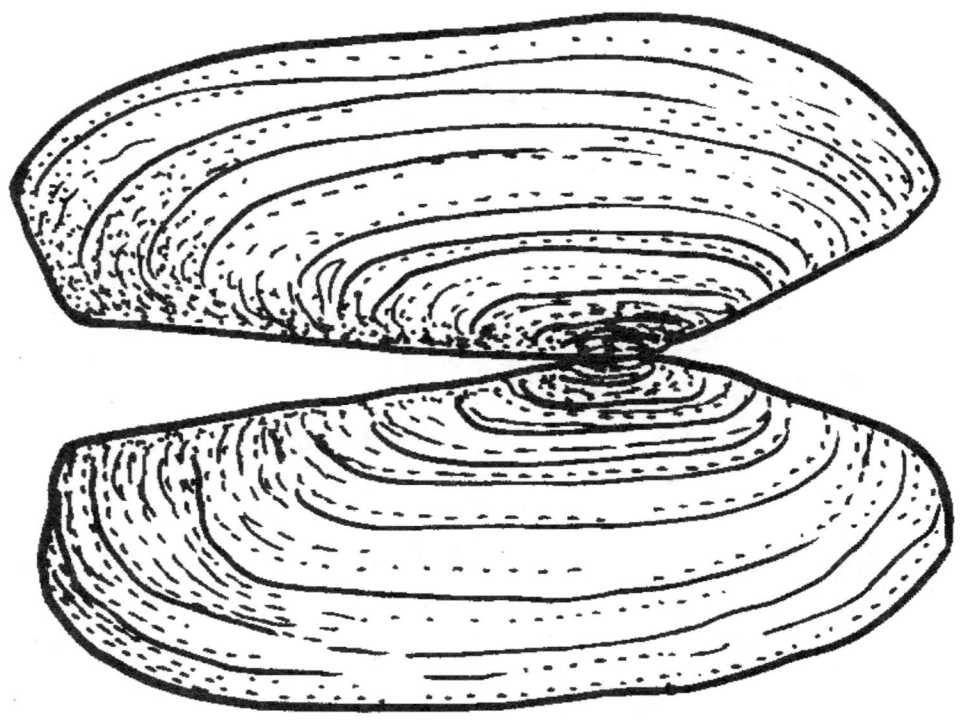

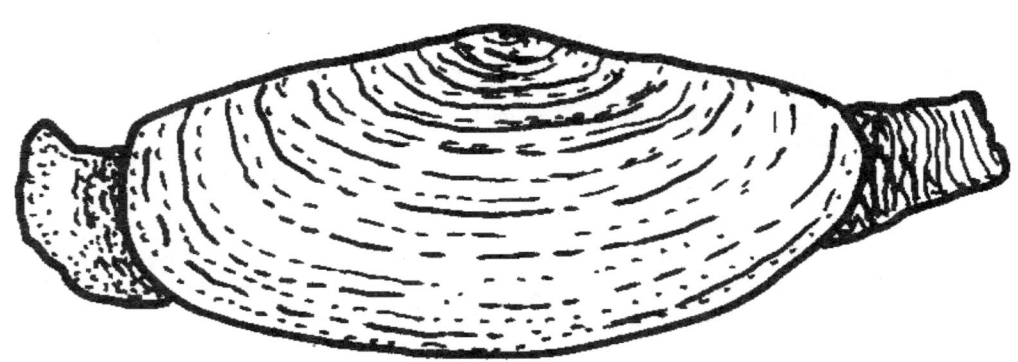

Under the Sand

Pismo Clams
I have a light brown shell with purple bands.
I eat plankton.
I live in the sand near the surface.
People and sea otters like to eat me.

Under the Sand

Bean Clam

I am very light in color.
I let the waves carry me up and down the beach.
I can burrow quickly in the sand to escape birds.
Birds, moon snails, and crabs eat me.
I eat plankton as I filter water through my siphons.

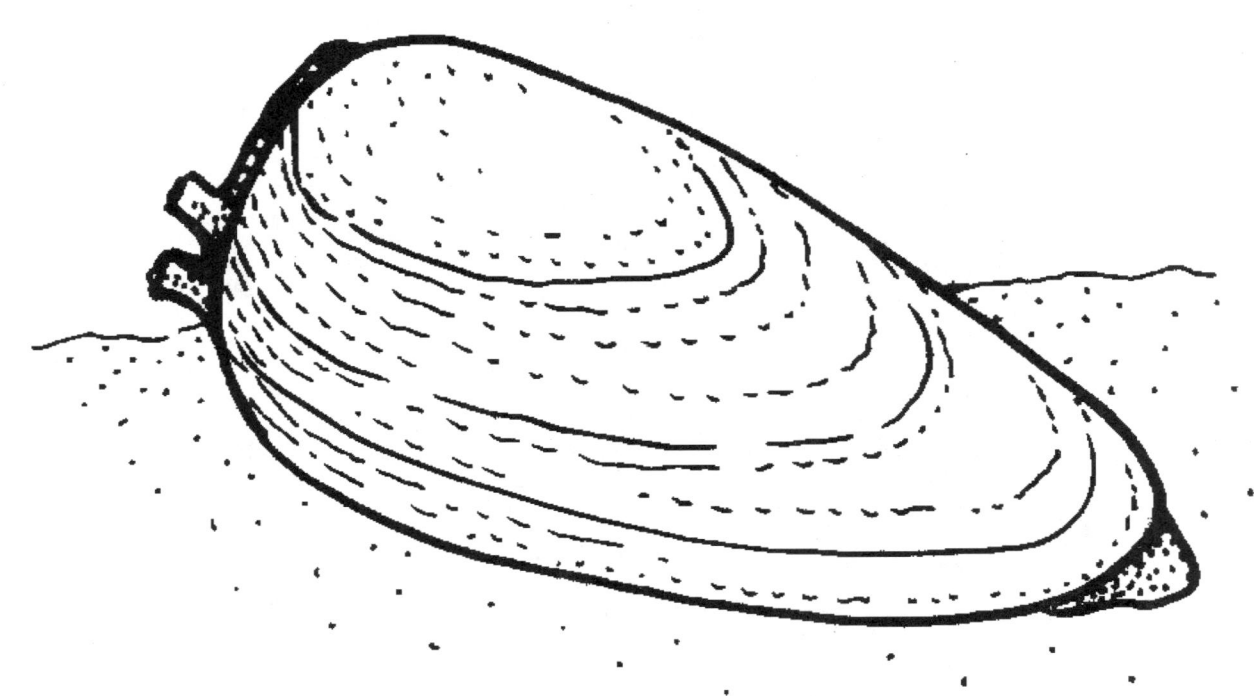

Beach Wrack

Beach Hoppers (West Coast)
I have a gray body and bright orange and pink antennae.
I live in burrows in the sand by the beach wrack.
I have long back legs to help me jump high.
I eat kelp.
Birds and rove beetles eat me.

Beach Hoppers (East and Gulf Coast)
I have an olive green or reddish brown body.
I live underneath driftwood or seaweed on the beach.
I eat algae.
Birds and ghost crabs eat me.

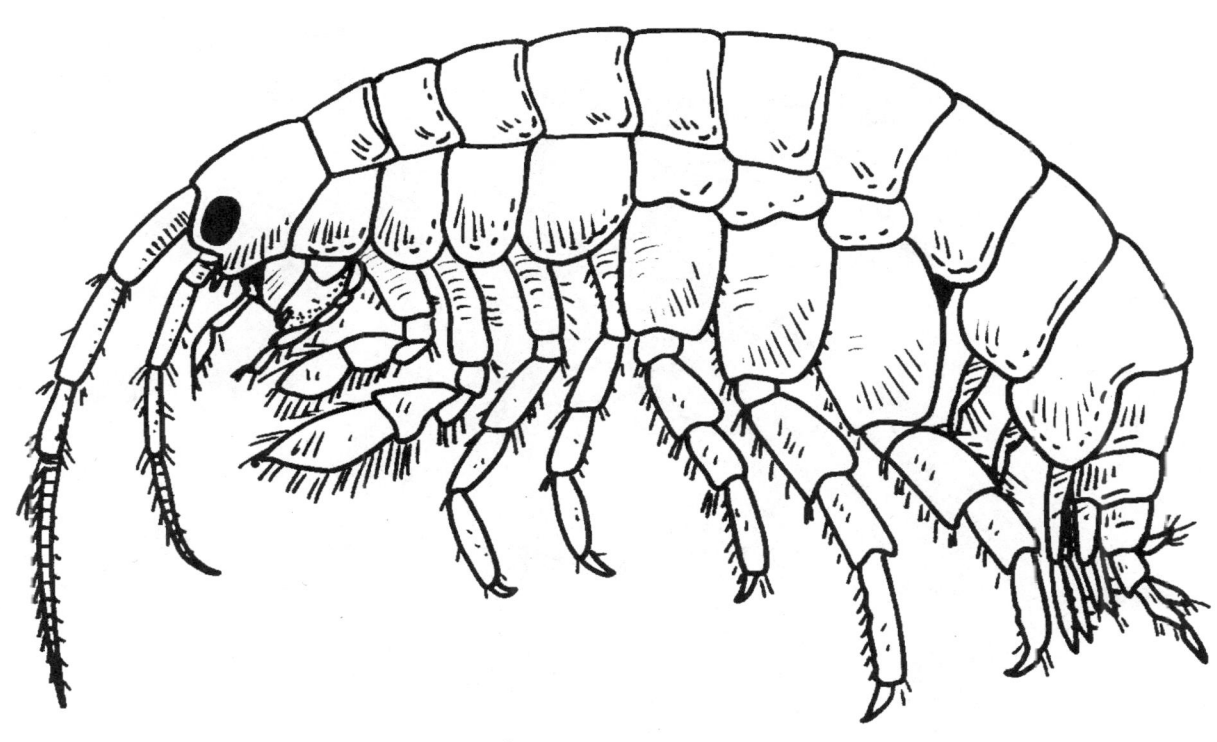

Beach Wrack

Pseudoscorpions
I have a brown head and yellow body with brown rectangles.
My legs are striped brown and yellow.
With my pinchers I catch kelp flies to eat.
I live in the kelp washed onto the beach.
Birds and rove beetles eat me.

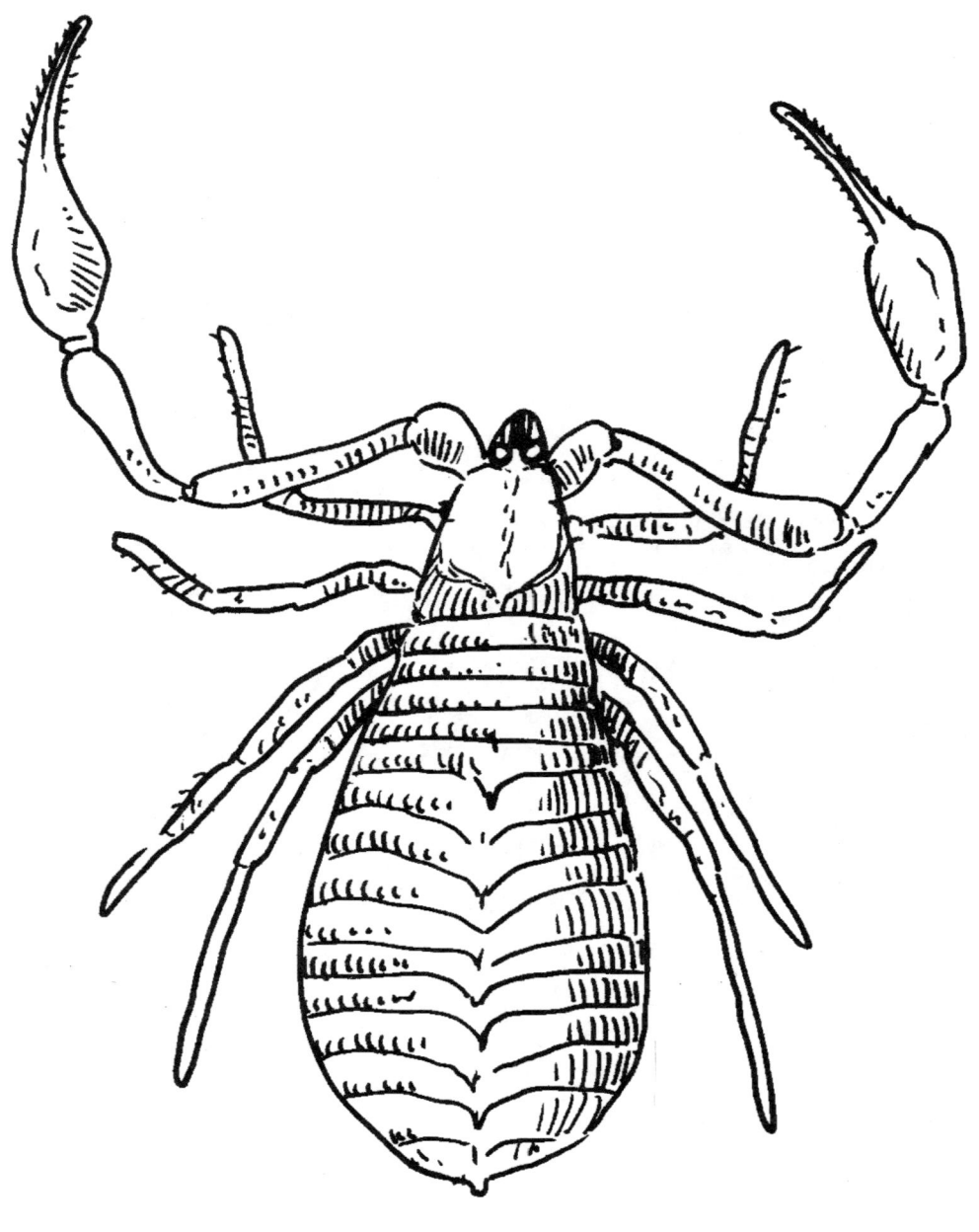

Beach Wrack

Rove Beetles
I am a super predator of the beach wrack.
I am yellow brown like the sand.
I have jaws like a knife to catch prey.
I eat beach hoppers.
Birds eat me.

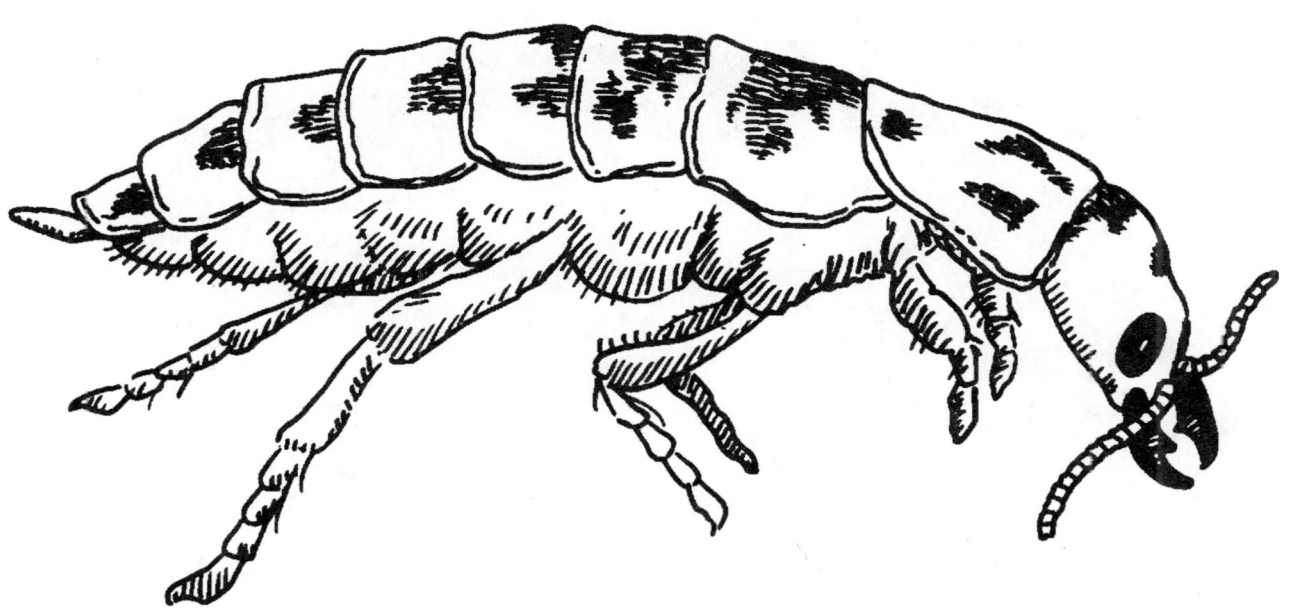

Beach Wrack

Kelp Flies

I have a hairy brown body with red legs.
I live my whole life in the beach wrack.
Rove beetles and pseudoscorpions eat my maggots.
I eat the kelp on the beach.

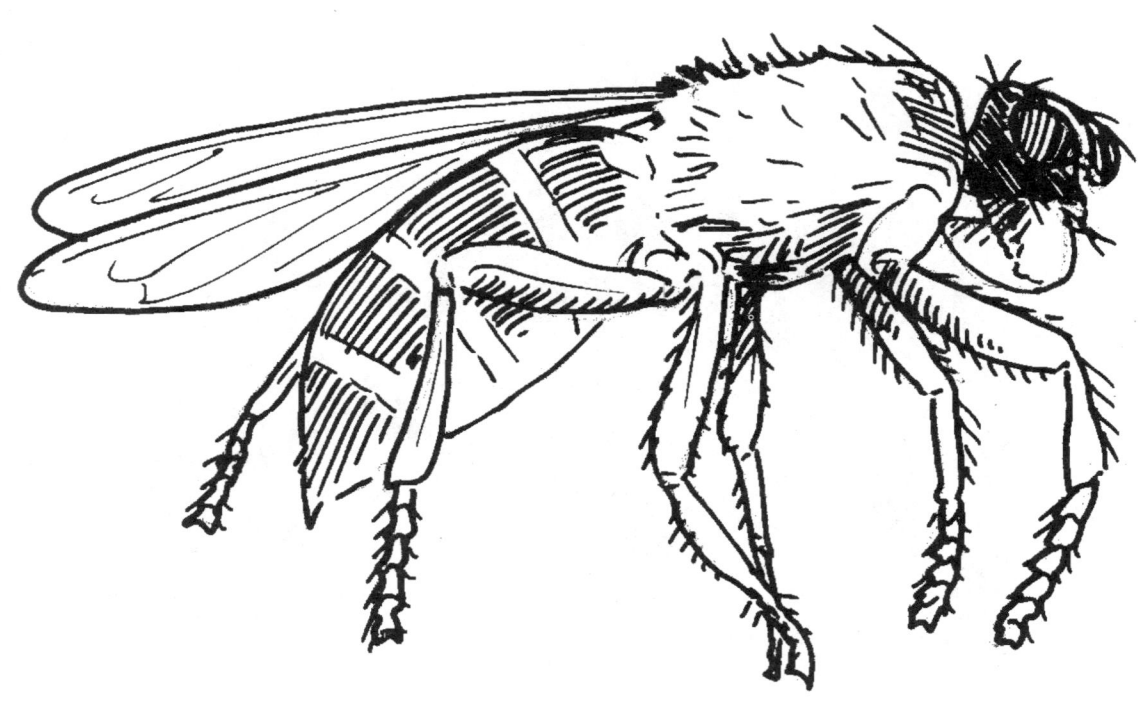

Beach Wrack

Giant Kelp
I make the giant kelp forests of the sea.
I am brown in color.
I can grow up to two feet a day.
Winter storm waves wash me onto the beach.
High tides push me higher up on the shore.
I am a habitat for many animals.

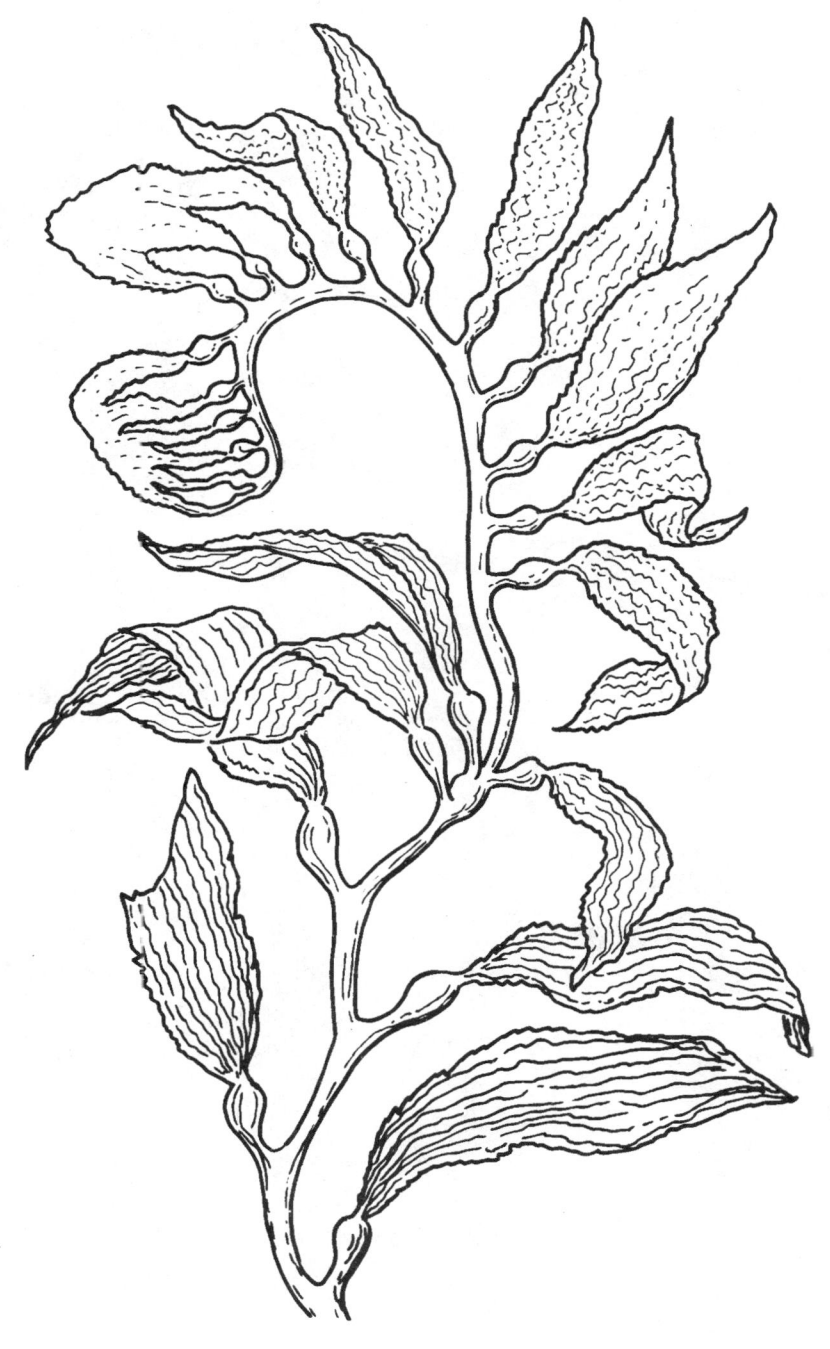

Beach Wrack

Gulfweed

Currents push me toward shore.
I form a huge mat of floating seaweed.
I am greenish brown in color.
I am a habitat for many animals.
I have air bladders that help me float.
Beach hoppers and kelp flies eat me.

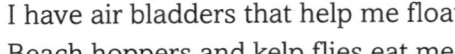

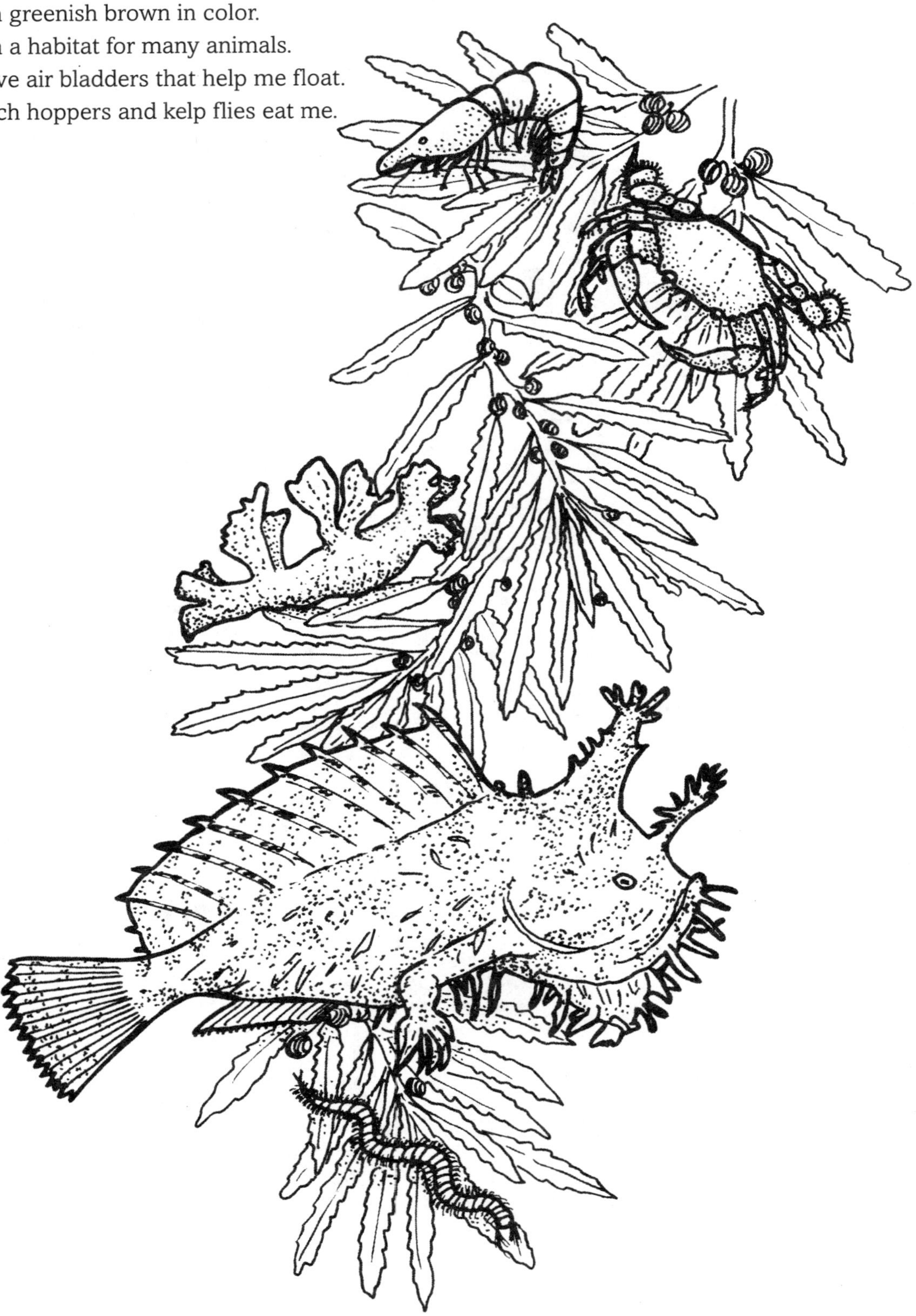

Beach Wrack

Bull Kelp
I am shaped like a whip.
I am olive green in color.
Native Americans had many uses for me.
Today, I am made into baskets and pickles.

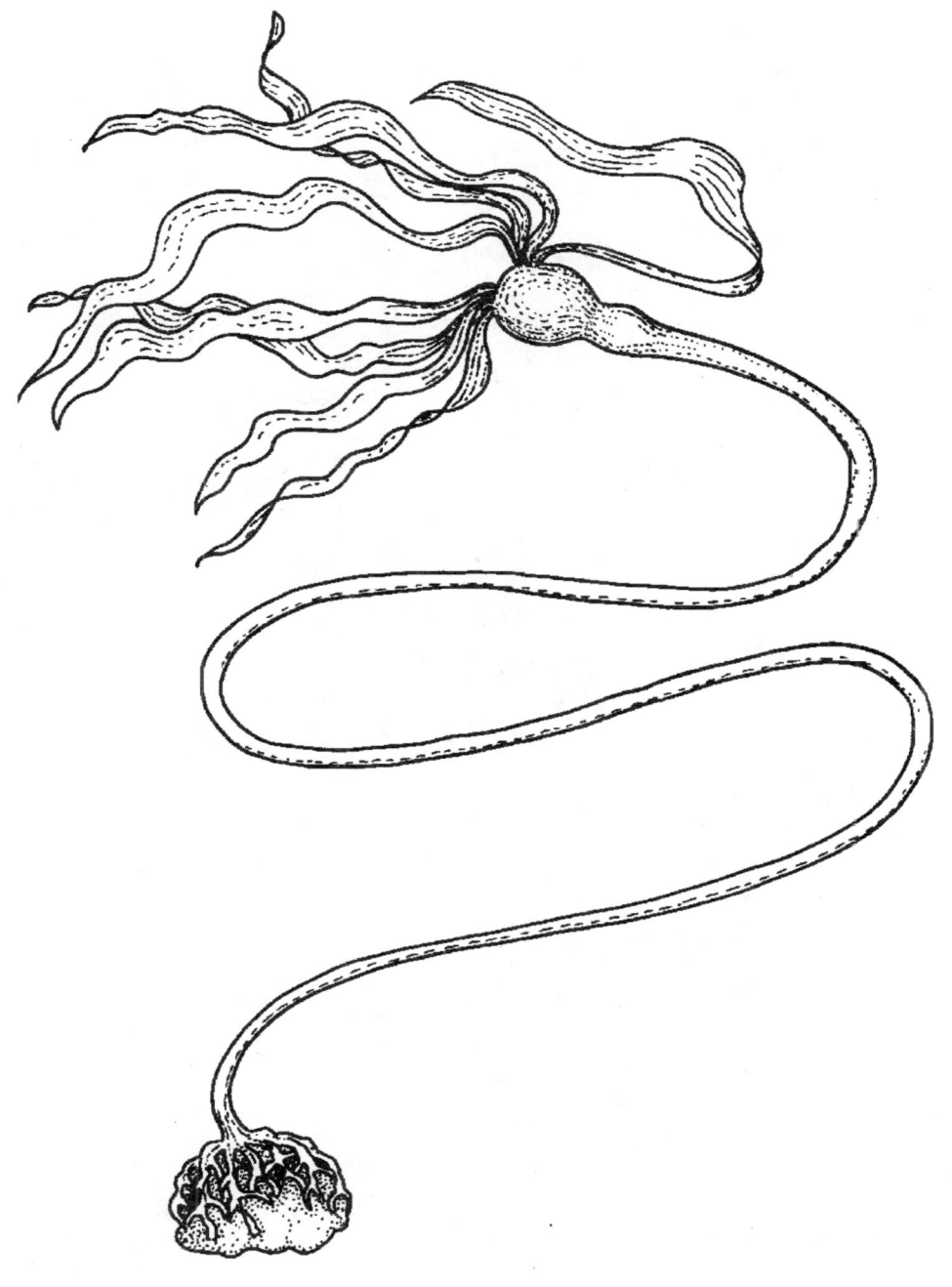

Beach Wrack

Kelp Holdfast

I am home to many animals.
I am light brown in color.
I act as an anchor for the kelp when it's growing in the ocean.
I am attached to rocks on the ocean floor.
I am washed onto the beach by storms.

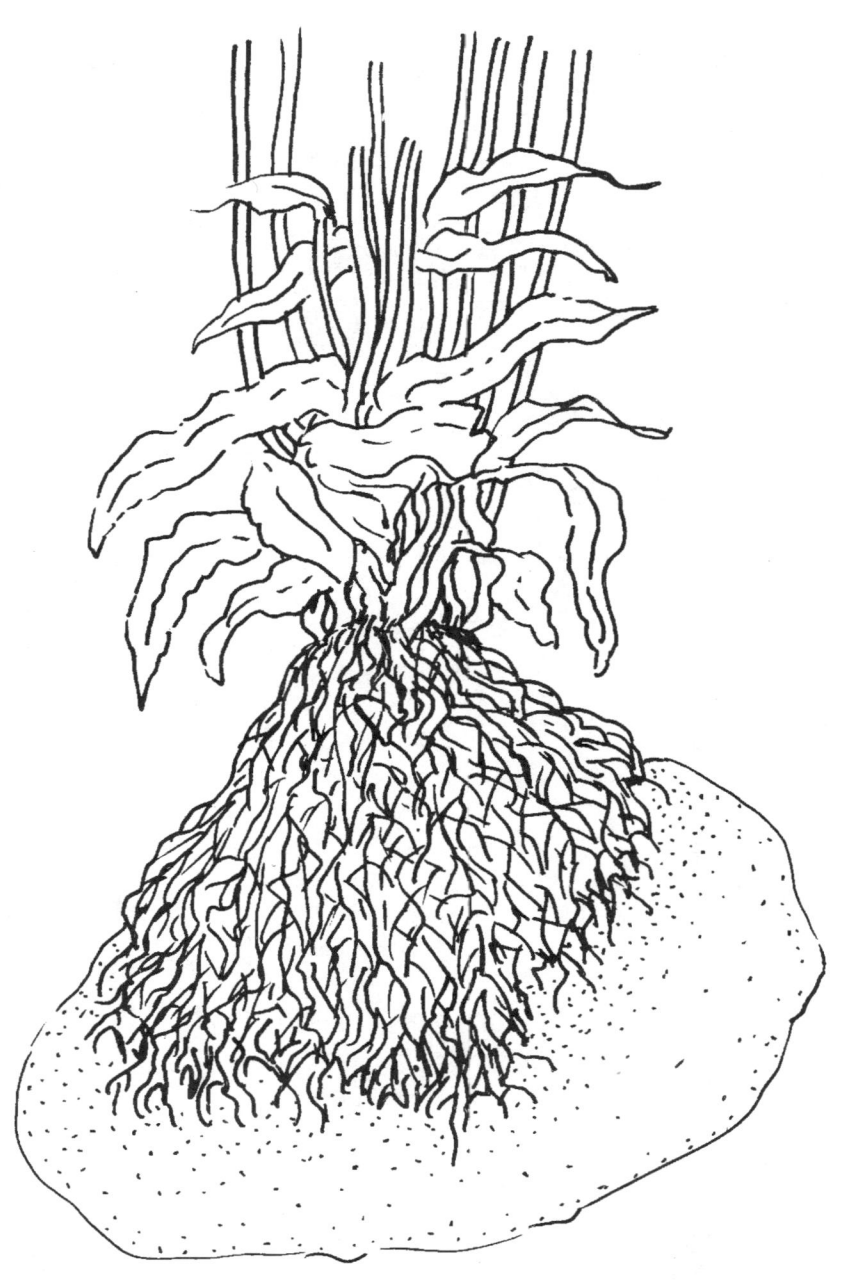

Beach Wrack

Barnacles
I am white in color.
I live attached to rocks.
I am shaped like a volcano.
I eat plankton.
I capture plankton with my feathery legs.

Beach Wrack

Bristle (or Red-lined) Worms
I have sharp black jaws to catch other worms.
I have many bristles on my sides to help me burrow.
I am a dark green color.
Birds eat me.
I can be found within holdfasts on the beach.